# Voices of Strong Democracy

## Concepts and Models for Service-Learning in Communication Studies

David Droge and Bren Ortega Murphy, volume editors

Edward Zlotkowski, series editor

A PUBLICATION OF THE

AMERICAN ASSOCIATION
FOR HIGHER EDUCATION

Published in cooperation with National Communication Association

The National Communication Association is a nonprofit organization of communication educators, practitioners, and students, with members in every state in the United States and 25 other countries. It is the oldest and largest national association promoting communication scholarship and education.

NATIONAL
COMMUNICATION
ASSOCIATION

Voices of Strong Democracy: Concepts and Models for Service-Learning in Communication Studies
(AAHE's Series on Service-Learning in the Disciplines)
David Droge and Bren Ortega Murphy, *volume editors*
Edward Zlotkowski, *series editor*

**About This Publication**
This volume is one of eighteen in AAHE's Series on Service-Learning in the Disciplines. Additional copies of this publication, or others in the series from other disciplines, can be ordered using the form provided on the last page or by contacting:

AMERICAN ASSOCIATION FOR HIGHER EDUCATION
One Dupont Circle, Suite 360
Washington, DC 20036-1110
ph 202/293-6440, fax 202/293-0073, email pubs@aahe.org
www.aahe.org

ISBN 1-56377-012-1
ISBN (18 vol. set) 1-56377-005-9

# Contents

# About This Series

by Edward Zlotkowski

The following volume, *Voices of Strong Democracy: Concepts and Models for Service-Learning in Communication Studies,* represents the 11th in a series of monographs on service-learning and academic disciplinary areas. Ever since the early 1990s, educators interested in reconnecting higher education not only with neighboring communities but also with the American tradition of education for service have recognized the critical importance of winning faculty support for this work. Faculty, however, tend to define themselves and their responsibilities largely in terms of the academic disciplines/disciplinary areas in which they have been trained. Hence, the logic of the present series.

The idea for this series first surfaced late in 1994 at a meeting convened by Campus Compact to explore the feasibility of developing a national network of service-learning educators. At that meeting, it quickly became clear that some of those assembled saw the primary value of such a network in its ability to provide concrete resources to faculty working in or wishing to explore service-learning. Out of that meeting there developed, under the auspices of Campus Compact, a new national group of educators called the Invisible College, and it was within the Invisible College that the monograph project was first conceived. Indeed, a review of both the editors and contributors responsible for many of the volumes in this series would reveal significant representation by faculty associated with the Invisible College.

If Campus Compact helped supply the initial financial backing and impulse for the Invisible College and for this series, it was the American Association for Higher Education (AAHE) that made completion of the project feasible. Thanks to its reputation for innovative work, AAHE was not only able to obtain the funding needed to support the project up through actual publication, it was also able to assist in attracting many of the teacher-scholars who participated as writers and editors.

Three individuals in particular deserve to be singled out for their contributions. Sandra Enos, former Campus Compact project director for Integrating Service With Academic Study, was shepherd to the Invisible College project. John Wallace, professor of philosophy at the University of Minnesota, was the driving force behind the creation of the Invisible College. Without his vision and faith in the possibility of such an undertaking, assembling the human resources needed for this series would have been very difficult. Third, AAHE's endorsement — and all that followed in its wake — was due largely to then AAHE vice president Lou Albert. Lou's enthusiasm for the monograph project and his determination to see it adequately supported have been critical to its success. It is to Sandra, John, and Lou that the monograph series as a whole must be dedicated.

Another individual to whom the series owes a special note of thanks is Teresa E. Antonucci, who, as program manager for AAHE's Service-Learning Project, has helped facilitate much of the communication that has allowed the project to move forward.

## The Rationale Behind the Series

A few words should be said at this point about the makeup of both the general series and the individual volumes. Although communication studies may seem a natural choice of disciplines with which to link service-learning, having roots in public speech and a focus on social problem solving, "natural fit" has not, in fact, been a determinant factor in deciding which disciplines/interdisciplinary areas the series should include. Far more important have been considerations related to the overall range of disciplines represented. Since experience has shown that there is probably no disciplinary area — from architecture to zoology — where service-learning cannot be fruitfully employed to strengthen students' abilities to become active learners as well as responsible citizens, a primary goal in putting the series together has been to demonstrate this fact. Thus, some rather natural choices for inclusion — disciplines such as anthropology, geography, and religious studies — have been passed over in favor of other, sometimes less obvious selections from the business disciplines and natural sciences as well as several important interdisciplinary areas. Should the present series of volumes prove useful and well received, we can then consider filling in the many gaps we have left this first time around.

If a concern for variety has helped shape the series as a whole, a concern for legitimacy has been central to the design of the individual volumes. To this end, each volume has been both written by and aimed primarily at academics working in a particular disciplinary/interdisciplinary area. Many individual volumes have, in fact, been produced with the encouragement and active support of relevant discipline-specific national societies. For this volume on communication studies, in fact, we owe thanks to the National Communication Association (NCA).

Furthermore, each volume has been designed to include its own appropriate theoretical, pedagogical, and bibliographical material. Especially with regard to theoretical and bibliographical material, this design has resulted in considerable variation both in quantity and in level of discourse. Thus, for example, a volume such as Accounting contains more introductory and less bibliographical material than does Composition — simply because there is less written on and less familiarity with service-learning in accounting. However, no volume is meant to provide an extended introduction to service-learning *as a generic concept*. For material of this nature, the reader is referred to such texts as Kendall's *Combining Service and Learning: A Resource Book for Community and Public Service* (NSIEE, 1990) and Jacoby's *Service-Learning in Higher Education* (Jossey-Bass, 1996).

I would like to conclude with a note of special thanks to David Droge and Bren Ortega Murphy, coeditors of the Communication Studies monograph. Not only have they demonstrated great skill and resourcefulness in putting it together, they have also maintained throughout the entire process a welcome flexibility and patience. I would also like to acknowledge the generous assistance of Gloria Galanes, director of citizenship and service-learning at Southwest Missouri State University, who provided valuable feedback on the manuscript.

May 1999

# Service-Learning in Communication: A Natural Partnership

by James L. Applegate and Sherwyn P. Morreale

The American Association for Higher Education (AAHE) series on service-learning in the disciplines is one current in a sea of change in higher education. As one of the fastest growing disciplines in the academy, communication is at the forefront of that change. Just as the original Morrill Act and its later application to historically black colleges defined land-grant universities and the service mission of higher education in the 19th century, a new outreach mission, a "Morrill for the Millennium," is sweeping across our institutions in the late 20th century. A commitment to integration and outreach is redefining our work within the sacred triad of teaching, research, and service (Boyer 1990). Even at research universities we are recognizing the need to link our work to the central challenges facing a global society. Such challenges include improving the plight of children, environmental preservation, economic development that mutes class stratification, and the rediscovery of civility and commitment as values in a humane society.

As a matter of both ethics and survival, American higher education must be about the business of creating a new compact for the next millennium. That new compact could energize and reorganize the talent and power we possess for the common good and for maintaining the support of our constituencies. As the compact develops in research, the distracting opposition between applied and basic research will be replaced by a commitment to all research as *praxis*. Theory and practice will become inextricably intertwined as we discover the best ways to teach, to research, and to serve the greater good. The social impact of research will assume greater importance in assessing its quality. Community-based research will take on new status, and disciplinary narcissism will not be tolerated.

The traditionally diffuse and unrewarded service mission will be recast with a new vision for community outreach that matches the expertise and values of the university with the needs of local, state, national, and international communities. Service efforts that create mutually beneficial partnerships with communities will be central to successful research and teaching efforts. And what will the scholarship of teaching look like within this new compact, this Morrill for the Millennium? Clearly, we will witness the continued growth of service-learning, as documented in the monographs in this

James L. Applegate is second vice-president and Sherwyn P. Morreale is associate director of the National Communication Association.

AAHE series. In this preface to the essays in this monograph, we will first describe service-learning, recognizing that differences in emphasis exist among practitioners. We will then discuss communication as a discipline in terms of its natural partnership with service-learning. We conclude with guidelines for incorporating service-learning in communication education.

# What Is Service-Learning?

The essays in this volume define service-learning by exemplifying its practice in various communication courses. But in brief, service-learning is what happens when students are afforded the opportunity to practice what they are learning in their disciplines, in community settings where their work benefits others. With service-learning, student learning is enhanced and meaningful service is provided to the community (Kendall 1990). As Erhlich notes, it is valuable both because it provides "practical experience" that "enhances learning" and because, as a form of service, it "reinforces moral and civic values" (Ehrlich 1995). Service-learning presents each act of learning as a resolution of the dialectic between the individual and society. Each successful resolution enhances both the perspective of the individual and the fabric of society by strengthening the link between the two. Students are reminded that the privilege of higher education brings an obligation to serve. Both faculty and students are confronted with a challenge to connect what they do to a larger social context. Faculty face the challenge in the design and implementation of curricula; students face it in the daily pursuit of the educational objectives of the course. Service-learning is about both service to the common good and individual learning. It focuses the scholarship of teaching on an outreach mission that is influencing every dimension of higher education.

Of perhaps even greater significance than what they are doing for individual students and for higher education, service-learning initiatives are countering some of the nihilistic forces in contemporary society. That nihilism has produced a "declining social capital" outlined in Putnam's (1995) portrait of Americans "bowling alone." Service-learning promises to enhance our social capital as a practice that: (1) embraces the productive dialectic between the individual and community in the course of social action; (2) serves to enhance our reflective understanding of who we are and how we are connected through common interests and moral obligations; and (3) holds the potential to improve the quality of our lives both morally and materially. As this volume makes clear, service-learning is a natural partner to teaching in the discipline of communication. Engaging in dialectic and connecting with others are inherently acts of communication.

# Communication and Service-Learning: A Reflexive Relationship

Communication is one of the fastest growing disciplines in higher education. During the latter half of the 20th century, a diversity of academic interests (e.g., rhetoric, speech communication, journalism, mass communication, telecommunications) has coalesced around a common concern for the role of oral, written, and electronic messages in defining self and community. The discipline's own historical literature (Benson 1985; Delia 1989) documents this convergence. From the work of the ancient Greek rhetoricians, to the influential writings of John Dewey and the pragmatists, to contemporary theories, the discipline has embraced a dual focus on understanding the practice of communication and improving it. Communication is the primary practice through which the individual and the community collaboratively develop or fragment. Hence as we study communication we are studying the process and the outcomes that service-learning is designed to enhance.

Craig (1989) offers a useful account of "communication as a practical discipline" that illustrates the natural affinity of the field for service-learning applications. Craig argues that the communication concepts we teach in our classrooms by nature reflect "a dialectical interplay between theory and [communication] practice." These concepts cultivate reflective and critical thinking about such practices. That critical reflection enables us to better address the problems and paradoxes inherent in the social reality created by the communication practices. Communication itself, Craig argues, is the method through which we define ourselves as individuals and create social capital. The study of communication, then, is a study of the methods that serve or undermine the ends of a civil and humane society. Habermas (1984; 1989), a critical philosopher, presents this search for the ideal communicative "method" as an effort to create uncoerced debates in which better ideas will prevail through a community's commitment to truth, critique, and rational consensus-building. Rorty (1987), a pragmatist, sees our efforts more modestly. Communication is aimed at assisting the continual "reweaving [of] a web of beliefs" that attains "an appropriate mixture of unforced agreement with tolerant disagreement" (48).

The discipline of communication is about the business of improving communication *praxis* (i.e., improving the quality of theory, the way it informs practice, and vice versa) at the individual and community levels. It is a study of how and why we argue and reflect as we do in the construction of social reality. Then what better way to allow our students to embrace the dialectics between communication theory and practice, and between the individual and the social, than through service-learning activities? By linking individual learning and public service, by offering the opportunity to put principles into practice and glean principles from practice, service-learning is a perfect pedagogical partner to the study of communication *praxis*.

Hence, there is a special reflexive relationship between the study of communication as the means for constructing social reality and service-learning as a pedagogy designed to enhance social life and communities. The student participates in the reflexive relationship by engaging in reflection activities. Communication theory is applied to practice, then the student reflects upon the results by thinking, writing, and speaking about what has been observed. Thus, service-learning deepens understanding of communication practice (why and how communication occurs and with what effect), while the study of communication practice informs the process of service-learning (why it succeeds or does not).

The essays in this volume dramatically demonstrate the ways in which service-learning has a natural affinity for communication as a discipline. For example, the chapter "Communication and Social Change: Applied Communication Theory in Service-Learning" describes a service-learning project that took place in a master's-level seminar at New Mexico State University in Las Cruces. The participating agency, a rape crisis center, sponsors an annual "Take Back the Night" event, part of a world-wide event protesting the prevalence of sexual violence. The service-learning project in the seminar highlighted two areas of communication theory: development communication (focuses on Third World community development issues) and the literature on communication campaigns. Students in the course took on the agency's event as their sole responsibility. They applied theory from the classroom to the challenge of promoting a successful event for the agency. Student groups were responsible for fundraising, media relations, campus relations, and promotion in the external community. Participation in "Take Back the Night" in Las Cruces quadrupled from the previous year and was double the participation in Albuquerque, NM, despite the fact that Las Cruces has one-fifth the population. Students applied theory to planning and promoting an event of social value, reflected upon their work and the results, and enjoyed success in so doing. This is but one example from this volume that illustrates the reflexive interaction of communication theory and practice.

## Some Guiding Principles for Service-Learning

The essays in this volume demonstrate some "best practices" for service-learning, in that they provide rigorous learning experiences for students and high-quality service to society. This point is crucial. Service-learning methodologies are not a less-demanding form of learning or teaching (Zlotkowski 1996). It is essential that: (1) students have high-quality knowledge to put into practice; (2) the learning context is structured to allow effective application; (3) there is opportunity to critically reflect on communication practices observed or enacted; and (4) the service provided the community is worthwhile. These expectations for service-learning may actually demand more of faculty and students than many have been accustomed to give to the educational process. But the result is the more genuine involvement in teaching and learning that is inherent in service-learning.

As we set about to expand service-learning in communication, there are some general principles that can guide us. These are lessons that have facilitated success for those already engaged in service-learning.

• *Integration in the Curriculum:* Service-learning must be integrated into the heart of the curriculum. It should not be an "add-on" course or activity. To "add on" negates the message that individual learning and service obligations are joined at the base. Full integration also will ensure that students have the time to talk, write, and reflect on the nature and effects of the communication practices they employ and observe.

• *Administrative Support and Resources:* Resources (time and money) are needed to recast traditional curricula into service-learning structures. Some administrators may think such substantive changes can occur with minimal tangible support. By contrast, successful programs have offered small grants to faculty willing to redesign courses. Those funds typically cover materials, student travel costs, etc.

• *Assessment of Impact and Outcomes:* Once implemented, service-learning initiatives must demonstrate that the criteria for learning are rigorous and the quality of service is high. That which is valued is that which can be evaluated. Fortunately, the work of Ernest Boyer has opened the academy to multiple forms of scholarship. Boyer's most recent work has inspired systematic assessment of scholarship, teaching, and application of knowledge. That work can inform the assessment of service-learning efforts in terms of its impact on the community and expected student outcomes (Glassick, Huber, and Maeroff 1997).

• *A Sense of True Partnership:* Service-learning must create a true partnership with the community. If faculty or students see service as the informed bringing wisdom to the "unwashed masses," then a major opportunity for learning from community members is lost and "partnership" is doomed to failure. Successful partnerships are based on mutual respect.

• *Dual Goals and Reflexivity:* Faculty and students must always keep the dual goals of enhanced individual learning and the support of moral and civic values at the forefront of the activity. Those in communication also must be aware of the reflexive way in which communication is the practice through which individual learning and civic engagement take place.

The exemplars and analyses provided in this volume embrace these guiding principles for service-learning. They also make clear the level of effort and attention to detail required of an efficacious service-learning pedagogy. They inspire us to make that effort as we see the outcomes of their good work. Service-learning in communication will remind our faculty and teach our students that the practice of communication is central to the social, moral, and material health of individuals and communities. Moreover, as members of this practical discipline, we have a special obligation to contribute to a healthy society through our research, teaching, and service.

## References

Benson, T.W. (1985). *Speech Communication in the Twentieth Century.* Carbondale, IL: Southern Illinois University Press.

Boyer, E.L. (1990). *Scholarship Reconsidered: Priorities of the Professoriate.* Princeton, NJ: Carnegie Foundation for the Advancement of Teaching.

Craig, R.T. (1989). "Communication as a Practical Discipline." In *Rethinking Communication: Vol. 1, Paradigm Issues.* Edited by B. Dervin, L. Grossberg, B. J. O'Keefe, and E. Wartella, pp. 97-122. Thousand Oaks, CA: Sage.

Delia, J.G. (1989). "Communication Research: A History." In *Handbook of Communication Science.* Edited by C.R. Berger and S.H. Chaffee, pp. 20-98. Thousand Oaks, CA: Sage.

Ehrlich, T. (March 1995). "Taking Service Seriously." *AAHE Bulletin* 47(7): 8-10.

Glassick, C.E., M.T. Huber, and G.I. Maeroff. (1997). *Scholarship Assessed: Evaluation of the Professoriate.* San Francisco, CA: Jossey-Bass.

Habermas, J. (1984, 1989). *The Theory of Communicative Action.* Translated by Thomas McCarthy. Boston: Beacon Press.

Kendall, J., ed. (1990). *Combining Service and Learning: A Resource Book for Community and Public Service.* 3 vols. Raleigh, NC: National Society for Internships and Experiential Education.

Putnam, R.D. (January 1995). "Bowling Alone: America's Declining Social Capital." *Journal of Democracy* 6(1): 65-78.

Rorty, R. (1987). "Science as Solidarity." In *The Rhetoric of the Human Sciences.* Edited by John Nelson, et al., pp. 38-52. Madison, WI: University of Wisconsin Press.

Zlotkowski, E. (January/February 1996). "Linking Service-Learning and the Academy." *Change* 28(1): 21-27.

# Introduction

## by David Droge and Bren Ortega Murphy

What is service-learning? How does this set of teaching and learning practices differ from internships or other kinds of experiential learning? Are we merely giving credit for volunteer activities? How can community service be academic? Do people who advocate service-learning also have a particular political agenda?

Regardless of our disciplinary identification, those of us who have worked in the service-learning arena have been addressing questions like these in countless conversations with our colleagues. This monograph, one of a series sponsored by the American Association for Higher Education, affords us the opportunity to compile and make available some preliminary answers to these questions. We welcome this chance to share some of the exciting, thoughtful work that has been done by teachers and scholars in communication studies with colleagues who may be less familiar with this pedagogy. Before providing an overview of the essays readers will encounter in this volume, however, we would like to offer a perspective on the relationship between service-learning and the study of human communication. Our major claim here is that service-learning instantiates one of the most important traditions of our field: education for democracy.

Although the contemporary service-learning movement was energized by a combination of organizational and governmental initiatives (Liu 1995), the roots of service-learning are intricately interwoven with one of the major traditions in American higher education. Bruce Kimball (1996) has argued that the history of liberal education can be viewed productively as the interplay of two major themes: privileging the unrestricted pursuit of truth, which he calls the *philosophical* tradition, and educating individuals for political participation and public leadership, characterized as the *oratorical* tradition. Although the philosophical tradition is currently ascendant in higher education, Kimball claims that contemporary criticisms of the academy lament the eclipse of the oratorical tradition. These criticisms center on four themes: (1) college graduates are inadequately prepared in the arts of discourse (writing and speaking); (2) colleges and universities give insufficient attention to questions of morality and ethics; (3) general education requirements are an incoherent collection of courses generated by academic power struggles rather than a coherent core; (4) faculty are often so concerned with their own specialized research that they neglect teaching. Each of these claims may, of course, be challenged. Kimball's thesis, however, is that these criticisms coalesce around an argument that contemporary higher education has overvalued the philosophical tradition and de-emphasized the oratorical tradition.

Kimball's analysis is particularly apt for communication studies. Although the field can lay claim to a historic role in providing rhetorical education as preparation for citizenship (see Cohen 1994, for an analysis of this theme in speech communication in United States higher education), contemporary research on unconscious psychological dimensions of persuasion as well as the pervasiveness of commercial mass media has led to widespread questioning of the relevance and efficacy of the oratorical tradition both by those within communication studies and by those outside the field. Even in institutions with large departments and strong student enrollments, some faculty and administrators continue to doubt the philosophical "legitimacy" of communication studies.

In addition, the oratorical tradition has been viewed as conservative, concentrating on the education of economic elites who can afford the luxury of an education that is not directly tied to career enhancement. Given the traditional ethnic and gender exclusiveness of economic elites, the oratorical tradition is thus encumbered with a set of antidemocratic connotations.

One of the key questions facing higher education in general and communication studies in particular, then, concerns the viability of democratic education at the turn of the millennium. Instead of an interest in democracy, which they see as disconnected from their everyday lives, these same students come to communication courses with an interest in marketable skills. At the same time, as communication scholars, we present ourselves to colleagues in other disciplines through, and ask to be judged by, the quality of our specialized research. It is not our intent as editors of this monograph to denigrate either scholarship or instruction in communication skills. Instead, we claim that activities like service-learning help to reconnect our classes, our students, our institutions, and ourselves with a tradition of democratic education while challenging us to think deeply about the broader mission of our work. As the essays in the current volume demonstrate, small nonprofit organizations and ad hoc community groups need people skilled in communication no less than do traditional employers.

Robert Putnam's (1995) "Bowling Alone" essay brings a sense of urgency to this challenge. Putnam summarized a series of indicators that pointed to a decline in participation in neighborhood groups, voluntary associations, and other "institutions of civil society." Although he may have overstated the case for this decline, Putnam's essay nonetheless highlights the importance of civil society in preserving and modifying democracy. As former Senator Bill Bradley (1995) has argued, these institutions — neighborhood and local voluntary associations — are necessary along with government and free markets for the preservation and transfer of strong democratic traditions. If

Putnam and Bradley are right, then the viability of democratic institutions requires the involvement of everyone, not just credentialed experts.

We see service-learning, then, as a pedagogy that addresses both our obligations as "institutional neighbors" in the communities in which our campuses are located and our historic role of preparing students for participation in civil society. We recognize, however, that the exigencies of academic life require articulation of the links between service-learning and the scholarly and pedagogical traditions of the discipline of communication studies.

And so we come to the present volume. We have organized the essays in this volume into three sections. First, we address broad programmatic and administrative issues. Paul Soukup's overview essay argues that service-learning pedagogy can prove useful across a range of courses by helping faculty and students examine some of the major dialectical tensions in the study of the human communicant. Christine Bachen describes an approach that integrates service-learning throughout a curriculum grounded in the Jesuit tradition of social justice. Bachen's essay is the first of many in which the authors incorporate statements about the value of service-learning in students' own words. Further, she offers a timely discussion of concerns about "romanticizing" this pedagogy and stresses the need for deep reflection by faculty as well as students as service-learning enters the curriculum. Mark Bergstrom and Connie Bullis recount the systematic institutionalization of service-learning by a group of faculty at a major research university. They argue that these institutions can meet their research obligations and enhance student learning through service-learning. Sally Perkins, Virginia Kidd, and Gerri Smith tell the story of their integration of service-learning at the graduate level. These authors found community-based education a valuable vehicle for problematizing the researcher's ethical standpoint regarding research "participants." Finally, Kathleen Stacey and Chris Foreman address the central problem of faculty incentives. Their research project demonstrates the importance of *internal* rewards (e.g., released time) rather than *external* rewards (e.g., grants and honoraria).

The second section of this volume focuses on specific courses that have utilized service-learning. Peggy Hashemipour's essay, the longest in the volume, is both a well-documented account of the integration of service-learning into a course on language and culture and a thoughtful tale of her planning, justification, and execution of service-learning. We commend it to any reader interested in a full account of the integration of service-learning into a course. Tasha Souza reports on a qualitative study of student learning in a course in interpersonal communication. Paul Yelsma offers a series of guidelines and tips for utilizing service-learning as an aid in teaching group problem-solving. Kristin Valentine documents an intriguing project in a course in the oral performance of literature that gives voice to a usually "voiceless" group of college and university stakeholders — those classified as staff members. Mark Pollock demonstrates the efficacy of service-learning in an introductory course on argumentation and advocacy. Sara Weintraub proposes ways of integrating this pedagogy into courses in public speaking.

A second group of essays in this section focuses on mediated or mass communication courses. Robbin Crabtree's essay provides a bridge between the two groups of essays, as she describes her own and her students' involvement in a public event for a local organization. Virginia Keller, Jeff Harder, and Craig Kois detail the incorporation of a community-based laboratory into media production courses. Eleanor Novek writes about two different kinds of teaching as she links service-learning with another innovative concept — civic journalism. Katherine Kinnick provides guidelines based on her experiences in integrating a community service project into a communication campaigns course. Lynne Texter and Michael Smith conclude this section with a practical orientation to service-learning in a public relations seminar.

The third section offers ideas for the future of service-learning and communication studies. Two contrasting essays, along with an annotated bibliography, comprise this final section. Angela Trethewey concentrates on the critical dimension of service-learning, arguing that feminism and critical organization theory provide a strong theoretical grounding for much of the work yet to be done in the pedagogy of service-learning. In contrast, April Kendall surveys the growing literature on service-learning and proposes an important role for communicant scholars in helping understand the role of communicant skills in community service work. These two essays underscore unresolved tensions in both communication studies and service-learning. How can academics as intellectuals committed to social change reconcile their commitments with some students' narrow drive for unreflective professional competence? Are service-learning activities another form of exploitation of the poor and oppressed in providing a "learning laboratory" for the next managerial elite? Given the overlap in service activities and reflective insights across the curricular offerings described in this monograph, how can communication studies faculty demonstrate that the discipline has — through service-learning — a unique contribution to make to higher education?

Benjamin Barber (1984), in the book whose title we have appropriated for this monograph, proposes "strong democracy" as an alternative to the impoverished models of democracy current in American political thought. Strong democracy privileges face-to-face interaction and community building as foundational elements in strengthening democracy. By giving voice to teachers and scholars who have engaged in community-based learning to enhance the teaching and scholarship of communication studies, we join with Barber in envisioning a multivocal democratic society. Service-learning seems to us an important, albeit imperfect, tool for strong democracy. We invite colleagues in the discipline to join us in celebrating the work of the authors whose essays comprise this monograph, and to join them in re-connecting our universities to the communities we all live in.

We would like to conclude by offering our appreciation to the American Association for Higher Education, particularly series editor Edward Zlotkowski, for making this volume possible. We also would like to thank the National Communication Association for its encouragement of the work of service-learning and for its cosponsorship of this monograph.

## References

Barber, B. (1984). *Strong Democracy: Participatory Politics for a New Age*. Berkeley, CA: University of California Press.

Bradley, B. (February 1995). "Civil Society." Address to the National Press Club, Washington, DC.

Cohen, H. (1994). *The History of Speech Communication: The Emergence of a Discipline, 1914-1945*. Annandale, VA: Speech Communication Association.

Kimball, B. (1996). *Orators and Philosophers: A History of the Idea of Liberal Education*. New York, NY: The College Board.

Liu, G. (1995). "Knowledge, Foundations, and Discourse: Philosophical Support for Service-Learning." *Michigan Journal of Community Service-Learning* 2:5-18.

Putnam, R.D. (January 1995). "Bowling Alone: America's Declining Social Capital." *Journal of Democracy* 6(1): 65-78.

# Service-Learning in Communication: Why?

by Paul A. Soukup

At a 1993 convention session honoring his work, Howard Giles recounted his attempts to introduce his students in a more practical way to accommodation theory. He would send them out from campus to visit nursing homes, where they would interact with elderly residents, paying particular attention to their own and their interlocutors' speech patterns. Such cross-generational discourse opened their ears to the accommodation normal in everyday speech. Seen in this way, communication should strike most people as a natural academic area for service-learning.

Service-learning — "a form of experiential education in which students engage in activities that address human and community needs together with structured opportunities intentionally designed to promote student learning and development" (Jacoby 1996:5) — systematizes Giles' insight by regularly connecting the students to the community beyond the boundaries of school and academy. As in Giles' case, many others have recognized service-learning's value as a pedagogical device (see Droge and Murphy in this volume). As a pedagogical device, service-learning provides a particularly apt instrument in the communication teacher's tool chest. In addition, it enriches the communication student, the communication department, and, one hopes, the community.

## Benefits for Faculty, Students, and Departments

Despite an impressive growth in theorization by communication scholars, communication study remains a fundamentally applied area. By its very nature, every kind of human communication, whether interpersonal, mediated, or even through the mass media, retains essential connections to practice. All communication students talk, interact nonverbally, act in groups, exist as family members, use the telephone, and consume the products of the mass media. The distinction between a "pure science" and an "applied science" simply does not fit communication study, for we can never divorce ourselves from our communication practice.

The first benefit of service-learning is that it makes the connection between theory and practice explicit. Within communication study, service-learning takes a variety of forms — ranging from students helping local girl scout units to working at homeless shelters, from visiting AIDS patients to tutoring children, from producing community video to translating in legal clinics. Some would even include internships at nonprofit organizations

(Cohen and Kinsey 1994). In every case, the communication student works not as a community volunteer but as a learner, seeking knowledge from the community and through reflection on experience, as well as from more traditional textbook study. This approach helps the teacher overcome the theory-practice divide by guiding the student to see practical communication both as worthy of study in its own right and as material that illustrates theoretical concerns. The approach helps the student by showing communication study as a unified area, with equally important poles of theory and practice. Finally, this approach helps the department integrate theory and practice in each course rather than erecting walls between the "theory courses" and the "hands-on courses."

For departments that grew out of disparate foundations — speech, radio-television-film, journalism, and so on — the divide between practitioners, theoreticians, and researchers can seem troubling. The integrative power of service-learning works to bridge gaps, moving the student from classroom theory and classroom practice to community experience and back to classroom reflection. This pattern helps departments come to grips with their own heritage and can lead to greater integration within the curriculum.

Second, service-learning is a corrective to both theory and practice. On the one hand, it adds concrete experiential practice to the theory-driven courses; on the other, its structured reflection on experience adds a theorizing step to a primarily technical course. More than this, it corrects both perspectives by anchoring them in the community, with its time constraints, unpredictability, human error, and conflict. Service-learning moves students to consider others and their needs as part of their education. All too often the educational experience focuses only on the student, leading to a kind of self-indulgence. By placing the student in the community, service-learning corrects both a potential disciplinary confusion and a personal temptation to self-centeredness.

Third, service-learning offers faculty and departments an important opportunity to teach communication research methods in an indirect fashion. Giving students the opportunity to reflect on their community experiences cultivates an ethnographic attitude. By taking the role of participant-observers, the students can develop a taste for empirical observation. Here, too, they begin to bridge the theory-practice divide.

Looking at the situation in another way, a service-learning placement can provide the students a fourth benefit — a realistic place of practice, especially in more applied cases. Through service-learning, students in journalism or public relations often find opportunities to write, conduct campaigns, and apply their own skill to the problems of the placement sponsors.

Fifth, service-learning benefits faculty, students, and departments by keeping us honest. As we have become more sophisticated in studying communication, we have honed critical skills through cultural studies, critical theory, varieties of deconstruction, and other valuable tools. But it is not enough for departments and faculty to see how communication works; we should also look for contradictions and manipulations. As students of communication, we should be skeptical and suspicious if we wish to avoid a naive acceptance of messages produced by economic, political, and cultural powers. What better deconstructive opportunities than those afforded by the mass media or by corporate communication? Yet at the same time faculty and departments happily send graduates off to these very industries, having taught them the skills they need to produce the very messages we criticize. To deal with tensions like this one, service-learning balances critique with participation. In other words, it changes a sequential experience in which most students move from study to critique to graduation to work in industry into a different experience, one that is more concurrent, in which they create messages and criticize them simultaneously. Service-learning gives students the chance to see how and why communicative contradictions occur by placing themselves in applied settings.

Finally, as many of its proponents suggest, service-learning facilitates the growth of students as citizens in a democracy (Cohen and Kinsey 1994). Students' community experience connects them at an early age with their fellow citizens, usually from a more diverse population than they would experience at home or in school. This encounter seems fitting for an academic tradition that traces its roots to Plato's and Aristotle's studies of rhetoric and government, to the long tradition of political persuasion, and to journalism's role in building and defining a community of citizens in the United States. Communication students particularly (though one hopes all students) should represent the ideal of the citizen-scholar, the one who sees knowledge in the context of community and political responsibility.

Service-learning, then, benefits faculty, students, and departments of communication by providing a connection between theory and practice, an integrating principle in our curricula, an introduction to empirical observation and reflection on experience, a corrective to an overemphasis on criticism, and an introduction to citizenship. Though it often goes without saying, service-learning also benefits schools and communities by drawing them together in possibly mundane yet new and significant ways.

## Practical Benefits

Even beyond these broad benefits to faculty, students, and departments, service-learning appears especially useful to communication study in a pragmatic way that addresses course content. This point will emerge more clearly if we look at the close fit between service-learning opportunities and the content of many communication courses.

Every service-learning placement requires some human interaction, and most require quite a lot, whether that consists of visiting the elderly, tutoring the young, talking with the homeless, answering phones at a crisis center, or teaching English as a second language. All of these experiences clearly relate in a concrete way to various communication theories: for example, accommodation, interpersonal development, interviewing, gender, persuasion. The chapters in this monograph represent a wide variety of introductory and advanced courses in which service-learning can be fully integrated.

Furthermore, many service-learning sites place students in contact with a much more demographically diverse population than they encounter on campus. Students have the opportunity to work with refugee groups, with documented and undocumented immigrants, with the elderly, and with the very young. Each of these experiences offers a chance to consider a range of communication theories and practices: intercultural communication, language and culture, minorities and media, representation, and identity formation. For most students, putting a human face on what they study changes their basic understanding of such theories.

Finally, many community situations give students the chance to utilize and sharpen already acquired skills in nonschool settings. Some tutor younger students and practice their own speaking skills. Others have the chance to write, design page layouts, do audio or video productions, or prepare websites. Some work on narrative construction and performance. Still others participate in local campaigns for fair housing or environmental protection. These campaigns are good places to practice argument and advocacy, test persuasion skills, and do applied research. Each community placement can offer students both learning and a sense of community participation.

## Other Benefits

Beyond its usefulness for communication teachers, students, and departments, service-learning also holds out many possibilities for communication researchers. Faculty doing the same kinds of community service as students can discover new research opportunities and methods. Adelman and Frey (1997), for example, used a community placement to develop research methods and analysis techniques needed to examine group interactions in a residential facility for people with AIDS. The setting — so different from campus or corporate research sites — offered them a privileged window into human interaction and community-making. They examined how communication constitutes community in a repeated way, as communities change over time, as people renew community in times of crisis and loss, and as people choose to stay together. To conduct research not only for the sake of theory development, not only for knowledge's sake, but for the communities in which we live and work adds a new dimension to our own self-understandings and commitments.

Several service-learning projects at my own institution have involved both student and faculty participation. In one, students and the instructor collaborated on a documentary on the homeless in downtown San Jose, California. The resulting video was shown with some success at local festivals. In another instance, several students worked with faculty to conduct research on behalf of a local school district, which wanted to increase its use of educational technology. In a similar project, another student carried out an assessment of the potential of a multimedia lab for a grammar school. In each case, students gained valuable experience in the community, benefited from close work with faculty, and saw communication study in a new light. They also came away from the term with a much better sense of grounded research.

Service-learning provides a great resource for communication study. Its imaginative use adds a great deal to the basic communication curriculum; its continued use prepares students well for later life. Its place in our departments makes them and us, the faculty, stronger and more understanding of our communities, our students, and ourselves.

## References

Adelman, M.B., and L.R. Frey. (1997). *The Fragile Community: Living Together With AIDS*. Mahwah, NJ: Lawrence Erlbaum Associates.

Cohen, J., and D.F. Kinsey. (1994). "'Doing Good' and Scholarship: A Service-Learning Study." *Journalism Educator* 48(4): 4-14.

Jacoby, B. (1996). "Service-Learning in Today's Higher Education." In *Service-Learning in Higher Education: Concepts and Practices*. Edited by B. Jacoby, pp. 3-25. San Francisco, CA: Jossey-Bass.

# Integrating Communication Theory and Practice in Community Settings:
## Approaches, Opportunities, and Ongoing Challenges

by Christine M. Bachen

Santa Clara University's undergraduate major in communication introduces students to humanistic and social scientific approaches to the study of mass and interpersonal communication and provides a grounding in the practice of communication through course offerings in speech, video production, and journalism. Several common goals are emphasized across the curriculum: the integration of theory with practice; the ethical responsibilities of communicators; the study of how communication is shaped by cross-cultural and cross-national factors; a critical examination of mass media industries and their practices with particular attention to perspectives left out by mainstream media; and teaching students to anticipate important social issues presented by emerging technologies. We hope students will emerge from our program as effective communicators, and that they will match their understanding of the communication process with their commitment to raising critical questions about access to and the performance of communication media.

Among other pedagogical tools, our department makes use of learning experiences in the community to sensitize students to the inequities and biases that persist in mass media and interpersonal communication among different types of communicators, and to reflect upon their own role in accepting or challenging the conditions that lead to these inequities. More specifically, through community-based learning we hope to achieve three related educational outcomes. First, we hope students will develop an understanding of the processes by which stereotypes are constructed, and the role the media play in perpetuating ideologies about such issues as poverty, ethnicity, and immigration. Second, by providing students with an opportunity to personally experience multiple subcultures within American society, we hope they will grow to appreciate the diversity and commonalities of human experience and the particular concerns of peoples whose voices are often not heard. Third, we hope that students will become more thoughtful communicators, sensitive to the needs and rights of those with whom they communicate, and more critically aware of their ethical responsibilities when representing people's experiences through a communication medium. These outcomes — particular to the field of communication — are consistent with the university's larger goals of educating for social justice.

# The Eastside Project

We are fortunate to have access to a university-wide program at Santa Clara that assists faculty in developing community-based learning components for their courses. The Eastside Project, originally named after the east part of San Jose where most of the program's efforts centered, "intends," as the *Project Handbook* declares, "to bring the life experiences of the marginalized members of society into the consciousness of students and faculty so that the concern for justice is fixed firmly within the teaching/learning experience at Santa Clara and not at its periphery."

The Eastside Project matches students with agencies in the community serving children and adolescents, elderly people, and recent immigrants through programs such as day care, health care, family shelters, and adolescent and adult education. The program was created in 1986 and functions as an academic support unit. Its four-person staff has identified about 40 local agencies that serve as placement sites for students. The Eastside Project places over 1,200 students from 75 different courses per year in these agencies, where each student will spend about two hours a week over the course of eight weeks.

The Eastside Project tries to situate itself outside more conventional models of student voluntarism or community service. Here, the goal is for students to enter the agency with the mindset of being a "learner," not a charity volunteer. The role of volunteer is in many ways easier and more comfortable for students, and we see many students struggle to see themselves learning from individuals who most likely do not have the same level of education or advantages as themselves. But the distinction between volunteer and learner is critical in achieving a core goal of the Eastside Project whereby students are challenged to bring into the classroom new questions that are grounded in the perspectives of the people they are meeting at their Eastside placements.

## Community-Based Learning in the Curriculum

Faculty in our department have been utilizing Eastside Project placements since the program was first developed. Although we have now identified areas of the curriculum where we believe community-based learning experiences are most effective, we continue to discuss the philosophical and pragmatic concerns raised by this approach. The partnership between classroom and community is not always easy, nor is a student's or faculty member's movement between those two worlds. But this unpredictability and real-world "untidiness" is, of course, ultimately part of the richness of the educational experience.

Preliminary findings from Eastside Project assessments indicate that more than one experience in the community seems to have a more powerful influence on students' rejection of stereotypes and their deeper understanding of issues such as poverty, welfare, and immigration (Sholander 1994). Consequently, we have identified at least two places in the curriculum — one more theoretical, the other more applied — where community-based learning is included as a required part of a course.

Students in our major first encounter an Eastside Project placement in the introductory communication course, which focuses on an overview of interpersonal and mass communication. By asking students to explore the process of communication — rules, language, nonverbal behavior — within a particular cultural context that differs from their own, we help them understand better the principles and practices of interpersonal communication. Their experiences enrich their understanding of cultural variations in communication styles, and they gain a sharper sense of the biases and preconceptions that shape interactions with others.

In this course, students gain more perspective on the process of mass communication as they learn more about the mediated experiences of other people and the meanings they construct through television or other media. Even students' notions of what constitutes "typical" media use may change as they come into contact with people who spend a lot of time listening to the radio or watching television programs broadcast in Spanish or Vietnamese. The research biases in the field surface during these placements as students recognize how little research exists about the populations with whom they are interacting.

In this introductory class faculty use a structured-journal approach to help students draw relationships between certain aspects of their learning experience and the study of communication. Over the typical eight-week placement, students choose from a list of course-related topics for their weekly journal entry. For example, in conjunction with readings on and discussion of interpersonal communication, students reflect on how their preconceptions about the people in their placement affected their initial interactions, or they may write about how cultural factors shape verbal and nonverbal communication. Mass communication journal questions focus students' attention on the media habits of those they're interacting with, how media use may strengthen or weaken cultural ties, and how patterns of media use within a placement affect interpersonal communication.

Faculty need to spend some time clarifying expectations with students about the journals they are keeping. We have found that journals work best as ongoing chronicles and opportunities for reflection, but many times students slack off on regular journal writing, especially given other demands that conform more to traditional categories of required class work. Frequent reminders and classroom discussion of the journal entries are important to get students to process their experiences on a regular basis. Additionally, it is common for students to limit their journal observations to surface summaries of what happened at the placement and how they felt, rather than deeper explorations that would be more conducive to analysis. Finally, without explicit encouragement and reminders from faculty, journal entries may not make connections to other theoretical material relevant to the class.

We have found that classroom discussions of what students are learning at their placements are also important, for they reinforce the connection between course material and the students' experiences, and provide a template for the kinds of public discussions of social problems that we hope students will continue to have long after their placement experience has ended. These class discussions also reinforce the centrality of this type of learning for the course, giving students an opportunity to bring the unique experiences and learning they have gained in the community to bear on more general topics in the class.

We also use community placements in advanced television production and journalism courses, where students are challenged first to learn from people whose voices are frequently misrepresented or ignored in mainstream media and then to come up with more responsible representations.

Students in the television production courses take on the role of participant-observers at their placements. Ideas for short productions emerge from these learning experiences and become the source of dramas, documentaries, and public service announcements for the agencies. Making these productions publicly available in the community and at the university ensures that students experience reactions to their work, especially by those at their placements.

Advanced journalism courses use community placements as sites for beat reporting or development of in-depth stories. In writing about such topics as homelessness or immigration, journalism students confront their own biases in their perception of the "problems" they choose to write about and their assessment of the causes and solutions of these problems.

Producing communications based on community experiences puts students in touch with the challenges involved in researching, interviewing, and developing a perspective about a complex social issue, and drawing upon human experiences as one important source of information. Respecting the privacy and confidentiality of individuals at the placements necessitates some adjustment of broadcasting and journalistic norms. But beyond this, students encounter more typical dilemmas as, for example, when they try to resolve questions of objectivity that arise when they move from the comfortable position of detached observer to building closer relationships with people. They may find themselves in an awkward situation as they deal with the clients at a placement and the placement's director or staff who may have very different views about the definition of a problem or the value of proposed solutions. Most important, students must deal with the issues involved in speaking for others. Even as they critique mainstream portrayals, they may find themselves questioning their own voices as well.

Faculty in our department have also made use of Eastside Project placements in other courses. In an upper-division elective course, Public Discourse and Poverty, students have direct experience with economically disenfranchised individuals and families in order to observe how they communicate about their poverty, thus comparing discourse *about* the poor with the discourse *of* the poor. Students spend two hours per week for at least eight weeks in a homeless shelter or other program where people are struggling with issues of dislocation and discrimination. During this time, they keep a journal to record and reflect upon their experiences as those experiences relate to the course readings.

Finally, some courses, such as Research Methods, have developed research projects in conjunction with schools, agencies, and community groups. Students and their community partners collaborate on the design of the study. Each student becomes responsible for working with a classroom or small group of respondents. The data are analyzed and presented at a joint session of the class and the interested community group. The key element here is the *collaboration* that leads to the identification of the research area, the design of the study, and the analysis and interpretation of results. With this element of collaboration, students learn more than an exercise in the application of research methods. They learn why research is important to a particular group of people and what the implications of the results obtained are for that group.

## Assessing Community-Based Learning

How do we know whether community-based learning projects, like the Eastside Project, are helping us meet the goals presented earlier? While we have not yet developed a formal assessment measure within the department, we can draw some conclusions based upon different types of student feedback and faculty evaluations of students' work. Together these measures suggest that some of our goals are being achieved, but they have also revealed the need for us to continue to think through the types of outcomes community-based learning can achieve.

Many students identify the community-based learning component as an important part of their course in their final journal entries or written course feedback at the close of the quarter. For example, the end-quarter feedback from students in the Poverty and Public Discourse course illustrates the importance of the experiential learning component in shaping their understanding of poverty — at both the cognitive and the emotional level:

> *This class, coupled with my placement experience, exposed a masked reality — a more complete, accurate, humanistic portrait of poverty.*

> *My favorite part of this class was my Eastside Placement. By doing it in coordination with taking this class, I was more aware of what exactly we were studying. The issue came alive, and was very real to me.*

Much student feedback from other courses is similar: The experience seems to heighten students' awareness of a set of issues, leads them to reflect more critically on their own patterns of interpersonal communication and on mass media representations, and helps them develop a sense of compassion for and commitment to the individuals and the problems they encounter. This outcome is especially characteristic of courses that make the experience central to the content of the course through regular discussions or assignments.

Alumni tell us that community-based learning has helped them develop ethical standards by which they judge their communications and those of others. As alumni relate stories about what they experienced in their placements, they often connect these with a decision they've just made — to fight against an oversimplified account of events, to challenge a stereotype, or to change jobs so they can work for something they believe in.

Even while at Santa Clara, many continue their relationship with their placement after the quarter's end. Some continue to work on a project related to their learning experience (e.g., further refining a video). Others simply want to continue to have contact with the people and the agency they were exposed to and see this additional contact as a time to "give something back," after feeling that they — in particular — benefited so much from their earlier experience.

Student feedback reveals another view, too. We know that not all students embrace the community-based learning experience. While there is no single type of learning experience that will appeal to or "work" with all students, there is some resistance to community-based learning similar to resistance to other pedagogical innovations that "add on" a time commitment (e.g., lab requirements in science or language-learning) or an unfamiliar course dimension. Students may complain that the two-hour commitment per week is too large, especially since many have outside jobs. Should students be taking another class that requires an Eastside placement, this concern only becomes magnified, although we try to allow a student to meet his/her requirements through a single placement wherever possible. Moreover, many students are uncomfortable with the idea of going into an unfamiliar environment and may bring fears and even prejudices to the placement. The best antidote to such resistance is clear communication by the faculty member as to the purpose of the placement and how it relates to the goals of the course. If the learning experience is demonstrated to be an important part of the course, most student complaints dissolve fairly quickly. However, if students have an experience where community-based learning is not brought into the course in a central way, they may approach the next course that uses this learning strategy with a dismissive or even hostile attitude.

Students' responses over the years highlight both the intended and unintended consequences of community-based learning. Some of the unintended consequences have challenged us to think further about the nature of the experience and of the role faculty should play in it.

From journal entries in particular, we find evidence of students moving through various stages of understanding as they try to sort through individual, situational, and structural explanations of complex social phenomena. Students often enter their placement with a less than compassionate view of the poor or marginalized. They may frame a person's condition as an individual problem (e.g., it's the person's fault for being poor). With more visits, students begin to demonstrate an understanding of structural factors that contribute to the situation (e.g., sociopolitical conditions that foster poverty). But in final journal entries, it appears that many move back to an understanding of the problem that is once again grounded in individual responsibility, but this time their own (e.g., the solution lies in their own attitude).

In faculty discussions of these responses, we find ourselves troubled by some students' inability to reconcile an understanding of the structural factors that shape many of the challenges marginalized people face with their own — often romanticized — ideas about how to be part of a solution. Journal entries bring this home most clearly, for they serve as a more unfiltered reflection of students' reactions than we are accustomed to receiving in more traditional academic papers. How and how much should faculty intervene in the students' learning experience when their knowledge is being developed in a more personal, individualistic way, and they are being encouraged to reflect more personally on this experience? It may be that in one or two 8-week placement periods, many students simply cannot achieve an integrated level of understanding of the individual differences among the people in the placement; the common social, political and economic circumstances that shape their situations; and their own role and commitment with regard to the individuals they have met and the social problems represented by their experience. But rather than see this as a limitation to be "fixed" within a course, we may need to accept that the faculty member's appropriate role is in providing important feedback to students on issues related to course material, and requiring a set of readings that help deepen their understanding of the complexity of these issues. How knowledge is translated into personal vision may be more of a lifelong process.

The second concern builds upon the "meanings" that students attach to their experience. Does the nature of the experience itself almost inevitably lead to a privileging of personal experience, especially in the feeling that a student has contributed to a "solution?" This question subtly changes the focus away from the placement and those served to the students themselves. By putting a human face on social problems, we risk a loss of focus on systemic reasons for conditions like poverty or illiteracy (McLoughlin 1994). Looking at the following examples of student feedback, we can ask whether opening of the heart in fact overwhelms critical understanding.

> This class and Eastside experience has opened my eyes, as Herman [a homeless person] said, 'opened' my 'heart' to homeless people and the problem of poverty in this country. I will never look at a homeless person the same again.

> The experience I got in these three months was so special that I wouldn't exchange it with anything . . . I write my last words in this journal today. Before I started writing, I went back and read what I wrote so far. It seemed like a journey. There are still so many things that can't be written, or I better say can't be expressed. . . . I can only say that it [working with the homeless] brings me joy, peace and calm.

The placement experience can construct a situation as "itself heroic; in keeping with the Christian message that the meek shall inherit the earth, the dignity that an individual can bring to an intolerable situation can easily be assigned to the situation itself. Poverty, homelessness, mental illness become a kind of test of strength, a place that can almost be admired for its ability to draw out the strength of character and will of those it affects" (McLoughlin 1994: 2-3).

Moreover, while Eastside placements are designed around a partnership model, McLoughlin (1994) identifies some aspects of the learning experience that preserve the status quo. Students leave campus to travel to another location where they encounter a situation they could not encounter at the university. Yet they return to the university, a safe and comfortable place, to process and make sense of the experience. Even when students raise issues from the perspective of the people in their placement, one can argue that their own location is never truly challenged, though they have taken an important step.

While we seek to have students represent others' experience in papers and discussions, it is important to recognize that the people from the placement sites very rarely travel to campus to represent themselves (and when they do, it's usually the directors of the agencies who come). McLoughlin (1994) argues that students must recognize the limitations in speaking *for* others, and that instead, we must provide opportunities for them to speak *with* others in the university setting, as well as in community settings, in order to achieve the partnership at the core of the Eastside Project. Some of the projects students work on in our department begin to bridge this gap by representing people from the placements directly in video or news stories, but this is not universally the case.

## Role of Faculty as Coparticipants in Community-Based Learning

A final issue that we feel needs more discussion deals with the role of the faculty member teaching a community-based course and how the experience of students going into diverse communities affects his or her own teaching and scholarship. To date, most faculty have not joined their students in going to the placements. But faculty who don't themselves engage in community-based learning are not in a position to understand their students' experiences; they are also missing out on ways to make the experience relevant to the subject matter they are teaching. It is appropriate for faculty to challenge themselves to become involved in teaching and scholarship connected to marginalized groups of people. In doing so, they take on the role of public intellectuals, "whose scholarly and pedagogical practice serve to educate students to become active citizens" (Scholle and Denski 1994: 34). Giroux (1991) also articulates this redefinition of the role of the faculty member:

> *Academics can no longer retreat into their careers, classrooms, or symposiums as if they were the only public spheres available for engaging the power of ideas and the relations of power. Foucault's notion of the specific intellectual taking up struggles connected to particular issues and contexts must be combined with Gramsci's notion of the engaged intellectual who connects his or her work to broader social concerns that deeply affect how people live, work, and survive (57).*

If social justice goals define a central — but not exclusive — part of the communication curriculum for our students, so should they be a central — but not necessarily exclusive — part of a faculty member's agenda as a teacher-scholar. Participation in a community-based learning experience is not the only way for faculty to engage in teaching and scholarship that actively serves the interests of those who are on society's margins. But if we do value this experience for our students, then it makes sense to engage in it ourselves.

While I have addressed some of the challenges presented by our continued involvement with the Eastside Project, I want to conclude by reiterating that our experiences with community-based learning have yielded outcomes that we value and find consistent with the goals of the department and university. Despite the risk of students romanticizing their role, or underestimating what it means to speak for others, or failing to appreciate all the structural underpinnings of complex social problems, without this experience they might remain even less knowledgeable and even more distant observers. According to the philosophy of the Eastside Project as described in a 1997 *Santa Clara University Bulletin*, people learn by doing: "We act ourselves into new ways of thinking — not the other way around." It must be recognized, however, that action must be supplemented by other pedagogical strategies to provide a framework that students learn to act, feel, and think their way through, with feedback from faculty and Eastside personnel.

It is important for faculty to think through decisions about when and where to implement community-based learning in the curriculum. We have learned that overuse tends to create burnout for students, yet too little use does not allow for students to move through different stages of understanding toward a more integrated sense of their experience. Our faculty have discovered that learning experiences in the community must be made central to the course curriculum or students tend to perceive them more as "service" than "learning." We have also realized that we need to challenge the model of community-based learning and push our operational definition of "partnership" further than we have often done. Creating a space on the university campus for the voices of others, not just encouraging students and faculty to more sensitively represent the voices of others, is a necessary next step toward achieving social justice.

### References

Giroux, H., ed. (1991). *Postmodernism, Feminism, and Cultural Politics.* Albany, NY: State University of New York Press.

McLoughlin, M. (1994). "Can We Talk About Justice From Here?" Presentation to the Speech Communication Association, New Orleans, LA.

Scholle, D., and D. Denski. (1994). *Media Education and the (Re)Production of Culture.* Westport, CT: Bergin & Garvey.

Sholander, T. (April 1994). "A Cross-Institutional Look at the Community as a Learning Environment for Postsecondary Education Students." Paper presented at the annual meeting of the American Educational Research Association, New Orleans, LA.

# Integrating Service-Learning Into the Communication Curriculum at a Research University: From Institutionalization to Assessment of Effectiveness

by Mark J. Bergstrom and Connie Bullis

Although the number of service-learning courses in higher education in general, and in communication in particular, is growing, service-learning is not being adopted as quickly at institutions that are defined by strong research missions. In this paper we first argue that service-learning is a pedagogical tool that is highly compatible with the research mission of such institutions. Moreover, as research-oriented universities struggle to adapt to current external demands for relevance and accountability, service-learning can provide persuasive evidence to external constituents as well as redefine the role of research institutions in their communities and in society. Second, we claim that the discipline of communication is particularly well-matched with the service-learning pedagogy. As a result, communication departments at Research I universities are ideal candidates for widely integrating service-learning into individual projects, courses, and curricula. Third, we provide a case study of service-learning adoption into a communication curriculum at a Research I university. Specifically, we describe our efforts to institutionalize service-learning into a central course in the Department of Communication at the University of Utah. Finally, we outline specific examples of service-learning projects, strategies for assessment of service effectiveness and student reflection, and review ethical and pedagogical issues that have resulted from the institutionalization of service-learning.

## Service-Learning as Pedagogy in Research Universities

We are all familiar with the common charges that research institutions reward faculty for narrow and esoteric research rather than for teaching and service to the community. In many cases, these charges are coupled with decreasing legislative budgetary support. Put simply, the public (often in the form of legislatures) is insisting that universities provide evidence of how they add value to community in concrete, identifiable ways. At the same time the public often expresses anxiety over the breakdown of society. Traditional justifications for the existence of research universities, such as the proportion of faculty who hold Ph.D. degrees and an appeal to liberal education, are increasingly scoffed at as costs and benefits are more concretely defined and measured. There is a growing demand that universities define the benefits they provide and illustrate how their operations and budgets are designed to provide these benefits. Outcomes are similarly scrutinized. The public often seems to be focused on job skills and economic benefits to the community as acceptable benefits toward which operations, budgets, and outcomes should be directed. The public perception is that technical schools provide concrete observable job skills more clearly and efficiently than research institutions. To the extent that research universities ignore these demands, and the increased funds and good will toward technical skill training, they risk increasing external coercion and decreasing support. On the other hand, to the extent that research universities accept these goals, adapt accordingly, and provide responses to anxiety over societal break-down, they can proactively participate in redefining their missions and roles in society.

Instead of choosing between noncompliance and compliance, research universities should seek ways to actively adapt to external demands (Boyer and Hechinger 1981) while redefining themselves by means that are consistent with their traditional missions. Altman (1996) argues that the primary focus of research universities has been *foundational* knowledge with a secondary focus on *professional* knowledge. He further argues that a third kind of knowledge, *socially responsive* knowledge, represents a meaningful alternative to foundational and professional knowledge.

Bonar, Buchanan, Fisher, and Wechsler (1996) summarize these concepts. *Foundational* knowledge includes basic concepts and the substance of a traditional discipline. *Professional* knowledge includes skills in vocationally oriented fields such as medicine, business, journalism, and law. *Socially responsive* knowledge includes fostering a sense of responsibility to others in a community through a commitment to community problem solving. In this paper we rely on these distinctions to describe service-learning as an alternative pedagogy that integrates the three kinds of knowledge and knowledge-generation processes.

By providing an observable service to the community while enhancing the academic curriculum, service-learning can mediate between current demands and a revised definition of institutional goals that includes producing citizens who are aware of and, it is hoped, committed to civic responsibility. Thus, integration of service-learning into the curriculum potentially provides higher education, and the discipline of communication in particular, with evidence of relevance and accountability consistent with public demands.

## Service-Learning and Communication

The rationale for service-learning is particularly strong in communication. Caught between public pressures to develop skills (professional knowledge) and academic pressures to function as a research discipline (foundational knowledge), communication curricula are often mixed. As a result, the discipline experiences tension between public and academic demands. Service-learning transforms this tension by focusing on communication as it functions in multiple ways and at multiple levels to foster civic responsibility (socially responsive knowledge). Communication is ideally situated to foster in students socially responsive knowledge. Service-learning allows students to combine foundational knowledge with professional knowledge in order to provide quality service to the community, thus producing socially responsive knowledge. In other words, students may provide service to the community in the form of skills that are richly grounded in theory. This may occur in the media as well as within interpersonal interaction in dyads, groups, organizations, and public arenas.

Nearly a decade ago we began to experiment with service-learning as the University of Utah provided information and resources for individual professors to develop service-learning courses. However, after experimenting with individual courses we recognized that a sustained, long-term commitment to service-learning was needed. When the Bennion Center invited proposals for institutionalizing service-learning, we worked closely with it to bring about such curricular integration.

## Institutionalization of Communication Research

We institutionalized service-learning in our curriculum as one means of redefining our goals in ways compatible with the mission of a traditional research institution, a definition of communication as an applied discipline, and current demands for relevance and accountability. Although any course at the University of Utah may include a service-learning component, institutionalization here is evidenced by a course's formally receiving a service-learning designation in the university catalogue, and requires that the course receive such a designation every term regardless of the particular instructor. In our case, we institutionalized service-learning in a required undergraduate research methods course, Communication Research.

Our goal was to broaden student conceptions of knowledge construction. Specifically, we wanted to change communication students' perceptions of research as abstract, nonpractical foundational knowledge to a view of such knowledge as essential in generating socially meaningful, applied professional knowledge. However, such curricular changes are not without financial cost. Thus, we sought means to effect these changes.

First, we consulted with the Bennion Center staff. All eight faculty members who teach the course met with center representatives to discuss the possibility of institutionalizing service-learning in Communication Research. A consensus emerged to pursue both service-learning and the resources needed to help with the transition. Second, we submitted a proposal to the Bennion Center's institutionalization initiative grant program and the center provided a small grant. With this combined commitment we were able to procure additional funding from our college dean. Third, we decided to use the monies obtained to fund graduate teaching assistants who were trained in the service-learning pedagogy. This was a particularly important need, as the faculty teaching Communication Research were novices in that pedagogy. Specifically, these graduate students would provide expertise in assessing socially responsive knowledge derived from the course, in establishing community linkages, and in facilitating service reflection activities.

In the winter and spring of 1996 several students agreed to participate in service-learning projects. One group agreed to conduct research for a large nonprofit organization that provides food to 212 distribution sites throughout the state. Students conducted on-site surveys designed to assess organization-site communication and the adequacy of each site's facilities. They investigated the correlation between the amount of food provided by the organization to each site and the total amount of food provided by each site to its clients. Another project tested receiver perceptions of a nonprofit organization's newsletter and made recommendations on message construction for the newsletter. The quality of the projects and positive student reactions to the course confirmed our interest in institutionalizing the course.

Communication Research was institutionalized in the fall of 1996. Students evaluated listener preferences for a public radio station. The entire class worked in independent groups that investigated various facets of programming including programming variety and fund drive pieces through focus groups, surveys, and minute-by-minute responses to messages.

During the following term, the class undertook several projects. One group worked with a local community action program to assess the feasibility of cooperative ownership of a mobile home park. Students surveyed tenants to determine interest and perceptions of owning part of the park. A second group worked with the American Cancer Society. It conducted focus groups with people from the cancer community in order to determine the extent of existing services, needs, and interest in support groups for cancer survivors' children. A third group worked with an agency concerned with homeless shelter providers. Students collected and analyzed data on the correlations among a decrease in federal funding, an increase in replacement funds from the state and the private sector, and actual levels of service provided by shelters. The last group investigated demographic characteristics of patrons at a local nonprofit garden and arboretum. The agency suspected it attracted a narrow spectrum of the population. It wanted to be an asset to the community as a whole, and demographic information assisted it in targeting its marketing messages. Subsequent classes have completed similar projects.

The institutionalization of service-learning in Communication Research and the early success of class projects have led to a surprising and exciting enhancement of the students' research experience and the service they provide to the community. Our graduate student service-learning teaching assistants have expanded the service Communication Research provides by coordinating research projects and their results with other service-learning courses offered by the department. For example, students who worked with a nonprofit organization conducted needs assessment surveys as these related to fundraising messages and public relations. The following term, students in a public relations class used the research to plan a public relations campaign while students in a corporate video class used the research to produce a video for the organization. As a result we can offer agencies research services during one term and assistance in implementing the research findings in subsequent terms, thus providing a more comprehensive and lasting service to the community.

## Assessment of Service Effectiveness and Student Reflections

Assessment of the projects is conducted on two levels: assessment of service effectiveness and reflection-based reports of student learning. Communication Research is unique in that assessment of service effectiveness is accomplished through established, objective criteria. That is, the end product of the service is a research report delivered to the agency. This report is evaluated according to traditional, widely accepted standards of what constitutes quality research.

Our strategy for student reflections involves written responses to reflection questions designed to assess affective, cognitive, and behavioral learning throughout the quarter. First, student journals include reactions to an article on service-learning (e.g., Parsons 1996). Students explain their understanding of, and expectations for, service-learning in the class. Later, students reflect on perceived links among the agency, its needs, and the material they are learning in class. They consider what kind of service they provide and why it is needed. Then students discuss issues or problems they are finding in their service area and analyze how research techniques may be used to help address these issues. Finally, at the end of the semester, students assess their progress and project in relation to what they have learned in class and how their service experiences impact them personally.

We are very enthusiastic about immediate student responses to this new approach. Traditional foundational knowledge seems far more interesting to students when it is combined directly with applied professional and socially responsive knowledge. Moreover, student reflections indicate that they internalize the importance of civic responsibility when they have the opportunity to engage in meaningful civic projects. Two reflections from student journals best illustrate this internalization. In response to a service-learning article one student wrote:

> I understand both the theoretical and practical meaning of poverty, having studied it and experienced it. The lofty language in the article — democracy, altruism, experiential learning — doesn't mean much to a person who can't get warm at night once the fire in the wood stove's gone out. It's not important for me to wrap [myself] up in self-congratulatory musing about how I'm helping my fellow human beings in ways they can't help themselves. It is important for me to do something. It's the whole reason I'm in journalism.

The second reflection illustrates connections linking the agency, its needs, and the course material:

> [The agency] is an organization dedicated to helping those less fortunate. Their goal is to try and get people on their feet and into a position of independence. It takes compassion to fulfill this goal. But along with this compassionate side of the agency there also has to be a more clinical side. Research has to be done to discover if the ideas are practical. Before [agency] implements policy they need to be sure that its policy will serve all interests. That's where research methods fit in.

Clearly, the value of service research is far more immediately evident than is that of basic research. However, service-learning raises different pedagogical and ethical issues than do other, more traditional approaches.

## Pedagogical and Ethical Considerations

Because service-learning includes socially responsive knowledge, it involves creating an experience that enables a student to participate responsibly and to reflect on that participation rather than to locate himself/herself as an observer. Service-learning, when used to teach research, requires several adaptations. First, although the methods remain constant, the research enterprise is chosen more for its role in serving society through socially responsive knowledge and less for its role in creating basic knowledge. We have historically taught students the logic of planned, systematic, social scientific inquiry; the methods involved in such inquiry; and how to implement logic and methods through a research project. We have positioned research in the scientific arena of creating new knowledge for the purpose of contributing to our understanding of human communication behavior. With service-learning, we reposition research as it is related to solving social problems and contributing to the formation of social policy. From a pedagogical standpoint, then, research and service are combined. Research is evaluated partially for its value in providing useful service. The service recipient, the teacher, and the learners/researchers together create such projects. The conceptualization and evaluation shift from a neutral scientific position to an engaged and applied position. A concomitant shift in the kinds of questions that are asked and the uses to which the results are put is thereby implied. Second, service-learning includes reflexivity as a basic component. Linkages among course content, individual participation in research, civil society, and individual students' roles as citizens are probed. As a result, the total class time devoted to learning traditional research epistemology and practice is reduced. Third, research occurs in the community and is connected to concrete, articulated community needs. This enables students to understand research as it is meaningful to clients and as it is used as a basis for decision making and planning. Fourth, service-learning entails creating partnerships with the community. These partnerships frequently entail multiple projects across academic courses and terms.

After many terms we have found that several changes have occurred in the way the course is taught. Historically, we emphasized research logic prior to the introduction of specific methodological tools. However, because service projects require additional coordination, we introduce methodological tools earlier in the term. In other words, we have to some extent changed from a pedagogy that first emphasizes the logic of research followed by an emphasis on practice to a pedagogy that emphasizes practice first and its logic later in the term. Second, we create time and assignments for reflection in order to facilitate the pedagogical linkage of learning, research, and service. The course now includes a substantial examination of the moral and social uses to which research is put as well as the ethical implications of research questions and the accompanying dissemination of research results. Third, the logistics involved in working with an external partner need to be considered. The project must be planned so that the course goals are accomplished *and* the partner's needs are met. This requires careful coordination. The final written report is tailored to the audience and, when possible, delivered orally to the partner.

An increased sensitivity to teaching and research ethics is also required. In general, this has meant more careful focus on the pragmatic ethics of research. However, the actual kinds of ethical concerns we face have changed as a result of incorporating service-learning. Previously, we considered issues such as the treatment of research subjects, the funding of research, and the uses to which results could be put. With service-learning, the initial purposes of projects and the intended benefits for particular audiences are far more evident and immediate. This ethical dimension of research, then, takes front stage when research is taught as service-learning. Students can readily see and consider the practical ends to which research is directed. The value questions that are often implicit in traditional research are more explicit in service research. Therefore, conflicts between students' personal values and assigned research projects could be more obvious than in the traditional course. Typically, the research projects we engage in have been designed to benefit such fairly noncontroversial clients as the homeless, a local arboretum, the poor, the American Cancer Society, the Easter Seal Society, the Ronald McDonald House, an emergency management agency, the Salvation Army, and a nonprofit radio station. However, by focusing on explicit needs, we may also encounter situations where the benefits and/or beneficiaries contradict some students' values. Or, we may find that the results of some projects could be used to make policy decisions that are considered harmful to groups such as the poor or homeless.

Thus, when possible, we include project alternatives. As Parsons (1996) notes, participating in the solving of a civic need does not automatically develop civic responsibility and sound moral values in a student. Regardless of how service-learning is presented and conducted, some students may perceive "learning by doing" as "learning *and* doing" what a particular instructor values. We attempt to avoid such a perception by offering students several options. Students either have a range of service projects from which to choose, or they may choose to engage in a traditional research project instead of a service project. However, the service-learning option remains quite popular — as evidenced by the overwhelming majority of students who continue to choose it.

Universities are often criticized for escalating costs, providing private benefits with public funding, being out of touch with the publics they serve, and being overly esoteric. The mission of Research-I universities compounds these criticisms because it clearly considers research a central operation. Service research is one potential means of addressing these criticisms.

## References

Altman, I. (1996). "Higher Education and Psychology in the Millennium." *American Psychologist* 54:371-378.

Bonar, L., R. Buchanan, I. Fisher, and A. Wechsler. (1996). *Service-Learning in the Curriculum: A Faculty Guide to Course Development.* Salt Lake City, UT: University of Utah.

Boyer, E., and M. Hechinger (1981). *Higher Learning in the Nation's Service.* New York, NY: Carnegie Foundation for the Advancement of Teaching.

Parsons, C. (1996). *Serving to Learn, Learning to Serve: Civics and Service From A to Z.* Thousand Oaks, CA: Corwin Press.

# Service-Learning at the Graduate Level

by Sally Perkins, Virginia Kidd, and Gerri Smith

Using a service-learning approach at the graduate level is both fruitful and challenging. Graduate students are more advanced than undergraduates and typically have more to offer in service; at the same time, graduate work inherently involves a higher level of theoretical content that service-learning does not automatically foster. This was the challenge we faced using the service-learning model to teach a master's level course, Assessing Communication Behaviors in Organizations, in the Department of Communication Studies. The course was designed to give students an opportunity to relate and apply communication theory to experiences in community service.

The three authors taught this class together, using a team-teaching approach. The idea for the class grew out of our separate but parallel experiences. During the two years preceding the course, each of us had engaged in fieldwork that included community service. We each independently had reached a common conclusion: that field experience was a powerful learning tool that illuminated readings and invigorated our interests, a tool we wanted to share with students. Thus, we set out to create a learning situation that would replicate that experience. We wanted our students to observe organizational communication firsthand, to be in situations where they could systematically recognize, and think critically about, the application of material that they had studied during their graduate education in communication.

Our course goals reflected that desire. Students would:
1. Become familiar with the concept of service-learning.
2. Provide a service to a community group or organization.
3. Become familiar with research in an area relevant to the service they were performing and/or the agency they were working with.
4. Synthesize theory and practice.
5. Become familiar with applied communication research.
6. Explore qualitative methods.
7. Engage in the study of communication in "bona fide" settings.
8. Learn about writing for both academic and nonacademic audiences.
9. Reflect on observations in a systematic matter.
10. Learn how to become ongoing learners.

The class was made up of nine students at different levels of graduate work, three of whom were "reentry" students returning to seek an advanced degree after establishing a career. All were pursuing master's degrees. We met twice a week for an hour and a half each time.

Because this course was at the graduate level, we presumed a degree of content knowledge about communication and therefore concentrated our readings on service-learning, on methodological issues revolving around qualitative research, and on varying writing formats for presenting information. We also wanted students to learn from one another, so we scheduled regular presentations in which they shared information about their service-learning sites and connected the class with a common email list.

Although we suggested service site possibilities, we allowed students to select their own. The final site selections and duties reflected a range of opportunities. One student helped the Nature Conservancy re-create photographic images lost in a fire; one served in a homeless women's shelter; one worked with the elderly in a nursing home; two worked together to put on workshops at a Campfire Boys and Girls teen conference; one helped the Society for the Blind create an identity through consistent brochure design and copy; two worked with an organization that had received a grant to unite multiple community groups to improve health care; and one worked with the Women's Wisdom Project, which helps abused women recover through art.

The team-teaching approach we used demanded an overload in teaching assignments, but allowed for a unique interactive teaching situation. Because the class was experimental from the outset, we kept our own field notes about it. Moreover, we videotaped some class sessions and audiotaped a final session of commentary from students at a potluck following the last class.

## Assignments and Integration of Service With Learning

Assignments were designed to help students make explicit ties between their service experiences and course content. Course readings were chosen to illustrate applied and field communication research. Individual student writing assignments were designed to help students make connections between communication theory/research and students' service-learning experiences.

The course content focused on diverse examples of applied qualitative communication research. The explicit ties made in class between course content and service featured applied and field research. For each class period, students were expected to complete assigned readings and prepare a written reading log in which they responded to thought questions posed about the readings. Students read John and Lyn Lofland's *Analyzing Social Settings* (1995) to learn techniques of qualitative research, specifically strategies for observational data collection, recording, and analysis. While learning about observational methods, students read essays reporting the results of this type of research, such as Adelman and Frey's report on their observations of an AIDS residential facility, published in *Group Communication in Context* (1994). They also read examples of applied communication research studies, many of which came from the *Journal of Applied Communication Research.*

Once students had collected most of their data, we asked them to examine alternative methods of reporting what they had analyzed. They read essays about writing and examples of different writing styles. They especially enjoyed a reading from Anne Lamott's *Bird by Bird: Some Instructions on Writing and Life* (1994), a selection from Tracy Kidder's creative nonfiction work *Among Schoolchildren* (1990), and Thomas Benson's "Another Shooting in Cowtown" (1981). The different essays challenged them to consider a range of styles, from personal to traditionally academic.

To help students apply the course content on qualitative research to their service experiences, we required them to keep journals in which they collected field notes. Simultaneously, we asked them to record their personal reflections. We encouraged students to divide each page in their journal into two columns, recording descriptive field notes in one column and personal reflections in the other. The "reflective" section of the journal assignment asked students to consider their experiences personally, recording their feelings, impressions, and initial inferences and questions. We hoped that dividing the page would help them distinguish empirical data from personal perceptions and feelings. Although many did not use the column strategy literally, they did include both sorts of observations in their journals (some more thoroughly than others).

In addition to the readings, reading logs, and journals, the students' primary task was to develop a research question(s) to pursue through their service organization, and then to conduct a qualitative study in the organization to answer that question. Through this project, individuals connected service experiences to communication theory and/or research. In the third week of the semester, they presented orally and in writing a detailed proposal for conducting research in their service organization. For this proposal, students were asked to identify the community groups with whom they were working, explain what work they would be doing, explain how they intended to relate their observations of the organization to the study of communication, identify literature they needed to read, describe the specific methodology they intended to use, and describe what they would produce in their final paper.

To assist students in making connections between their service experiences and communication literature, we required each to produce an annotated bibliography of relevant research on the communication issue at hand, examples of similar research, and studies of the type of organization in which the fieldwork took place. Students turned in installments of their bibliography when they gave their two oral progress reports. These oral reports provided them with an opportunity to talk through their discoveries and explain any roadblocks they faced in identifying appropriate literature. It also allowed peers and instructors to help them clarify the focus of their research and identify relevant literature to explore. At the end of the semester, students presented orally and in writing a final report in which they analyzed the data they collected and drew conclusions about both the communications in their service organization and the applicability of communication theory in the field.

Ultimately, the service orientation of the experience led many students to question the place of the researcher in the process of collecting, analyzing, and reporting about qualitative data because they saw the influence of their personal feelings and perceptions on their data. When they read various examples of writing styles, some including the author's voice and others excluding it, they were challenged to think through the implications of such choices in their own writing.

The final reports differed considerably. Some were highly narrative and personal while others were impersonal and traditional. Some students concentrated on the relationships between their field observations and their personal experiences. Others wrote strictly traditional research reports based on their data, leaving out personal experiences and feelings. Students also applied vastly different lines of communication theory and research, ranging from small group theory, to research on communication and the aging, to Burkean theory.

One student, for example, volunteered her time in a nursing home. As she observed the interactions between residents and staff, as well as her own interactions with residents, she noticed patterns of invasion into the residents' personal space. She then began reading existing literature on communication and the elderly, aging, and nursing home life. Her own observations led her to argue the thesis that "verbal and nonverbal messages sent by the physical environment and staff promote homogenization and dependent behavior" rather than individualism and autonomy in the residents. Her analysis critiqued the ways in which staff communication created these conditions to achieve organizational efficiency.

Another student volunteered at the local Society for the Blind. Because he had skills in graphic design, the organization's leaders assigned him the task of redesigning their brochures. The existing brochures, designed to present different branches of the Society to different audiences, lacked coherence. Thus, the student redesigned and standardized the brochures by creating consistent logos, graphics, and text. The process led him to observe that the organization lacked a clear identity. In his final paper he used

Burkean theory to ground his choices in redesigning the brochures, explaining how he altered the language, visual images, and tone to create an organizational identity that would help unify the organization and better appeal to its audiences.

## Benefits of the Service-Learning Approach

At the end of the semester, we asked students to complete a short questionnaire regarding their experience in the service-learning course. We found that while there were some problems, generally they benefited in ways that differed from their experiences in traditional graduate courses. Moreover we, as instructors, found the process enriching and advantageous.

Linking course assignments and class discussions to actual organizational involvement was academically beneficial. Students had the opportunity to relate course content to their service-learning sites in particularly meaningful ways. In response to the questionnaire, one student wrote, "Through my service-learning I was able to be very involved and to identify with the organization. It allowed me to have insights in interpreting the data that I would not have had through a less involved perspective." Another student found the opportunity to engage in a project that "really mattered" even more compelling:

> I have spent the last year of graduate school loudly protesting academe's separation from the community as seen in research projects completed for the benefit of the researcher rather than for the community. Service-learning does a great deal to begin bridging the gap between academe and the community.

Since the students were required to provide a service to their organizational settings, rather than simply to engage in data collection, most of them were regularly immersed in daily organizational activities, which ultimately enabled them to make observations as "insiders" or as real organizational members. Academically, these observations provided a rich source of data both for their writing and for classroom discussions.

Students benefited from mutual support. Since they were required to give oral "progress reports" throughout the semester, they became keenly aware of their peers' service-learning sites, the challenges encountered, and the focus of individual projects. In turn, they became supportive of one another's work and emotional responses. In one case, for example, when a student reported feeling stress at her task, another replied, "I feel bad for you. I know what it is to be stressed. I'm the Stress Queen." Another added, "Remember we're doing service. [Now] we're thinking about our grade, so we focus on our report but no matter what we focus on, we're giving service."

Some of the students chose to work in teams of two, where peer support and cooperation was experienced even more acutely.

While at times a cause for student anxiety and uncertainty, service-learning stretched student minds in ways that went beyond their normal academic experiences. These mind-stretching experiences occurred on several levels. First, the service-learning requirement forced students to carefully consider where and in what ways they could best serve the community. Although some students thought first about convenience, their other commitments, and how most easily to fulfill the requirement, the majority approached their service delivery in very thoughtful and personally meaningful ways. Second, the course readings exposed students to nontraditional approaches to research and writing. Moreover, these readings pushed them to reflect on their service-learning sites and research projects. One of the unanticipated foci for several class discussions centered on the process of writing. Students struggled with the notion of voice and style in their writing, questioning whether to write from their own perspective, from an organizational member's perspective, or even from the perspective of the silent walls of the service-learning site. Whereas in most graduate seminars the final written product consists of a very traditional research paper, the papers here took a variety of approaches. Furthermore, regardless of the form the final papers took, students were exposed to alternative ways of knowing and modes of expression. They read work by established scholars who have adopted a more creative approach in their writing, and they shared their own work with each other, demonstrating a willingness to move into an arena that students considered risky, exciting, and new.

By far the most potent benefit for students was their increased awareness of and exposure to some of the social problems and issues facing our communities. The power of such learning was heightened when students were working in settings that had personal relevance and offered opportunities for reflection and personal growth. The student who worked in an organization where creative arts were used to empower disadvantaged and homeless women had a particularly powerful experience:

*In order to understand the organization I took the classes and personally benefited by feeling the expansion and power of my own creativity. My most recent realization is that I now have a different view of poor women. My research taught me that they are usually subject to harsh and stereotypical judgments. While I do not think I judged them harshly, I had no idea I would find the women thoughtful, articulate, and friendly. The women I met have been working very hard on themselves to improve their lives and it shows.*

This student continues to volunteer for the organization and currently serves on the board of directors.

Such intensity of personal growth was further articulated by a student who provided service in a homeless shelter for women:

> There were times, especially during my first weeks at the shelter, that I would drive home upset and distraught. I was horrified and repulsed at the levels of social and economic deprivation that I was witnessing. I spent a lot of time asking myself why I had been so blissfully unaware of these problems previously. In the end, I realized that these experiences were necessary. Talking to the women and hearing their stories has raised my awareness in a way that would be impossible to experience without having served them.

Finally, one student created a visual image for his readers in a short narrative on his feelings during his first meeting with an organization that serves the visually impaired. He articulated how a course requirement can turn into a self-reflective and personally revealing activity:

> The tiny lobby smells like a junior high cafeteria, the overwhelming odor of cheap food so thick you could gag on it. Nearby, two tables of elderly people, half-blind, half-sighted, sit and spoon brown mush into their mouths as a man talks about the beauty of cooking for yourself with a Braille microwave. Jeannie cuts through the miasma, pleasant and unperturbed, her hand extended in greeting about forty-five degrees south from where I am standing. Our relationship had been established by two phone conversations, so it is a mild shock to discover that she is blind. I take two side steps, place my hand in hers, and do my best to direct my gaze at her eyes as I greet her. I am asked why I am here. In truth, I don't know. I blurt out something. . . . Several seconds of silence pass. I fear I have said something taboo in the world of serving the blind. I'm beginning to get worried. I had not expected such scrutiny, thinking they would take whoever they could get. I actually begin to sweat and for the first time I fear that I may not get this gig.

In each of these examples, students challenged their preconceived notions by engaging in self-reflection and ultimately experienced personal growth as a result of their service-learning activities. The classroom discussions and activities further reinforced, and at times intensified, their personal and community revelations.

Finally, teaching the service-learning course provided a unique and intense opportunity for personal and professional growth for us. We were able to experiment with service-learning in the classroom, a technique on the cutting edge in higher education. Further, we explored our own preconceived ideas about students' abilities and desires to engage in a different, nontraditional learning environment. Finally, through our ongoing discussions and reflections, we were encouraged to develop a service-learning course at the undergraduate level with 50 students. By working in a cooperative and trusted team environment, we planted new seeds. Fresh ideas continue to bloom as we engage in an ongoing exploration of alternative forms of teaching and learning and continue to explore service-learning in other contexts.

## Problems Encountered

Despite the positive outcomes of this class, we encountered a number of problems teaching via the service-learning process. First, students had difficulty with two intellectual tasks: (1) some displayed an excellent grasp of detail in data collection and observation but did not take the next step of tying these observations back to communication constructs; and (2) some failed to distinguish between personal reflection and service-site observations. These problems were reflected in field notes and journals, in class discussion, and, in some cases, in final papers. Even after a semester of discussion about the issues, some students made very weak associations between what they observed and what research or theory about such occurrences might note. In weaker papers, those associations seemed forced, as if students had written their observations first and then flailed about for a theoretical tie-in. The stronger papers interwove such literature with observations to create convincing interpretations of the data.

Second, site selection needed coordination with pedagogical goals. Because students in this class were expected to study organizational communication behavior through field research methods, they needed a service site where they could observe ongoing communication. Stronger analytical work seemed to emerge from sites where students could make regular, ongoing observations about communication as it occurred in meetings, conversations, memos, and nonverbal displays. Students contributing service at sites where they worked alone and/or in brief spurts at varying intervals were less successful at producing insight into communication practices. For example, the student who photographed scenes for the Nature Conservancy engaged in somewhat isolated work. While the placement allowed him to contribute lovely images for use by the Nature Conservancy, it did little to illuminate communication behaviors among organizational members. In a second case, a team of two that participated in a youth conference led workshops on team-building that were highly successful. However, much of the planning for these workshops was between the two students alone, making it difficult for them to observe the organization's recurring communication patterns.

Third, learning abstract concepts from applied fieldwork demands a certain level of maturity. Some of the less mature students seemed to interpret their work as simply completing their service-learning project and keeping field notes of what they saw, rather than conceiving of the service-learning project as a vehicle for understanding concepts of communication. In the team-building example, for instance, the two students could have expanded their observations greatly by attending optional meetings that did not directly affect their section of the conference but related to the conference as a whole. They chose not to. Two other students in a similar context chose to attend a variety of meetings and gained greater insight into the communication network of the organization with which they worked.

Fourth, student interests changed the focus of the class. Students did not define the class in the same way we did, nor did the class energy flow into the areas we expected. To us this was a class on gaining insights into how theories of communication explained or failed to explain actual communication situations. To many of the students it became a class in writing up qualitative research. As students kept notes on their fieldwork and read other authors who had written about their experiences in applied communication, a very large percentage of the class grew much more interested in these authors' writing styles than their substantive contributions. The issue of writing grew to absorb students in their discussions, their informal interactions, their email exchanges, and their final comments about the class.

We were both perplexed and delighted by this. Discussions with students as to what led to this shift generated several tentative conclusions. First, graduate students, who had to this point in their academic careers read extensively both theoretical material and research results, and who had perceived the forms of such material to be the correct writing format for advanced work, reveled in the freedom to write in less constraining forms. The challenge of re-creating a site they had observed and wanted to share verbally excited them. At the same time, the necessity of threading vivid, detailed examples through a discursive, conceptual frame seemed intimidating. This tension generated much dialogue.

Second, they had something to say. Their papers were genuine expressions of their own experiences, not abstract reports based solely on reviews of literature that cited work by others. Their ability to convey experiences grew in significance to them as the importance of their experiences grew.

And third, we had inadvertently encouraged this interest through readings that described ways to write up fieldwork, posed questions about creative nonfiction as distinguished from scholarly work, focused on how different audiences demand different authorial stances, and explicitly discussed the writing process.

# Ethical Considerations

An additional set of problems grew from ethical concerns. First, as students became immersed in their service-learning activities, they began to question the degree to which they should be open about the "study" part of their projects. That is, since each student was required to complete a research project and to record field notes, the ethics of how much to tell and how much not to tell people at the service site became a topic for classroom discussion. This issue was handled in a variety of ways depending on the service-learning site and its organizational members. Some of the students were never questioned regarding a potential writing project. Some students were asked to utilize their expertise in communication to provide feedback to the organization, and some students made their supervisors aware that they would be writing a paper about the organizational communication while guaranteeing confidentiality to organizational members. This issue of confidentiality was raised further as students learned personal life stories of their organization's clients and agreed to protect the confidentiality of these clients when discussing them during class.

A second concern surrounded the perceived need of some students to provide a "final report" to their service-learning organization. Students explored whether their final papers should be shared or if a shortened "executive summary" would be more beneficial and appropriate, since some revealing data would likely surface in the final analysis. Again, individual situations and organizational settings were taken into consideration as we considered the ethical implications of these decisions. Students were discouraged from providing materials that would potentially have any negative impact on organizational members or on the organization itself.

Finally, students were concerned about the ethics of attempting to publish or publicly present their final products. Again, we provided ethical guidelines stressing the importance of confidentiality.

# Conclusion

For many students graduate education is distant from their lived experiences. The personal often is severed from the professional in order to train graduate students to become "professionals in the field." Whereas undergraduate literature such as textbooks makes explicit references to students' daily lives, graduate literature, based largely on primary sources, makes few such references. Many graduate students find this transition from secondary to primary sources daunting and disappointing. The service-learning experience provides a useful bridge for graduate students, helping them merge their personal growth with their professional growth. Service-learning itself is not the end of graduate education, but it is a powerful tool.

## References

Adelman, M.B., and L.R. Frey. (1994). "The Pilgrim Must Embark: Creating and Sustaining Community in a Residential Facility for People With AIDS." In *Group Communication in Context*. Edited by L.R. Frey, pp. 3-22. Hillsdale, NJ: Lawrence Erlbaum.

Benson, T. (1981). "Another Shooting in Cowtown." *Quarterly Journal of Speech* 67:347-406.

Kidder, T. (1990). *Among Schoolchildren*. New York, NY: Avon.

Lamott, A. (1994). *Bird by Bird: Some Instructions on Writing and Life*. New York, NY: Pantheon.

Lofland, J., and L.H. Lofland. (1995). *Analyzing Social Settings: A Guide to Qualitative Observation and Analysis*. 3rd ed. Belmont, CA: Wadsworth.

# Faculty Incentives:
## A Necessity for Integrating Service-Learning

by Kathleen H. Stacey and Chris Wood Foreman

For service-learning initiatives to be successful on college campuses, there must be a shared understanding of what service-learning is and a commitment by at least some faculty to use it as a teaching methodology. Faculty are ultimately responsible for providing service-learning experiences for students, and developing and maintaining a faculty commitment to do so is an issue for many colleges and universities. Studies have looked at faculty involvement and development from two perspectives: (1) what barriers exist that keep faculty from using service-learning; and (2) what incentives could be offered to encourage faculty to develop and maintain service-learning courses? We will first examine the barriers.

To incorporate a service-learning experience within a course, faculty must reconceptualize their current teaching methodologies and use nontraditional teaching methods. Seeman (1990) observes that "faculty are used to beginning with their own notes. We need to help them go beyond the old epistemological heritage and pedagogy, to be comfortable with the nontraditional style of going from student experiences to analysis and on to new generalizations" (163). This prospect is scary for many faculty who like to be in total control of the classroom. They must change from being the sole providers of information to becoming facilitators in a process in which students are also responsible for generating learning. For some faculty, using service-learning raises a series of personal dilemmas or barriers that include: (1) surrendering sole control of the teaching-learning process, (2) teaching in settings requiring different pedagogical skills, and (3) responding to students rather than presenting prepackaged academic material (Chesler 1993: 32).

In addition to initial fears regarding control and reconceptualization, faculty also have pedagogical and professional concerns that include: apprehension about academic quality, lack of familiarity with techniques for assessing experiential learning, confusion about how experiential learning helps students test course concepts, the belief that application is only useful when it follows theory, limitations of the 50-minute course, fear of the world outside the campus, and concern whether involvement in experiential education helps with tenure, promotion, and merit increases (Kendall et al. 1990).

Many of the barriers or reservations that faculty have about using service-learning stem from an unfamiliarity with it. Some faculty are reluctant to use it because they are unsure how to implement such an experience for their students, while others are unsure how it will affect the learning process. Many of the barriers discussed here might be overcome if the appropriate incentives were given.

Levine (1994) discusses his experiences with service-learning and what helped lead him to adopt it. He cites the following incentives as being instrumental in this: being asked, receiving financial support in the form of a summer grant that allowed him the time to adapt his course, finding respect for service and service-learning colleagues at other universities, obtaining support to attend conferences and professional meetings related to service-learning, discovering connections between service-learning activities and both scholarship and faculty development, and seeing recognition and rewards given for incorporating service-learning.

Kendall et al. (1990) have identified "21 things to do to increase faculty involvement" in service-learning. These include: organize informal discussion groups, let students speak for the value of service-learning, conduct workshops, give away money and authority, arrange faculty internships, establish a library of resources for faculty about using service-learning methods in courses, and have a summer study group of faculty focusing on service-learning.

The National Center for Service-Learning, ACTION puts faculty incentives into two major categories: (1) time or money and (2) technical assistance. While money may be an effective incentive, for most faculty time is even more attractive. In terms of technical assistance, some useful ideas include providing workshops, logistical support, assistance in finding research populations for study, and help in writing grant applications.

In addition to those incentives that help initially attract faculty to service-learning, the National Center for Service-Learning, ACTION identifies incentives useful in maintaining faculty interest. These include recognition by the institution, the media, and/or the community. Peer recognition is also important. Providing opportunities for faculty who use service-learning to share experiences allows them to energize and support each other. It also gives them the chance to meet faculty from other academic areas.

Hammond (1994) surveyed 250 faculty in the state of Michigan who currently use service-learning to find out why. He discovered that the strongest motivators were curriculum issues; i.e., whatever brings greater relevance to course content, encourages self-directed learning, improves student satisfaction with their education, and/or provides an effective way to present material (24). One university's attempts to increase faculty involvement in service-learning led to our own research project.

# Evolution of a Research Question

In 1994-95, Dale Rice, a special education professor at Eastern Michigan University (EMU), received a federal grant from Learn and Serve America and additional funding from the university to build an infrastructure for service-learning opportunities on campus. During that academic year, the Office of Service-Learning consisted of a project director, two faculty, and two graduate assistants.

To increase faculty involvement with service-learning, the Office of Service-Learning at Eastern Michigan University offered faculty the opportunity to apply for a Service-Learning Faculty Fellowship in the form of a mini-grant or released time. The mini-grant was a monetary honorarium and the released time consisted of one course for both fall and winter terms. In return, selected faculty members were required to attend a weekly seminar during the fall term to learn how to integrate service-learning into one of their courses and were expected to implement the service-learning component during the winter term. During the same term, they were expected to meet every other week to discuss issues and problems that arose during the implementation. Six full-time faculty members were chosen.

During one of the weekly seminars, faculty members discussed the need for faculty incentives. Participants asked themselves whether they would be doing service-learning if they weren't receiving special support. Furthermore, would they continue using service-learning next fall without incentives? This raised interesting issues about why faculty engage in service-learning and what kind of support or incentives are necessary to offset additional time and resource demands. Arguments supporting faculty incentives included:

1. Developing/revising courses and syllabi to incorporate service-learning is challenging work.

2. Training is necessary to help faculty integrate service-learning, and this training is itself time-consuming.

3. Incorporating a service-learning component into a class often requires lengthy coordinating efforts with community agencies.

4. Faculty already feel overworked and overwhelmed by their normal responsibilities; without incentives, they have little motivation to add to their list of obligations.

However, the case *against* providing extra faculty incentives was also considered. Arguments here included:

1. Faculty are expected to be effective classroom instructors, and this expectation includes looking for ways to improve their teaching; therefore, faculty should integrate service-learning as part of their regular teaching responsibilities.

2. Faculty should want to use service-learning to increase their own sense of accomplishment. A job well done should be its own reward.

3. If one rationale for service-learning is to increase civic mindedness, why should faculty need incentives to be civic-minded?

4. Through incorporation of service-learning into their courses, faculty may receive other rewards, such as better relationships with community agencies that might provide job opportunities for their students, positive student experiences that might increase future enrollments, and increased scholarship through papers submitted to conferences and academic journals. Shouldn't these rewards suffice?

This discussion and the issues it raised laid the groundwork for our first research question:

RQ1: *Are faculty incentives a necessity for integrating service-learning?*

# Data Collection

Data collection for this research project came from three sources: (1) discussion notes from a panel presentation at the Second National Gathering of College Educators and Service-Learning; (2) a questionnaire sent to 98 recipients of Learn and Serve grants for the 1995-96 academic year; and (3) a questionnaire administered to the approximately 700 full-time, tenure-track/tenured faculty members at Eastern Michigan University.

## Data Source 1

Intrigued by issues raised among the faculty fellows at EMU, the two authors and one graduate assistant facilitated a panel discussion at the Second National Gathering of College Educators and Service-Learning held in Indianapolis on June 21, 1996. They opened a discussion of the necessity of faculty incentives by raising points on both sides of the issue.

Among the 20 participants at this panel discussion, there emerged no real consensus about whether faculty should receive incentives for integrating service-learning into their courses. On the one hand, most agreed that there should be incentives for faculty "to reward what we value, and value what we reward." On the other hand, there was a general consensus that additional incentives for faculty are not necessary because incorporating new pedagogical tools into the classroom is part of the faculty job description. If service is part of a university's mission statement, then it should also be part of core teaching responsibilities.

We then asked participants to talk about what each of their universities was doing to encourage service-learning. At some universities, no faculty incentives were given (either because there were no funds or because service-learning was simply expected of faculty). At other universities there were multiple forms of faculty incentives, including released time, mini-grants, team teaching, teaching assistant collaborations, and the use of new informational technologies. At universities where some grant money had been received to incorporate service-learning, most provided mini-grants, small annual awards for teaching innovations, and some released time. Universities where additional monies were not available offered either no incentives or incentives in the form of technical and logistical support.

Even though there was no unanimous view as to the necessity of faculty incentives, there was a clear consensus that faculty would have to be motivated in "some way" to get them to adopt service-learning. The discussion prompted the authors to further investigate this issue. We decided that, in addition to our original research question regarding the necessity of faculty incentives, it would also be useful to collect data regarding the best types of incentives to use if incentives are given. This led to our second research question:

RQ2: *What types of incentives would best motivate faculty members to integrate service-learning into their classes?*

## Data Source 2

Questionnaires were sent to the 98 institutions receiving Learn and Serve grants for the 1995-96 academic year. Respondents were asked to respond to the following questions about faculty incentives and the goal(s) of service-learning:

• *In what ways does your college/university administration support service-learning?*

• *To what extent are faculty involved in service-learning?*

• *Does your college/university provide any incentives for faculty members to incorporate service-learning into their courses?*

• *If yes, list the types of incentives. Describe all forms of incentives (e.g., released time, honorarium, mandatory, etc.).*

• *If yes, state reasons why faculty incentives are provided.*

• *If no, state reasons why faculty incentives are not provided.*

• *Based upon your service-learning mission, is service-learning viewed more as an improved teaching methodology or as a means to increase student citizenship? Explain your position.*

Of the 98 questionnaires mailed, six were returned by the post office as undeliverable, three respondents were not campus-based, and 23 respondents answered the questionnaire. Rather than make generalizations that may not be statistically significant, the following are qualitative summary accounts of those 23 responses.

Responses to question one (regarding the level of college/university administration support) ranged from "not very supportive" to "very support- ive because it is part of our mission statement." Most respondents indicated some level of support in the form of monies provided to support service- learning efforts campus-wide.

When asked to what extent faculty were already involved in service- learning, some responded that 10 percent, 15 percent, 25 percent, or even 80 percent of the faculty were involved. One respondent indicated that "faculty have no choice [because they must] learn, grow, and change or they will not have a workload." Another responded that the number of faculty involved is growing; "however, it tends to be among younger, nontenured, or recently tenured faculty." Another responded that "faculty have been reluctant to participate for obvious reasons (too much work, status quo, philosophical opposition)," a response that led us to question again whether incentives were a necessity.

Of the 23 respondents, 14 indicated that incentives for faculty were pro- vided and eight indicated that no incentives were provided.

### Types of Incentives

The question about types of faculty incentives provided generated a number of specific examples. Careful analysis of the responses revealed that specific responses fell within one of four general categories or incentive types: (1) monetary awards, (2) released time, (3) logistical assistance, and (4) tenure/promotion considerations.

*Monetary awards:* Twelve respondents indicated that some form of mini- grant or stipend was given to motivate faculty members. Most mini-grants were in the $500 to $1,000 range and were applicable for such things as con- ference travel, books and publications, software, and videos. One university even provided money for student travel to community sites, as well as to purchase materials and supplies.

*Released time:* Only five of the 23 respondents indicated that faculty released time was provided as an incentive. And all five indicated that the released time was only available for developing a new course. Included in this category was one university that provided a "little more credit for load calculation," amounting to partial released time for piloting a service- learning course.

*Logistical assistance:* Eight universities saw assisting faculty in the devel- opment of service-learning courses as an incentive. Four provided learning seminars and faculty development workshops and one staffed two service-learning trainers to assist faculty in developing syllabi. Two talked specifically about providing technical support and assistance in helping contact agencies, while one other provided undergraduate coordinators to help with logistics.

*Tenure/promotion considerations:* Seven respondents mentioned proposed and pending changes to tenure and promotion guidelines for faculty members where, as one respondent put it, "service-learning is increasingly viewed favorably in the rewards structure." Three indicated that proposals were pending that would support the pedagogy as a significant component of promotion and tenure guidelines.

### Reasons for Incentives

Respondents indicating that some form of faculty incentives was provided were asked to state reasons why. Nine respondents acknowledged that because course development takes additional time, incentives were seen as a way to acknowledge and reward that extra work. Beyond the issue of extra effort, 15 of those responding indicated that incentives were necessary to encourage faculty. As one person put it, "it is hard to challenge the status quo without some incentive." Another noted that "we get more response" when the institution provides incentives to the faculty. Yet another viewed it as "a courtesy that is motivating." And as one respondent noted, since "service-learning is not perceived as important as research," incentives are necessary to enable the work. A final reason given for incentives was that the institution philosophically supports service-learning. As one respondent put it, "if you teach here, you teach service-learning, [and] incentives are a way to show institutional support."

### Why No Incentives

Two primary reasons were given for why there were no faculty incentives: (1) because the administration did not support service-learning, and (2) incentives were not necessary because curriculum development and service were part of the university's mission. Five respondents indicated that no incentives were provided due to lack of institutional support. One noted that "the administration does not see service-learning as central to [the university's] mission." For three others, incentives were not viewed as necessary because, as one respondent put it, "service-learning is an integral part of the university culture, [and] faculty are eager to participate."

This data indicates general support for faculty incentives but doesn't clarify what faculty really want. Data from our third source sheds light on that particular question.

## Data Source 3

To collect additional data about the use of incentives to motivate faculty to incorporate service-learning components into their courses, we sent questionnaires to approximately 700 full-time, tenure-track/tenured faculty members at EMU. This survey on incentives and service-learning asked faculty to indicate whether or not they had ever included service-learning as part of a course they had taught, and if not, would they ever consider doing so. In addition, a list of possible incentives was given and faculty members were asked to rate the incentives as to how important ("very important," "important," "somewhat important," or "not important") they thought each would be in motivating a faculty member to integrate service-learning into a course. The list of incentives included:

- Released time to develop a course that includes service-learning
- Monetary incentive or honorarium
- Graduate assistant to coordinate and monitor students' service activities
- Reduced class size to enable closer interaction with students
- Summer salary supplement to develop a course that incorporates service-learning
- Workshops on how to incorporate service-learning into your teaching
- Increased weight given to teaching and service in promotion, tenure, and salary decisions
- Increased recognition of faculty who provide opportunities for service-learning
- Having your department supportive of service-learning
- Assistance in locating appropriate agencies
- Help with designing a course outline and assignments
- Help with how to evaluate and grade service-learning assignments.

Respondents were also provided with an opportunity to indicate other incentives that might motivate them to include a service-learning component in their course(s).

Seventy-six questionnaires were returned by faculty members at EMU. Of those, 34 percent (26) had included service-learning as part of a course they had taught, and 65 percent (49) indicated they had not. As indicated in Table 1, released time to develop a course that included service-learning was viewed as the most important type of incentive. A closer look reveals that incentives that provide assistance and alleviate time pressures were viewed as more important than incentives that provide additional monies or recognition.

Overall, these results lead us to theorize that faculty view "intrinsic" incentives more favorably than "extrinsic." *Extrinsic* rewards are those that occur apart from the work process, such as salary, benefits, bonuses, and special privileges. *Intrinsic* rewards are more closely related to the work itself, such as a chance to be creative or the challenge of the work. In most cases researchers have found that intrinsic rewards are more effective and longer lasting than extrinsic ones (Guzzo 1979; Pinder 1977). Why, then, when we look back at the data collected from Learn and Serve institutions, was more emphasis placed on providing mini-grants and honorariums (extrinsic rewards) and less given to providing released time and logistical assistance (intrinsic rewards)? It would seem as if the incentives being offered may not have been viewed as sufficiently motivating by faculty. A closer look at the results of our faculty survey further supports this conclusion.

As shown in Table 1 (on the next page), the five most important types of incentives deal less with financial or recognition gains and more with time and logistical issues. Released time is closely followed by assistance in locating agencies, which according to many faculty members is one of the most time-consuming functions involved when integrating service-learning. The third most important incentive, a summer salary supplement, may at first glance seem to fall within the extrinsic reward category. However, at EMU, teaching during the spring and summer semesters is very common, and receiving a summer salary supplement would be the same as having released time from teaching. Having a graduate assistant coordinator and reduced class size are also incentives that would reduce time constraints on faculty members.

The three types of incentives that were viewed as not as important were a monetary incentive/honorarium, increased weight for promotion, and increased recognition of faculty. Each of these incentives is more extrinsic in nature, because it is a reward that lies outside the realm of the creativity of the work itself.

Even more emphasis was placed upon intrinsic incentives (e.g., released time, assistance in locating agencies, and summer salary supplement) when we look only at those faculty members who were not currently incorporating service-learning into their classes but said they would (see Table 2, page 57). Released time was almost unanimously viewed as very important or important, while monetary incentives, increased weight for promotion, and increased recognition were relatively unimportant. Even those faculty members who said they would not consider using service-learning in their classes (see Table 3, page 58) believed that the more important incentives were reduced class size, a graduate assistant coordinator, and released time, rather than increased weight for promotion or increased recognition of faculty.

**Table 1: Ratings of Incentives by Faculty Members (n = 76)**

| Type of incentive | "Very important" or "Important" | "Somewhat important" or "Not important" | No response |
|---|---|---|---|
| Released time | 80% (61) | 19% (14) | 1% (1) |
| Assistance in locating agencies | 72% (55) | 27% (20) | 1% (1) |
| Summer salary supplement | 71% (54) | 28% (21) | 1% (1) |
| Graduate assistant coordinator | 67% (51) | 30% (23) | 3% (2) |
| Reduced class size | 67% (51) | 29% (22) | 4% (3) |
| Service-learning workshops | 63% (48) | 36% (27) | 1% (1) |
| Supportive department | 62% (47) | 35% (27) | 3% (2) |
| Help with how to evaluate | 55% (42) | 42% (32) | 3% (2) |
| Help designing course outline | 50% (38) | 47% (36) | 3% (2) |
| Monetary incentive, honorarium | 42% (32) | 58% (44) | 0% (0) |
| Increased weight for promotion | 42% (32) | 54% (41) | 4% (3) |
| Increased recognition of faculty | 42% (32) | 54% (41) | 4% (3) |

**Table 2: Ratings of Incentives by Faculty Members (not currently using service-learning, but interested) (n = 35)**

| Type of incentive | "Very important" or "Important" | "Somewhat important" or "Not important" | No response |
|---|---|---|---|
| Released time | 91% (32) | 9% (3) | 0% (0) |
| Assistance in locating agencies | 83% (29) | 17% (6) | 0% (0) |
| Summer salary supplement | 83% (29) | 17% (6) | 0% (0) |
| Reduced class size | 77% (27) | 17% (6) | 6% (2) |
| Supportive department | 74% (26) | 23% (8) | 3% (1) |
| Service-learning workshops | 71% (25) | 29% (10) | 0% (0) |
| Help with how to evaluate | 72% (25) | 25% (9) | 3% (1) |
| Graduate assistant coordinator | 63% (22) | 34% (12) | 3% (1) |
| Help designing course outline | 57% (20) | 43% (15) | 0% (0) |
| Monetary incentive, honorarium | 43% (15) | 57% (20) | 0% (0) |
| Increased weight for promotion | 37% (13) | 54% (19) | 9% (3) |
| Increased recognition of faculty | 37% (13) | 57% (20) | 6% (2) |

**Table 3: Ratings of Incentives by Faculty Members (not currently using service-learning, and not interested) (n = 14)**

| Type of incentive | "Very important" or "Important" | "Somewhat important" or "Not important" | No response |
|---|---|---|---|
| Reduced class size | 64% (9) | 29% (4) | 7% (1) |
| Graduate assistant coordinator | 64% (9) | 29% (4) | 7% (1) |
| Released time | 57% (8) | 36% (5) | 7% (1) |
| Assistance in locating agencies | 50% (7) | 43% (6) | 7% (1) |
| Summer salary supplement | 43% (6) | 50% (7) | 7% (1) |
| Service-learning workshops | 43% (6) | 50% (7) | 7% (1) |
| Monetary incentive, honorarium | 36% (5) | 57% (8) | 7% (1) |
| Help designing course outline | 29% (4) | 64% (9) | 7% (1) |
| Help with how to evaluate | 29% (4) | 64% (9) | 7% (1) |
| Increased weight for promotion | 21% (3) | 72% (10) | 7% (1) |
| Supportive department | 14% (2) | 79% (11) | 7% (1) |
| Increased recognition of faculty | 14% (2) | 79% (11) | 7% (1) |

# Discussion

Are faculty incentives necessary for integrating service-learning? According to faculty members at EMU, the answer to that question is a resounding "Yes," and might best be summed up by this response from one faculty member: "Time and assistance are the two most important factors to me. I know I could improve what I am already doing." The most important question, however, might be our second research question: What types of incentives would *best* motivate faculty members to integrate service-learning into their classes? According to our findings, the incentives viewed most favorably by faculty members (i.e., released time, graduate assistance) are not those most typically provided (i.e., mini-grants and honorariums). After the first year of awarding faculty fellowships at EMU, the Office of Service-Learning made two major changes to the incentives it offered faculty. First, mini-grants were no longer offered because very few faculty chose that option, and those who did wished that they had taken released time instead. Second, the released time granted was reduced from two semesters to one. It was decided that only one semester was needed to train faculty on how to integrate service-learning into a course and that in this way the office could offer 12 faculty fellowships a year instead of only six.

Our findings lead to several other research questions worth pursuing: Among colleges and institutions that have service-learning missions, is service-learning viewed more as an improved teaching methodology or as a means to increase student citizenship? If increased student citizenship is the primary goal, is providing faculty with incentives counterproductive to this goal? Do those faculty who find more motivation in intrinsic types of incentives see the primary purpose of service-learning as internalizing citizenship?

We suggest the pursuit of these and other lines of inquiry may better position the service-learning community in its dual pursuits of improved teaching *and* increased citizenship.

### References

Chesler, M.A. (1993). "Community Service-Learning as Innovation in the University." In *Praxis I: A Faculty Casebook on Community Service-Learning.* Edited by J. Howard, pp. 27-40. Ann Arbor, MI: OCSL Press, University of Michigan.

"Carrots for Faculty." (1990). In *Combining Service and Learning: A Resource Book for Community and Public Service, Volume II.* Edited by J. Kendall and Associates, pp. 137-163. Raleigh, NC: National Society for Experiential Education.

Guzzo, R.A. (1979). "Types of Rewards, Cognitions, and Work Motivation." *Academy of Management Review* 4:75-86.

Hammond, C. (1994). "Integrating Service and Academic Study: Faculty Motivation and Satisfaction in Michigan Higher Education." *Michigan Journal of Community Service-Learning* 1(1): 21-28.

Kendall, J., J. Duley, T. Little, J. Permaul, and S. Rubin. (1990). "Increasing Faculty Involvement." In *Combining Service and Learning: A Resource Book for Community and Public Service, Volume II.* Edited by J. Kendall and Associates, pp. 137-163. Raleigh, NC: National Society for Experiential Education.

Levine, M.A. (1994). "Seven Steps to Getting Faculty Involved in Service-Learning: How a Traditional Faculty Member Came to Teach a Course on 'Volunteerism, Community, and Citizenship'." *Michigan Journal of Community Service-Learning* 1(1): 110-114.

Pinder, C.C. (1977). "Concerning the Application of Human Motivation Theories in Organizational Settings." *Academy of Management Review* 2:384-397.

Seeman, H. (1990). "Why the Resistance by Faculty?" In *Combining Service and Learning: A Resource Book for Community and Public Service, Volume II.* Edited by J. Kendall and Associates, pp. 137-163. Raleigh, NC: National Society for Experiential Education.

# Learning Language, Culture, and Community

by Peggy Hashemipour

When I was hired at California State University, San Marcos in 1992, I received as my teaching assignment a Language and Culture course. While this appeared to be a typical teaching assignment for a beginning assistant professor, several considerations caused me to consider how to teach this class in a fashion that not only discussed social, cultural, and linguistic issues but also offered the course content in a way that would help students to think critically about issues such as language rights and bilingualism. An initial consideration in the development of the course was the fact that the university was new, having admitted its first students in 1990. It was open to different curricula and teaching philosophies. One such belief that the school had established from the very beginning was that it endorsed "an international perspective that addresses the global community in its distinctive social, political, and economic terms" (University Mission Statement). Much of the new curriculum focused on global issues and problems. One such issue was the establishment and maintenance of the linguistic rights of the United States' ethnically and linguistically diverse communities.

Traditional courses that deal with the connection of language, culture, and thought offered correlations to the multicultural mission of the university. However, I was also concerned about students' limited understanding of the field of linguistics and a need to make course material both accessible to learners and relevant to their lives and experience. Through the five years that I have taught the Language and Culture course, it has evolved into an interactive class with a highly integrated service-learning component. In this paper I will discuss some of the pivotal questions that have guided me in developing this successful course. These questions have focused on determining the overall theme of the course while drawing on background literature; preparing for service-learning; and creating organizational components in the course that allow students to benefit maximally from community learning. The end result has been a unique approach to learning language, culture, and communication.

## Determining the Overall Theme of the Course

Several common themes appear in most language and culture courses typically offered within anthropology, communication, and linguistics departments. Most study the extent to which language and culture have a causal effect on a community's view of the world and how its members construct meaning. In addition, most combine this general topic with a study of how languages vary and are similar within the confines of culture. Such courses may also contain additional content, like the nature of language — syntactic, morphological, phonological — or the structure of interpersonal or cross-cultural interactions, language acquisition and socialization, or multiculturalism and multilingualism. These areas correspond to the overall theme as a demonstration of the variation of linguistic behavior across cultures. For example, class participants may investigate the contrasting systems of discourse patterns or the use of space in different cultures. Courses may also share a common method or technique.

The connection of language, culture, and meaning has been studied for nearly a century, and is commonly recognized in the work of ethnologists such as Edward Sapir and Benjamin Whorf. A broader course perspective would encompass the types of work, analyses, and findings of anthropological linguists such as Franz Boas, Edward Sapir, Leonard Bloomfield, and Benjamin Whorf in the first part of the 20th century. These scholars brought benefits to the language communities with which they worked.

One of their contributions was to transform linguistic studies in a way that brought benefits to indigenous groups whose rights were not being upheld. One change occurred in their expansion of the types of languages relevant for study. A second modification appeared in how modern linguistic analysis was conducted.

For example, Boas was known for his stance against racism and pseudo-scientific support of white supremacy within both academic and political circles (Hyatt 1990). He believed that research should be used "in the interest of freedom" (Beardsley 1973: 55). The linguistic research of Boas, Sapir, and Whorf also broke away from earlier studies of language, providing both enhanced understanding and other benefits.

Linguists such as Bloomfield, Boas, Hockett, Sapir, and Whorf applied a comparative method (Lehmann 1992) to American Indian languages. Their work compared contemporary languages using oral traditions and from this comparison they reconstructed early language forms — all without written texts. This action was important in establishing that the communication forms of indigenous people in the Americas (and also Africa) were in fact systematic. Sapir stated:

> Is there any reason to believe that the process of regular phonetic change is less applicable to the languages of "primitive" peoples than to the languages of the more civilized nations? This question must be answered in the negative. Rapidly accumulating evidence shows that this process is just as easily and abundantly illustrated in the languages of the American Indian or of the Negro tribes as in Latin or Greek or English. If these laws

*are more difficult to discover in primitive languages, this is not due to any special characteristic which these languages possess but merely to the inadequate technique of some who have tried to study them. (1949: 74)*

Researchers demonstrated that language represents a creative ability possessed by every speaker, an "essential part of the human mind" (Robins 1980: 174). With assertions such as these, American linguists and anthropologists countered claims that "primitive" peoples did not have systematic languages as had been proposed by racist "scholars" such as de Gobineau, Chamberlain, and Galton (Nye 1966; Hyatt 1990). By showing that indigenous languages were in fact systematic, Boas, Bloomfield, and Sapir proved that the notion of "civilization" was ill-defined. Their work represented a break from the norm and did much to foster the development (albeit over time) of modern linguistics and anthropology.

Another important transformation initiated by early American linguists was the development of a discovery method commonly used in both modern and contemporary linguistic research. At the time, linguists in the United States based their work on de Saussure's founding ideas of *langue* (competence) and *parole* (performance) (Robins 1980). Knowledge of language or competence is subconscious, and speech or performance is the overt product of competence in action. Today this distinction is the basis for linguists' well-known claim that speech is governed by often covert rules of grammar. Based on de Saussure's conceptualizations, linguists since the beginning of the 20th century have seen their work as uncovering the nature of *langue*. Yet their only means has been through observation and description of *parole*. One of the contributions of Bloomfield, who was instrumental in founding structural linguistics, was in the establishment of criteria for linguistic analyses: assumptions must be posited, details of analysis stated, and conclusions drawn. This pattern is still largely followed today.

While this approach may be linked to the scientific method, it also compares with methods of acquiring knowledge posited by the American pragmatic philosopher John Dewey. Dewey's proposal called for educational renewal founded on the idea that an individual learns through attempting to do something, followed by her/his undergoing the consequences of that action (Dewey 1916). Dewey set out a process of learning through encountering and formulating a problem, gathering information, and then making and testing hypotheses. In his approach to the learning process Dewey proposes a model of experience that resembles the experientially based fieldwork conducted by American linguists.

This approach parallels Freire's recommendation that education be conceived of as a kind of problem-posing (as opposed to a kind of information "banking") based in *praxis*, action, and reflection. The methods of knowledge acquisition proposed by Dewey, Freire, and early 20th century American linguists were most influential in my decision to adopt a learning modality that would engage students experientially in the content of the Language and Culture course. Moreover, the connection between this focus, the contributions of language and communication studies to language users, and the discovery method strengthened my theoretical justification for including service-learning.

However, incorporating service-learning into the course posed another question: what community issue (related to language and culture) should the students address? In struggling with this question, I considered additional factors such as the linguistic makeup of the communities surrounding the university. The local economy is partially dependent on agriculture, which attracts a primarily Spanish-speaking workforce. The area also has a number of ethnically and linguistically diverse communities such as Filipino, Samoan, Farsi, and deaf groups. Many of these groups face issues regarding language that resonate with Dewey's remark that: "There is more than a verbal tie between the words common, community, and communication. [People] live in a community in virtue of the things they have in common and communication is the way in which they come to possess things in common" (Dewey 1974: 113). Some of the community-identified issues relevant to language are literacy development in both children and adults, and the design and implementation of materials and curricula for limited-English individuals.

Another variable that influenced the course design was the likely constitution and characteristics of the students. Those who had previously enrolled were liberal studies majors, many with aspirations for the teaching profession. The California State Department of Education requires that all preservice students complete coursework in language structure and language acquisition in order to place out of a national education exam. The Language and Culture course had to meet the standards of the state requirement. Students were eager to find out what teaching was really like from their own experience. They wanted to know what it was like to teach children who spoke a language other than English and whose world view might be different from their own.

An amalgamation of many elements determined the final theme and objective of the Language and Culture class: the university's mission statement and the state's need for citizens and teachers who understand and appreciate language and culture combined with the contributions of American linguists to the study of language and culture and the speech communities they studied. My desire to tap into the students' motivation and my interest in providing an educational experience where students were active in their learning opened the door to the community as the optimal setting for learning. Hence, the overall theme of the Language and Culture course was — and is — to study the interaction of language and culture in ways that demonstrate for citizens (mostly prospective teachers) the situation in our increasingly multilingual and multicultural communities.

## Precourse Preparation: Placements

In the same fashion in which the selection of a textbook to some degree determines the quality of the learning experience in a traditional class, so the selection of a community site governs much of the success and quality of a service-learning experience. Random placement produces random success. To minimize randomness I considered several options, the first being a single placement site at which all class participants perform their community work. For some of my service-learning colleagues this has been appropriate. However, there are some factors that must be considered in such a placement. For example, specifying that all students attend the same community site requires logistical planning. They need to be notified amply in advance in order to accommodate their different schedules. Indeed, schedule conflicts may require that community times be arranged during the normal class period, a less-than-optimal expedient especially if class meetings are less than an hour in length. In addition, the community service site must be large enough to support the number of students enrolled.

For the purposes of the Language and Culture class, with an enrollment of 25 students, a single community site would not accommodate the course goals. Using dialogue as a learning paradigm (Freire 1970: 73), I wanted students to engage in exchanges with bilingual or multicultural community members. This type of interaction would require special accommodations; e.g. students would need some degree of autonomy in selecting their community setting in order to match their prior experiences and interests with the environment. In short, I needed multiple sites to support the number of students involved.

To guide selection of community learning sites, I established specific criteria (Howard 1993: 6). These pertained to:
(1) the overall goals of the class;
(2) the clientele served by the community organization;
(3) the type of service the organization requested;
(4) the number of hours and time frame requested;
(5) safety considerations.
The first and second criteria were perhaps the most critical since "course content circumscribes the community service site" (Howard 1993: 7). Initially, the learning goal of the class was broad: to study the interaction of language and culture in ways that demonstrated for citizens (mostly prospective teachers) the aspects of our increasingly multilingual and mul-

ticultural communities. The fact that this goal could be met through a number of smaller learning objectives was intentional. Students could develop their own individual objectives, and these they would find more motivating than objectives set by the instructor. For example, students could look at the cultural variation of language behavior in cross-cultural communication; study the acquisition of a second language in children or adults; investigate the extent of support for bilingualism in American society; or even examine the controversy over bilingual or second language education.

However, I did not want students to study these issues passively and mechanistically, but rather through sensitive interaction with individuals directly affected by them. Students needed to have dialogues with service clientele who were bilingual, learning a second language, or had experienced culture and/or language shock or language loss. Interactions with multilingual individuals could "stimulate course-relevant learning" (Howard 1993: 7).

As the third criterion implies, the type of service students provide must be appropriate to the content of the course. Hence, it was not sufficient that students be in any agency serving a multilingual clientele. In this class successful student learning required settings where students could assist service recipients (both children and adults) with their language needs.

Time was another important issue. On the one hand, I had to consider the limitations of the students and the extent to which service-learning figured in the course as a whole. The number of hours required had to be manageable for students who are typically financially self-supporting, many with families. Ultimately, I chose to make the service-learning a core component of the course (all of the assignments are connected to the service experience). The course description in the university catalogue would indicate that fieldwork was required.

In addition, I had to make sure the number of hours provided was sufficient to benefit the community organizations involved. For example, many organizations do not find commitments of one hour per week for five weeks beneficial, since 8-10 hours may be needed initially just for the student to become acclimated to the community environment. Moreover, low hours can result in low expectations and low-level tasks — tasks that did not meet the learning goal of the class.

Weighing the students' need for flexibility, the organizations' time requirements, and my desire to have every student participate, I finally decided that each student would complete a minimum of 30 hours of service between the third and 13th week of the 16-week semester. Service hours would be verified through time logs initialed each week by the community supervisor. Students would be responsible for completing the log and submitting it to the instructor at the end of the semester.

A final consideration concerned the safety of the service recipient, the student, and the community supervisor. I looked for sites that were handicapped-accessible, clearly stated their expectations, and provided an orientation that included what to do in the case of an emergency. In addition, each organization had to assign a supervisor to work with each student. To promote both safety and clarity, I required that all students sign a contract that specified project expectations and limitations as well as what their learning objectives were.

Among the organizations that met my criteria, local schools were a significant resource. I also looked for other sites that served bilingual and limited English adults: adult education classes, job-training programs, adult literacy agencies, and programs such as those offered by Head Start. The Office of Community Service-learning assisted me through its centralized database. However, I remained involved throughout the entire process so I could experience firsthand what my students would experience later and would be better able to answer questions they posed.

## Course Construction and Delivery

The syllabus of the Language and Culture class reflects a multitiered approach to service-learning. Unlike traditional courses where the topics of discussion are ordered according to theme or chronology, the organization of this course can best be thought of as three-tiered: The first two concern skills development and progression through the community experience. The third, which includes a discussion of linguistic topics such as connections among language, culture, and thought; language acquisition (monolingual, bilingual, and second language); the structure of language; and the ethnography of communication, is determined by the students' own interests. Because each student has individualized learning objectives, a preset order will not accommodate them. After the seventh week of the semester, the students themselves decide the order of subsequent discussions, which the instructor facilitates and occasionally directs.

Students receive a coordinated reading list. However, they also receive the following two cautions:

(1) They are instructed and encouraged to read ahead. Indeed, in my feedback to their projects, I often indicate which pages deal with the issues they have encountered. Bonvillain's (1997) consolidated review of communication theory works well in this situation.

(2) As class discussion changes according to student interests, so also does the order of the readings. Since students suggest the changes in class discussion, they also suggest the changes in the readings. I should note here that students also do library and electronic research, especially using references cited in Bonvillain.

Chickering and Gamson (1987), Shumer (1987), and Howard (1993) stress the importance of changing students from passive to active learners. Service-learning not only gets students actively involved in addressing real problems with real solutions, but also makes them responsible for their learning. Giving students the option of deciding the order of discussion topics and what they should be reading places the power and responsibility to learn in their hands, not in those of the instructor.

**Orientation to Community Service-Learning and to the Community Site.** Community service is the basis of the second tier of the course. This level consists of an orientation to the community setting, development of cross-cultural understanding, expansion of service-learners' roles in the community, and closure. In other words, this track proceeds throughout the semester as a means of consciously guiding students through the service-learning experience. Students begin working on their placements from the first day of class through an assignment titled the Identification Report. This assignment seeks to accomplish several tasks including establishing the student's point of departure for learning, setting initial learning objectives that will be refined during the semester, analytical reflection, and orientation to service-learning and the community site.

To start this assignment, students investigate the list of possible placements I have established, which includes the names of organizations, contact persons, phone numbers, addresses, and service descriptions. Each class participant is responsible for setting up an interview with a designated organizational representative and for conducting an interview through which she/he can gather information about the site, the service recipients, and the type of assistance needed. During the interview, the student shares with the contact person the goals of the service-learning class and discusses her/his skills. If the student agrees to the placement, she/he must set up a service schedule. Subsequent to the interview, each student completes the identification assignment by filling in the necessary information on a registration form and addressing the five sections described below.

In the first section, the student provides information about the organization, such as its location and address. She/he must note the number of its staff members and volunteers and the size of its physical plant. The purpose of this exercise is to help students appreciate the extent to which her/his involvement will make a difference to the organization. Similarly, the student is required to list the goals and mission of the organization and the types of services it provides. Finally, the student provides a profile of the clientele served, including its distribution according to age, gender, and ethnicity.

In section two, each student writes about the types of activities in which she/he will participate. Examples would include tutoring in mainstream classes (language arts, social studies, mathematics, reading), assisting teachers in bilingual and English as a Second Language (ESL) classes, helping with homework in after-school programs, participating in activities such as Friday Night Out at Boys and Girls Clubs.

Students are also instructed to write about the significance of these activities. This assignment is intentionally left open-ended. Many students respond with their own ideas. Others ask the agency supervisor or a service recipient. In other assignments throughout the semester students return to this question in an effort to help them "to notice, reflect on, and participate in dialogues about differences in defining, interpreting, and expressing concepts of 'responsibility,' 'action,' and 'common good'" (Cruz 1995).

In the third section of the Identification Report, students are required to list the responsibilities and requirements the community organization has defined for them. These may include training, attendance, TB tests, etc. Students are also required to submit a general schedule of when they will be present at their community sites. It is important in a service-learning context for students to be fully aware of requirements like these since they are not common in traditional classes. Such an awareness also helps to minimize the risks to the student, community supervisor, and service recipient.

The fourth section serves as a pretest of the student's multicultural and multilingual understanding. In it, she/he identifies the cultural group with which she/he would like to work and what motivates her/his interest. While the selection of a cultural group is intentionally left to the student, every student is required to interact with a multilingual group of which she/he is not a member. Because in some cases students are mistrustful of a particular ethnic community, I ask each to give an honest appraisal of her/his motivation and to recount any prior impressions or experience with the selected group. This appraisal serves as one of the initial opportunities for critical reflection and provides what Freire has called "a means of understanding more clearly what and who [learners] are so that they can more wisely build the future" (Freire 1970: 65). From this point of departure, each student can enter into a critical dialogue about learning and the issues of linguistic and cultural identity.

In the final section of the Identification Report students brainstorm about what they want to learn in the Language and Culture class. Having them identify their learning goals means they must also assume responsibility for their learning and for their actions both in class and in the community. Students are alerted to the fact that early in the semester their objectives may be vague and unclear — in part because many have never previously had a linguistics class and are unfamiliar with course concepts. However, in order to build a framework for self-directed learning, students list their initial objectives with the understanding that their ultimate goals may change as the semester and their community experience progress. Later refinement of initial learning goals is expected.

The next point in the orientation track centers on the students' journals, their written record of and reflection on what occurs in the community experience. Through this assignment I am able to assess their personal level of involvement. This record also indicates the extent of their personal and academic development. Fieldnotes are collected twice during the semester — in weeks five and nine.

A subsequent stage of this phase consists of a one-on-one conference with me during weeks seven and eight. In this meeting we discuss the student's community placement, problems, questions, and topics that she/he has raised in her/his first set of fieldnotes. We also consider the initial learning goals given in the Identification Report and define them more narrowly. As a result of this meeting, each student achieves a clearer sense of how she/he is relating to and learning from the service-learning experience. Although these one-on-one conferences are labor-intensive, their results justify the effort. Commonly at this point, i.e., after four to five weeks at their service sites, students have begun to uncover the richness of the service-learning experience. Some may even feel overwhelmed at the prospect of attaining their learning goals. Yet because each student is working toward different goals and at different service sites, it is difficult to answer questions adequately and provide clarity in class. Conference time is effective and efficient.

The final phase in the community orientation track involves a series of in-class activities where students work with fellow classmates solving problems, discussing and reflecting on their community experience. Here I use collaborative frameworks such as "think-pair-and share" and "round robin" as well as report-outs where students explain to one another what they are learning at their sites. This occurs during weeks 9 to 13, with at least one oral assignment that requires each student formally to brief peers on her/his progress toward meeting her/his learning objectives.

**Fieldnotes.** In preparation for writing fieldnotes, each student receives an instruction packet explaining observation techniques and the art of taking fieldnotes. I direct students (1) not to presume that they know which events or interactions matter the most; (2) to be observant of everything that is transpiring around them; (3) to take note of their surroundings, all people present, and the time taken by events; and (4) to attempt to look at the setting or situation through the eyes of the community (Richlin-Klonsky and Strenski 1994). Because students are expected to participate interactively, they are encouraged to remain observers only until they feel comfortable with the setting. Then they should become participant-observers, directly involving themselves in activities. Several factors mandate such involvement. First, by becoming directly involved, students actively experience the topics they are learning. Second, through participation and responsible action, they may develop rapport with the community group they are learning from and providing service to. Thus they will be able to gather richer data.

We also discuss in detail the art of writing fieldnotes. Students are encouraged to describe vividly both their social interactions and their own reactions, paying attention to the mundane as well as the dramatic. From samples distributed in class, they learn that fieldnotes involve describing specific gestures, sounds, smells, reactions (both their own and those of others). (See Emerson, Fretz, and Shaw 1995 for further use of fieldnotes.)

One in-class activity that helps students acquire observation and note-taking skills utilizes films and videos of nondramatic interactions; e.g., home videos, news segments. After viewing a brief clip, students are required to write down what they have seen. They do so individually and then discuss their notes in groups of three to four, seeking to explain differences among group members' notes. Then they are assigned to take notes on an event outside of class (such as interactions within another class or a ride on an elevator).

Students are also introduced to the practice of making jottings as an expedient way to record initially notes that they can later turn into full fieldnotes after the experience is over. Ethnographers commonly use jottings as a means of recalling events. Two points are emphasized. First, the writing up process will probably take as long as the actual activity observed. As Emerson, Fretz, and Shaw note, ". . . every hour spent observing requires an additional hour to write up" (1995: 39). Second, students are instructed to write their full fieldnotes as soon as possible after their time in the community, principally because most people tend to forget the details of interactions as time passes.

**Feedback.** Although fieldnotes typically are private, noninteractive writings, in this case, they frequently serve to frame the dialogue between a student and me. There are, of course, both benefits and disadvantages to having an individual's notes open to review. With regard to academic development, one assumes that feedback from the instructor will provide direction and support. However, with regard to personal development, especially in the case of students who are coming to question their own beliefs, considerable tact and understanding on the part of the instructor are necessary to ensure that sharing does not lessen the level of intimacy and revelation.

**Error Analysis.** Another skill Language and Culture students develop involves error analysis (Corder 1981; van Els et al. 1984; Ellis 1990). In this technique students first examine a problem area for a second language learner, contrasting an actual utterance with an intended or target utterance. Then, they identify the basis of the discrepancy (e.g., syntactic, morphological, phonological, semantic, pragmatic factors), following this with a description and explanation of the learner's difficulties. They next compare the grammars of the language learner's native and target languages, or ask the learner about her/his target language.

As a final step, students evaluate and reflect on the severity of the language error or problem. This involves making connections between what has been attempted and what has happened as a consequence (Dewey 1916). In considering the connection between a language learner's attempts and its consequences, students are led to appreciate the effects of linguistic prescriptivism and discrimination upon language utilization.

# Findings

**Combining Tools and Reflection Within Linguistic Analysis.** The commonly defined categories of competence vs. performance and subconscious vs. conscious can be the basis of an experiential teaching of language and communication, whereby sensitization to the experience of speech production leads to understanding the rules of language. A case in point is in the study of articulatory phonetics.

Teaching phonetics at an introductory level entails demonstrating that sounds are composed of physical features according to where they are produced (place of articulation), how they are produced (manner of articulation), and status of the vocal cords (voicing). However, the description that derives from explanation of these constructs typically has little meaning for the beginning student; e.g., the sound [b] is a bilabial, voiced, stop. For this reason, I ask Language and Culture students to figure out the properties of phonetics by actually producing sounds and then describing them using a minimal number of features.

Working in groups, students use diagrams to determine the place of articulation and hands-on techniques to determine voicing and manner of articulation. In active, collaborative groups, they struggle to develop the system of speech sounds of English through producing, sounding out, viewing, and timing. By the time they have finished, they have inferred the system.

However, the learning does not end here. The next step is for them to connect their knowledge with their community experience. Hence, they are now required to collect examples of problems in pronunciation from the service recipients with whom they are working. In class, using error analysis, they work to uncover the nature and source of these problems. Since many of the service recipients are Spanish-speakers, common examples include Estefanie for Stefanie, dey for they, and [wek] for weak [wik]. Students learn to compare a service recipient's pronunciation with the target pronunciation. Using references such as Smith and Swan (1991) and Thonis (1983), they discuss the fact that most learners' difficulties are not random but systematic, and that the basis of stereotypes and language attitudes in this area are ill-founded.

At this point, the Language and Culture students are learning to draw on resources to explain language phenomena, test assumptions, and question faulty beliefs. Through reflection they question the extent to which the learner and her/his teacher should be concerned with these types of errors, and what they as members of the community can do to help language learners resolve difficulties and stereotypes.

Finally, I should note that I use the same problem-solving model to teach syntax and morphology — introducing subject matter experientially, with students inferring the system and then applying their knowledge to data collected through their community experience. Students complete their knowledge base through research and finally determine ways of addressing the difficulties they have identified. Although I am concerned that students acquire a knowledge base, I am equally concerned that they learn steps to increase their understanding and solve problems. These problem-solving skills will make possible future learning.

**Reflection Within the Learning Process.** Using theories concerning the nature and the value and basis of reflection proposed by Dewey (1974), Freire (1970), and Kolb (1984), I incorporate a variety of reflective components into the course, with reflection occurring at both the personal and the analytical level and in both written and oral modalities. This multileveled incorporation suggests Dewey's position that knowledge gained within the classroom has no particular privilege over knowledge gained from outside it:

> We live not in a settled and finished world, but in one which is going on, and where our main task is prospective, and where retrospect — and all knowledge as distinct from thought is retrospect — is of value in the solidity, security, and fertility it affords our dealings with the future. (Dewey 1974: 151)

Accordingly, *every* assignment has some reflective component to it. Class participants reflect in their conferences with me, and within their journal assignments they not only include the details of their field experience, they also respond to weekly reflective prompts regarding their impressions and questions that intrigue them. In addition, they are required to reflect in collaborative work groups within the classroom. These sessions are held throughout the semester.

Still another opportunity for reflection occurs in the final poster presentation, where each student is required to present two critical incidents that occurred during the semester as well as an overall reflection on the community service-learning experience. For their critical incidents, students are instructed to write about instances when they understood the importance of assisting someone or when there was a critical problem in at least the sense that it was not immediately obvious to the student what to do or say. Students also discuss what it was that led them to judge or deem an incident "critical."

Finally, I should note that my use of several modalities of reflection represents an effort to draw upon different learning styles; that is, while some students may enjoy writing in prose or even in a poetic format, others appreciate oral or visual interaction. Hence, instead of limiting reflection to one form, I incorporate opportunities for students to experiment with several and learn what works best for them.

## Conclusion

The Language and Culture course I have described represents a multifaceted venture. From the viewpoint of the researcher of language, culture, and communication, it is an opportunity to examine and create ways that knowledge in these areas can be used to address community needs. From the viewpoint of the student, it is an opportunity to discover data and apply knowledge. From that of the learner, it is a chance to reflect on the connection between disparate experiences and consequences. My students themselves best characterize the effects of the course's unique structure:

> *Encouraged higher, and more comprehensive learning.*

> *Very rewarding and allowed us to learn on our own about what we were studying in class.*

> *Based on what we wanted to learn. Allowed for discussion and sharing set up to have us facilitate our [own] learning.*

Still another student wrote:

> *The class was very enjoyable. For me, the service work was the best part. There is so much to be learned through the personal interactions and further explanations given in class and in our fieldnotes. It was very helpful. Great experience. Thank you.*

If this is not enough to make someone want to facilitate the learning of language, culture, and community, I don't know what is.

# References

Beardsley, Edward H. (March 1973). "The American Scientist as Social Activist: Franz Boas, Burt G. Wilder and the Fight for Racial Justice, 1900-1915." *Isis*: 50-66.

Bonvillain, Nancy. (1997). *Language, Culture, and Communication: The Meaning of Messages*. 2nd ed. Upper Saddle River, NJ: Prentice Hall.

Chickering, Arthur W., and Zelda F. Gamson. (March 1987). "Seven Principles for Good Practice in Undergraduate Education." *AAHE Bulletin* 39(7): 3-7.

Corder, P. (1981). *Error Analysis and Interlanguage*. Oxford: Oxford University Press.

Cruz, Nadinne. (1995). "Multicultural Politics of Difference in Service-Learning." In *Service-Learning in Higher Education: Concepts and Practices*. Edited by B. Jacoby, pp. 248-267. San Francisco, CA: Jossey-Bass.

Dewey, John. (1916, 1974) *Democracy and Education: An Introduction Into the Philosophy of Education*. New York, NY: Free Press.

———. (1938). *Experience and Education*. New York, NY: Free Press.

———. (1974). *On Education: Selected Writings*. Chicago, IL: University of Chicago Press.

Ellis, Rod. (1990). *Instructed Second Language Acquisition: Learning in the Classroom*. Oxford: Basil Blackwell.

Emerson, Robert M., Rachel I. Fretz, and Linda L Shaw. (1995). *Writing Ethnographic Fieldnotes*. Chicago, IL: University of Chicago Press.

Freire, Paolo. (1970, 1997) *Pedagogy of the Oppressed, 20th Anniversary Ed*. New York, NY: Continuum Publishing.

Howard, Jeffrey. (1993). "Community Service-Learning in the Curriculum." In *Praxis I: A Faculty Casebook on Community Service-Learning*. Edited by J. Howard. Ann Arbor, MI: OCSL Press, University of Michigan.

Hyatt, Marshall. (1990). "Franz Boas Social Activist: The Dynamics of Ethnicity." New York, NY: Greenwood Press.

Kolb, David. (1984). *Experiential Learning: Experience at the Source of Learning and Development*. Englewood Cliffs, NJ: Prentice Hall.

Lehmann, Winfred P. (1992). *Historical Linguistics*. 3rd ed. London: Routledge.

Nye, Russel B. (1966). *This Almost Chosen People: Essays in the History of American Ideas*. East Lansing, MI: Michigan State University.

Richlin-Klonsky, Judith, and Ellen Strenski. (1994). *A Guide to Writing Sociology Papers*. 3rd ed. New York, NY: St. Martin's Press.

Robins, R.H. (1980). *A Short History of Linguistics*. 2nd ed. London: Longman.

Sapir, Edward. (1949). "The Status of Linguistics as a Science." In *Selected Writings of Edward Sapir: In Language, Culture, and Personality*. Edited by D.G. Mandelbaum, pp. 160-166. Berkeley, CA: University of California Press.

Shumer, Robert. (1987). "Spring Into Action." *Field Studies Development Newsletter.* Los Angeles: University of California, Office of Instructional Development.

Smith, B., and M. Swan. (1991). *Learner's English.* Boston, MA: Cambridge University Press.

Thonis, Eleanor. (1983). *The English-Spanish Connection.* Northvale, NJ: Santillana Press.

van Els, T., T. Bongaerts, G. Extra, C. van Os, and C. Janssen-van-Diete. (1984). *Applied Linguistics and the Learning and Teaching of Foreign Language.* London: Edward Arnold.

# Service-Learning and Interpersonal Communication: Connecting Students With the Community

by Tasha Souza

Ernest Boyer concluded his survey of undergraduate education with "the uncomfortable feeling that the most vital issues of life — the nature of society, the roots of social injustice, indeed the very prospects of human survival — are the ones with which the undergraduate college student is least equipped to deal" (Boyer 1987: 283). Higher education needs to encourage students to see beyond themselves and better understand the interdependent nature of society. Service-learning can provide this opportunity and offer an antidote to the separation of college students from the wider community.

Consistent with research suggesting that service-learning is useful as a pedagogical strategy (Conrad and Hedin 1991), this chapter describes the need for service-learning in interpersonal communication courses, provides a description of a research project that sought to determine the effectiveness of a service-learning assignment in interpersonal communication courses, and discusses the results of the analysis.

## Service-Learning in an Interpersonal Communication Course

In an interpersonal communication course service-learning can enhance students' understanding of communication skills and help them to apply course content by bridging theory and practice. Service-learning can provide students with opportunities to apply newly acquired interpersonal communication skills and knowledge; furthermore, students can benefit from interacting with a population with whom they otherwise might not communicate. From an interpersonally oriented, social constructionist perspective, the service-learning experience can help students acquire a deeper understanding of the service recipients, develop a recognition of the collaboratively constructed nature of interpersonal communication, and foster a sense of caring for others and the community. In addition to learning from the application of skills and theory, students simultaneously benefit by reflecting on what they have learned and discussing those reflections with others. Given that communication is inherently process-based, it makes sense for students "to learn about communication by participating in a process-oriented activity" (Beck 1995: 7).

Despite the inherent logic of approaching interpersonal communication from a service-learning perspective, Krupar (1994) contends that there is very little service-learning currently available in interpersonal communication courses. The few interpersonal communication courses I am aware of that have integrated service-learning have done so by requiring students to work in the community for a specified number of hours in order to meet specific instructional goals related to interpersonal communication. For example, students have been required to provide service one time (for three to five hours) or throughout a semester (for one to three hours a week), apply course concepts to the experience (e.g., negotiating identity, dialogic listening, perception), and provide written analyses in the form of a journal, short papers, or a term paper. However, there exists as yet minimal research that explicates the benefits of using service-learning in such courses. Therefore, I decided to not only implement a service-learning component in my interpersonal communication courses but also gather from the students data about its effectiveness. I wanted to determine if they could see the connection between service and learning in their assignments.

In an attempt to explore students' perceptions, I analyzed essays written by interpersonal communication students who participated in a particular service-learning assignment. The following specific research question guided my analysis:

RQ: What did students enrolled in an interpersonal communication course indicate that they learned as a result of their service-learning experience?

The next section describes the nature of the service-learning assignment and the procedures used to analyze the essays written by 65 students who had taken my introductory interpersonal course during the 1995-96 academic year.

## The Project

The introductory interpersonal communication course in which the students were enrolled was grounded in the theoretical perspective of social constructionism. The basic contention of this perspective is that reality is socially constructed and that researchers must analyze the processes by which this construction occurs (Berger and Luckman 1966). The underlying assumptions of this approach are that people constitute themselves and their worlds through their conversational activity (Shotter 1993) and that when people communicate, they are offering definitions of themselves and responding to definitions of the other(s) whom they perceive (Stewart 1978).

Service-learning from a social constructionist perspective focuses on the complex, dynamic, context-dependent communicative transaction or relationship (Stewart 1978). This theoretical perspective provides students with the opportunity to focus on the role of communication in creating, constituting, and sustaining relationships and reality. Rather than being an activity that merely seeks to satisfy the needs of the service recipients or the goals of the service providers, the experience is conceptualized in terms of "dialogue."

Students were asked to spend three to four hours working in the community in order to gain new insight and perspective on communicative interactions with others while meeting community needs. The students before and after the service-learning experience voted on the amount of time spent at the service site. Although three or four hours during the quarter is a small amount of time, the majority of students agreed that (1) they were able to gain useful insights in the amount of time they were present at their service site, and (2) additional hours would be difficult to coordinate given the limited time available for service. I worked in coordination with the service-learning center at the university to provide students with appropriate service-learning sites. Because the center identified numerous such sites, there were no difficulties with site selection. Students were asked to choose a site that was of interest to them and that allowed them to engage in dialogue with members of the community they were serving. Students participated in activities such as taking blind people sailing, serving food to the homeless, going horseback riding with mentally disabled youth, and assisting at a rest home.

Students wrote a term paper that described their service experience according to the theories and concepts presented in the course. In addition, they were asked to reflect on their service-learning experience and describe what, if anything, they had learned from it. The section of the student essays that described their learning was the focus of my investigation. Although most essays provided detailed descriptions of the application of course concepts and theories, some did not provide much detail regarding what they had learned specifically as a result of their service. For a majority of the students, the section describing what they had learned consisted of only a short paragraph. However, on the day the term papers were due, I dedicated the entire class session to reflecting on and discussing the service-learning experience. Students' comments in class were consistent with the descriptions and perspectives they included in the essays.

## Data Analysis

A thematic content analysis was used to analyze the section of the students' essays that described the learning that took place through their service-learning experience. According to Montgomery and Duck (1991), "content analysis is the process by which the researcher represents one set of meanings in terms of a second system of symbols, the coding categories to which numerical representations are ultimately assigned" (240). Permission was gained from the students to use their essays in this investigation (n = 65).

The data were analyzed using a detailed, line-by-line approach, which Strauss and Corbin (1990) characterize as the most detailed and generative type of analysis. The discourse was segmented into thematic "thought" units. These "thought" units were main ideas contained in a phrase, sentence, or paragraph. A sentence could be given two or three codes if it contained more than one main idea. In addition, two or three sentences could have been given a single code if the main idea did not change. The thematic analysis consisted of five steps similar to the steps used by Peterson et al. (1994). These include:

1. Searching for individual themes in the transcripts and field notes;
2. Developing each of the themes identified in step one;
3. Determining relative significance of themes;
4. Searching for groupings and thematic hierarchies;
5. Determining which respondents produced specific data within the categories.

After several readings of the text for conceptual patterns, I created the codes. I also created tags or labels (codes) to assign units of meaning to the text (Miles and Huberman 1994). I started with 11 themes and, after following the steps described above, narrowed the data to five final themes.

# Results

This section describes and explicates each of the five themes: (1) application of interpersonal communication skills to contexts outside of academia, (2) a positive view of service-learning, (3) heightened awareness of interpersonal communication concepts and theories, (4) understanding agency in communication, and (5) change in perspective about self and/or service recipient.

**Application of Interpersonal Communication Skills to Contexts Outside of Academia.** The theme students mentioned most frequently in their service-learning essays was their application of communication concepts to contexts outside the classroom. Thirty-nine students commented that they learned that the skills, theories, and concepts discussed in class applied to the "outside" or "real world." Several students described how useful it was to be able to see and apply the concepts of interpersonal communication rather than just reading about them in a book. One student wrote that she had studied the interpersonal communication principles, "applied them to role-play exercises, and participated in discussion about them. But it wasn't until after this experience that I actually learned them. . . . They're practical life skills that can be applied to and enhance everyday lives." Another wrote: "I think that applying newly learned information you've learned to [service work] is a really positive experience. . . . Applying interpersonal skills to an experience and then writing about that experience is a good way of reinforcing the skills learned." In addition, this student stated his belief that he will get more out of his future volunteering experiences by using the skills learned in the course. Several students described how the experience helped them to develop their skills as well. For example, one student wrote that his experience "truly helped me better my interpersonal communication skills."

**Positive View of Service-Learning.** Twenty-eight students stated that due to this assignment, they now felt positive toward service and service-learning. Students frequently wrote about wanting to return to their community site because they had had such a positive experience. Several students described the experience as positive because it helped them gain insights that they would otherwise not have had. For example, one student remarked that he had thought that our text was not believable prior to his service-learning experience. Afterward, however, he asserted that "seeing is believing" and claimed to recognize the importance and validity of the concepts described in the text. Another student wrote that service-learning "helped to broaden my mind in a way that could not have happened from anything except the direct contact that occurred." After describing the experience as a challenge, a third student commented, "I learned more from this one activity than I did in all of the other activities combined." A fourth student noted that his

> . . . outlook on [service] work has changed. . . . Although I was initially skeptical about doing community service, I am glad I did it. . . . Several ideas that pertain to interpersonal communication study . . . were even more obvious under a new light such as community service.

**Heightened Awareness of Interpersonal Communication Concepts and Theories.** Twenty-five students described an increase in their awareness of the interpersonal communication theories discussed in class. One student asserted that the greatest thing she gained from her service-learning experience was a heightened awareness of interpersonal communication concepts. She wrote, "Now that I am aware of the factors that go into making communication more interpersonal I will continue to make my interactions fall where they should on the impersonal/interpersonal continuum." Another student noted that because she was very focused on the impact of her communication, "I was therefore aware that I was constantly redefining myself with every interaction, and that my words had an effect on others."

Several students described the impact of their heightened awareness from the service-learning experience. For example, one student claimed, "When communicators are aware of how they cocreate meanings within every interaction, they are able to recognize the distinctive characteristics of everyone, including themselves. This awareness brings about equality as you realize every individual deserves respect" for his/her uniqueness. However, whereas most students described how their heightened awareness contributed to positive outcomes, one student confessed that although "my awareness was heightened regarding the concepts above and I enjoyed reflecting on them, I didn't experience much improvement in the interpersonal communication with the youth." This student recognized the disconnect between understanding and effectiveness.

**Understanding Agency in Communication.** A theme that recurred 18 times was that of agency in communication. Prior to their service-learning experience, some students seemed to believe that interpersonal communication "just happens." After the assignment, students discussed how their conceptions of agency in communicative encounters changed because of their service-learning experience. For example, one student noted that he learned that "interpersonal communication and its existence in my life must begin with me." Another student claimed, "in order for me to communicate on an interpersonal level, I have to change." A third student wrote, "the main thing I learned about interpersonal communication is how much of a choice it truly is."

From a social constructionist perspective, the recognition of participation and joint action is central to understanding interpersonal communication. One student asserted:

> I learned that I have the ability to decide on the quality of my conversations and that this decision can also encourage others to contribute to the conversation on a more interpersonal level. We are all active participants in molding our interactions.

**Change in Perspective About Self and/or Service Recipient.** The service-learning experience was described by 14 students as causing a shift in some of their perspectives about themselves and/or the service recipient. For example, one student who worked at a senior center for the needy asserted that "I learned that these people, many without homes, most without money, some without family, are not lazy alcoholics. They are people we can learn from." Another student who served at the center claimed, "This service-learning project got me out in the community and successfully broke down my stereotype of all senior centers being 'institution-like' and unpleasant." Still another student wrote that this experience allowed her to emerge with "a new understanding and respect for different types of people."

Many students who worked with the homeless wrote about their realization that any person can be homeless and had a change in perspective about people without homes. One student wrote, "A major lesson I learned is that homeless people are real people. . . . They are smart and funny and they all have something to offer this world."

Several students described how they had learned about themselves and changed as people thanks to the service-learning experience. One wrote, "This experience was in complete contradiction to many of my long-standing beliefs. In these three and a half hours, I realized more about myself and communication in general than I have in a long time." This same student also described how the experience caused her to reflect on her own biases and "reinforced the importance of the cliché, 'never judge a book by its cover.' You never know what's inside until you open it, until you 'communicate' with it."

## Discussion and Limitations

It is important to understand the students' perspectives on their service-learning experiences and the effects of service-learning on understanding human communication. One thing that became apparent was that the learning described in the student essays was consistent with the arguments people have made advocating service-learning in higher education. Service-learning helped these students to understand the relevance of interpersonal communication and enabled them to test theories and skills against the reality of the world around them.

In particular, the experience seemed to facilitate and advance student understanding of interpersonal communication from a social constructionist perspective. Engagement with others in unfamiliar settings highlighted negotiation of identities and coconstruction of realities. Students described their recognition of their participation in joint actions and realized the value of viewing communication as a collaborative process. This perspective helped them to move beyond their preconceived notions of the service recipients and service sites and revealed to them the multiple layers of social meaning. As they worked to make a difference in the lives of others, they discovered the power to make a difference in their own lives.

Students were also able to reflect on their service experience and describe these reflections both in their essays and in class discussion. Reflection gave students the opportunity to carefully analyze, synthesize, and evaluate their service participation and create connections with the course content. As a key component of the service-learning experience, reflection is consistent with Dewey's contention that "education is the reconstruction of experience" (1938: 3).

Given the assignment's focus and the minimal number of hours that were spent in service, one might, however, question whether any substantive service was done. Although many students stated that they thought they had made a meaningful contribution, most were focused on what they had *received from* the experience. On the one hand, it could be perceived as solely utilitarian and egocentric. On the other, it could be considered socially positive since it helped to break down the barrier between service provider and service recipient, allowing the former to learn from the latter. This move beyond a bifurcation between student and service recipient can be seen as reinforcing the connection between students and the community.

Clearly the analysis left several important questions unanswered. For example, did the service really meet the needs of the community? What was its impact on service recipients? What are the implications of middle-class young adults going out to "serve" people of different classes, abilities, ethnicities, and ages? Do students come to recognize the complex dynamics of power, race, class, and gender during their service experience or their later reflections? What are the ethical considerations that attend such brief encounters? What will be the long-term effect of service-learning on the students? Are students more likely to participate in the community or become active politically because of their service experience? Although many students stated that they would continue to serve, the actual consequences of their intentions have not been identified. These and other questions need to be explored.

In addition, there are several limitations to this research methodology in this context. I encouraged students to be candid about their opinion of the service assignment both in their essays and in class discussions. However, I recognize that because ultimately I (as instructor) was the one who would give the students grades, they may have felt a need to foreground the positive aspects of their experience. Therefore, it is important that future researchers collect anonymous data regarding students' opinions in this area.

This research is also limited in that the amount of service provided was minimal. Although most of the students commented that they believed the number of hours spent in the community was appropriate for the assignment, research that examines long-term service assignments can provide a more in-depth analysis of both the benefits of service-learning and the effect it has on service recipients and the community.

## Conclusion

The results of my analysis shed light on the link between service and learning from the students' point of view. Although the usefulness of this analysis is limited, I contend that, given student reflections on their service-learning experience as articulated in their writing and class discussions, this approach can be an effective and valuable strategy in helping students learn more about interpersonal communication and the community. Their service experience helped to enlarge their connections — connections with the course content, connections with experience, and connections with the community. It also seemed to result in a linking of thought and feeling that, in turn, can encourage students to discover even more complex ways to understand and act in the world.

## References

Beck, C.S. (1995). *Putting Our Knowledge to Work: Integrating Service-Learning Component Into Advanced Interpersonal Communication Course.* Paper presented at the annual meeting of the Speech Communication Association, San Antonio, TX.

Berger, P.L., and T. Luckman. (1966). *The Social Construction of Reality.* New York, NY: Anchor Books.

Boyer, E. (1987). *College: The Undergraduate Experience in America.* New York, NY: Harper & Row.

Conrad, D., and D. Hedin. (1991). "School-Based Community Service: What We Know From Research and Theory." *Phi Delta Kappan* 72(10): 743-749.

Dewey, J. (1938). *Experience and Education.* New York, NY: Macmillan.

Krupar, K. (1994). "Service-Learning in Speech Communication." In *Building Community: Service-Learning in the Academic Disciplines.* Edited by R. Kraft and M. Swadener, pp. 103-114. Denver, CO: Colorado Campus Compact.

Miles, M.B., and A.M. Huberman. (1994). *Qualitative Data Analysis.* Thousand Oaks, CA: Sage Publications.

Montgomery, B.M., and S. Duck. (1991). *Studying Interpersonal Interaction.* New York, NY: The Guilford Press.

Peterson, T.R., K. Witte, E. Enkerlin-Hoeflich, L. Espericueta, J.T. Flora, N. Florey, T. Loughran, and R. Stuart. (1994). "Using Informant Directed Interviews to Discover Risk Orientation: How Formative Evaluations Based in Interpretive Analysis Can Improve Persuasive Safety Campaigns." *Journal of Applied Communication* 22(3): 199-215.

Shotter, J. (1993). *Conversational Realities.* London: Sage Publications.

Stewart, J. (1978). "Foundations of Dialogic Communication." *The Quarterly Journal of Speech* 64:183-201.

Strauss, A.L., and J. Corbin. (1990). *Basics of Qualitative Research.* London: Sage Publications.

## SERVICE LEARNING TERM PAPER
Interpersonal Communication/Souza

### Service Learning Defined

Service learning is a method in which students learn and develop through community service that: (1) is conducted in and meets the needs of a community; (2) helps foster civic responsibility; (3) is integrated into and enhances the academic curriculum of the students enrolled; and (4) includes structured time for students to reflect on the service experience.

### Paper Description

Your term paper should be approximately 6 double-spaced, typed pages. For this paper, it is necessary to spend 3 to 4 hours volunteering in the community. Possible sites to volunteer will be provided. We will agree upon the site in which you volunteer in order to assure that the site will be able to fulfill the requirements of the assignment. The site should thematically relate to the issues that this course addresses. The service learning experience should engage you in the complex issues of the diverse communities and human endeavors that continuously create our world and give you some new insight and perspective on communicative interactions with others. **Be sure that you will** *engage in dialogue* **with others in the community during your service experience.**

First, provide a description of the context and address the 5 "W's" (who, what {your role} when, where, why) and the 1 "H" (how long). The "W's" will help me to identify the site and situate it in context. The "how" will tell me the length of your experience (please be honest).

In your paper, please respond to the following questions by relating your experience to the concepts described in the text and discussed in class:

- What were the communicative interactions like (use the social/cultural/interpersonal continuum as a reference)? What degree of interpersonal communication occurred between you and those with whom you had contact (refer to the five components)? Why? What was your reaction to the communicative interactions?
- Choose three topics (e.g., negotiating selves, verbal & non-verbal, perception, expressing selves, dialogic listening, etc.) What were the dynamics of your communication with others in relation to each of the three topics? Be specific.
- What, if anything, did you learn about interpersonal communication from this experience?

This paper will be evaluated based on your understanding of the concepts discussed in class and your text. Your analysis should identify how these principles contribute to the achievement of interpersonal communication. Weave in the course content throughout your paper. Please be thorough in your analysis and use the book's terminology correctly. Be sure to include **clear** details and examples in order to provide a full analysis and allow me to "see" what it is you are describing.

* Please proofread your paper before submitting it to me and include an introduction, conclusion, and transitional statements (as well as proper grammar, punctuation, and spelling).

# Small Group Problem Solving as Academic Service-Learning

by Paul Yelsma

The communication dimension in group problem solving is complex. Thus most of us understand its dynamics more fully when given opportunities to study principles and then apply them to solve tangible tasks and socio-emotional problems. Life experiences alone are insufficient to facilitate understanding the complexities of small group communication. If such experiences alone were sufficient, we would have little reason to continue to research and study group communication. Furthermore, our individual communication skills are enhanced when we experience the results of our own efforts and receive feedback about our own behaviors. Optimal learning appears to take place when both academic insights (constructs, abstract principles, and theories) and application of these insights are fully integrated (Howard 1993).

Service-learning projects are particularly valuable learning experiences in group communication classes because as students become aware of concepts, theories, and principles, they have opportunities to apply these in their group interactions and with the people for whom they provide services. When faced with real challenges that affect group members and people in the community, students seem more compelled to learn methods of working together as team members. Although service-learning projects vary from group to group, the amount of academic learning that occurs in the problem-solving class remains substantial.

Many communication researchers recognize the importance of studying real-life, bonafide groups, versus studying zero-history groups (no previous experience of working together) in order to learn about group behavior. In a similar manner, providing students with opportunities where they can immediately apply some of the principles of group problem solving to real-life situations offers unique benefits. However, little information exists on ways of inaugurating service-learning within small group problem-solving courses (Yelsma 1994).

The objectives of this chapter are to examine several perspectives for integrating academic concepts, principles, and theories of group problem solving with procedures for engaging in service-learning. Such engagement has at least four advantages. First, students enhance their group communication skills by engaging in issues affecting others in the community. Second, students become aware of major theoretical issues associated with the dynamics of small group communication. Third, students experience the satisfaction of providing meaningful services to others within the community. Fourth, students frequently report an increased sense of confidence and interest in providing service to others.

Service-learning, at least as it pertains to small group communication in higher education, is a new educational phenomenon. The following section is intended to introduce some of the theoretical and developmental issues associated with implementing service-learning practices in small group problem-solving courses. The reactions of students experiencing community service-learning in this context will also be shared.

## An Overview of the Group Problem-Solving Course

Traditionally, the study of small group communication within the communication discipline has provided two avenues of learning. First, students learned principles about more effective ways of working with peers in group settings. Second, they learned about their own attitudes and values by interacting with others who often were similar to themselves. In service-learning, a third type of learning, civic responsibility, occurs as students select issues to problem solve within the community. By combining service-learning activities with principles of group problem solving, one can provide students with opportunities to learn more about the attitudes and values of people who often are different from themselves (Hammond 1994).

During the last 15 years, students in my problem-solving classes have engaged in more than 200 group projects in the community.[1] These projects have resulted in a wide variety of services. Most projects have been undertaken by five-member groups, and in almost all cases, were completed within a single semester. However, some groups found their projects so exciting that those projects were handed on to successive groups in following semesters. In these cases, continuity of service was established by having a few students from the original groups continue with portions of the project until others could assume the responsibilities necessary to complete the projects.

*Changes in Academic Classroom Pedagogy.* Students typically contribute from 10 to 40 hours of their time participating in service projects; they attend 20 to 22 lectures, engage in three problem-solving demonstrations in class (a part of the decision-making process for their projects), complete midterm and final examinations, write individual research papers, and write group communication analysis papers, which are about the communication processes they have used to solve the problems they addressed.

Early in the semester, they are given two choices for doing their group work: either a library-oriented problem-solving experience or a community-based project. This choice of options appears to reduce their hesitations about investing time and energy in service-learning. Over the last several years approximately 92 percent of the students in this class have become involved in community-based projects. The 8 percent who have embraced library-oriented projects have slightly lower grades on the academic evaluations used in the class (tests, papers, and classroom demonstrations). Class attendance is also slightly lower for the students who have selected library rather than service-learning projects. Approximately half of the students who participate in service-learning projects have engaged in some form of service activity elsewhere.

*Making Changes in Classroom Teaching Strategies.* Early in the development of this course, I discovered that I needed to make changes in the lecture materials I presented. Students needed a more pragmatic orientation because they would be expected to learn about communication constructs and then implement aspects of those constructs as they problem solved in their groups. In most cases, the application of course materials would occur as groups engaged in community service.

# Principles of Effective Small Group Interaction

This section outlines principles of group dynamics that help group members utilize their resources and complete their projects. I have divided these principles into two sections: first, central principles of group dynamics essential for effective service-learning in group problem solving; second, important guidelines related to class structure and instructor duties. Exploration of these materials is necessarily brief due to space constraints.

## Principles of Group Dynamics

*Teamwork Is Essential.* The ability to work together effectively to solve problems is a core concept within the course. Thus, a considerable amount of information on ways to promote teamwork within small groups is essential. "If we are to solve the enormous problems facing our society, we need to learn how to collaborate more effectively. We need to know how to set aside individual agendas so that a common understanding of a problem has an opportunity to develop" (Larson and Lafasto 1993: 7). Teamwork that emerges with knowledge of group dynamics and skilled practice becomes a way of life.

*Peers Learning to Empower Peers.* Without receiving substantial support from peers and teachers for their ideas, commitment, time, and energy, some students are apprehensive about working on projects that appear to be almost impossible for a small number of people to complete in one semester. Furthermore, students who are accustomed to thinking in individualistic ways frequently find group work challenging. Thus, a major concern facing most peer groups is providing sufficient socioemotional support for one another. Another challenge students often face when participating in complex service projects is overcoming the tendency to rely on leaders (prior experience often has conditioned them to rely upon teachers and coaches) to guide task completion as well as provide much of the needed socio-emotional support. In many service projects, group members need to learn to empower one another as they move from leader-directed problem solving to peer-member problem solving. Fox (1994: 58) provides an important perspective associated with empowering others: "Teaching empowerment, then, would have to mean holding back, accepting students (peers) as they are, listening with interest and compassion to their experiences and points of view."

As peers learn how to empower one another, they complete projects more effectively than when those projects involve advice or criticism from authorities. Ongoing service to others is clearly contingent upon peers empowering one another. Principles of empowerment and self-efficacy (Fox 1994) help students learn how to empower each other and utilize the human potential of all group members. Indeed, service can provide two types of rewards: satisfaction with the service task and praise by peers.

**Assembly Effect.** A key element of effective small groups is utilization of the talents available to the group. Groups perform best when the talents of each person are effectively coordinated into a whole. But the communication abilities of group members are often unknown or untested, and it takes the efforts of the entire team to cultivate the "natural" talents of each member. Hence, the essential communication functions (role behaviors) needed to help group members perform effectively should be addressed before groups are formed. An effective combination of previously learned communicative roles, such as those of initiator, gatekeeper, devil's advocate, harmonizer, and information giver, helps problem-solving groups utilize the resources of each member (Yelsma 1994).

Larson and Lafasto (1989) note that it is imperative to select persons with complementary talents to develop competent teams. Two communication talents necessary for small groups to be highly effective are task skills to achieve desired objectives and personal relationship skills required to work well with others. Thus, before individuals form groups or engage in any task work, an attempt should be made to help them form groups consisting of several different communication strengths. Teachers using small groups for service-learning should help prospective group members join those teams where their previously learned or "natural" talents will be best utilized. Effective assemblage of group members' skills and abilities enhances each individual's self-confidence as well as the group confidence or "synconfidence" of all.

At this point two kinds of problem groups should be noted. "Leftover groups" are composed of persons who, for a variety of reasons, just do not work well with one another. Some of the group members lack motivation to work on selected tasks, have inadequate social skills, or simply were assembled into groups that selected projects in which they have no interest. Leftover groups often lack one or two major group communication strengths, such as an initiator or gatekeeper. Members of leftover groups frequently possess different work ethics and value different levels of academic and problem-solving effort. These groups require more one-on-one instruction, feedback, and correction if they are to work through the diverse issues present within them.

"Super-star groups" often have the opposite problem. These groups have too much motivation and want to achieve too many things given the time and energy available for the task. Super-star groups may have two or three initiators who spend much of their time vying for leadership and recognition. This leadership struggle, or "shakedown cruise," can consume much of the group members' energies and inhibit them from accomplishing their tasks.

**Curbing Social Loafing.** In groups where there is low accountability for each member's actions and an outside evaluator is not present, social loafing may occur more frequently than when students work independently. Group members often expend less effort when they work collectively on a task than when they work alone but in the presence of others (Jackson and Williams 1989). When social loafing is reduced by increasing the identifiability of each individual member's contributions (Williams and Karau 1991), fewer group member complaints or grievances occur. In most small groups, individuals are willing to exert effort on task projects when they get credit for doing their work.

Williams and Karau (1991: 580) suggest that social compensation for others' lack of efforts is likely to occur when the following conditions are present: (1) when the group's task accomplishment is especially important and meaningful to an individual, (2) when an individual must remain in the group working collectively, (3) when the group is at the beginning stages of negotiating who does what, (4) when the group's size is relatively large, and (5) when individuals believe others cannot be trusted to work hard on the task or to contribute their fair share.

**Lieutenanting in the Group.** Likert (1961) developed the concept of "linking pins," a means of linking a group of individuals of one team with members of other teams at the next higher organizational level. Linking influential members together within an organization facilitates sharing information across teams as well as validating information exchanges within teams.

In recreational swimming, the procedure used to ensure each person's safety is known as the "buddy" system. Each buddy is responsible for watching out and protecting his or her partner. In small groups, a similar principle of peer protection is known as lieutenanting (Ellis and Fisher 1994). Protecting your partner by enhancing his or her communication implies that each group member facilitates the communication process of another person. When groups are working well, each member's communication will be facilitated by at least one other group member. Lieutenanting is a process of interpreting, explaining, extending, critiquing, and defending the communication practices of another person. In small groups, where errors of expression or lack of expression may frequently occur, lieutenanting greatly enhances the effectiveness of small group communication.

Within service-learning groups, where team structure is less likely to be imposed by outside "leaders" or teachers, the assistance of a lieutenant can be invaluable. Group members are more task-effective and have higher group satisfaction if each person has his/her lieutenant in the group.

**Need for Supportive Feedback and Avoidance of Negative History.** Hedin and Conrad (1990) suggest that one of the most important aspects of the service-learning experience is reflection on interactive processes that occurred during the service project. In the realm of small group behavior, feedback on members' effective and less than effective communication behaviors remains the primary reason for students enrolling in the class. Instructors must provide feedback pertaining to students' effectiveness and ineffectiveness in working with others on the projects.

Positive feedback is usually the most important means of encouraging and empowering individual behaviors. However, forms of critical feedback are useful when given effectively. Results from Davies and Jacobs' (1985) research suggest that positive comments can be given within the group, but that negative comments are best received when given in private. Critical comments are often received as blocking statements and frequently result in a loss of both productivity and group cohesion. Haslett and Oglive (1988), as well as others, offer several suggestions for providing feedback to problem-solving groups: (1) be specific and clear; (2) support comments by providing evidence; (3) separate the issues from the people; (4) soften negative messages by providing relational support to receivers; (5) sandwich negative comments in between positive messages; (6) pose the issues as a mutual problem; (7) employ good timing in presenting messages; and (8) use an effective manner in presenting the message.

One principle useful when working with small groups is to keep negative group history to a minimum. Negative talk about a group's past experiences seems only to add confusion and block effective future interactions. Most people are in task groups to manage and solve problems rather than to process relationship difficulties. Providing effective feedback to group members is one way of enhancing their communication skills and helping them successfully reach their goals.

***Principle of Incrementalization.*** Service-learning projects that are divided into small work units or tasks are often the most successful. When less-experienced group members encounter complex issues affecting the lives of other people, problem solving must be kept at a manageable level (Yelsma 1994). One important principle of effective decision making is the use of incrementalization. Lindbolm (1959) observed that in real-life decision making, effective group members tend to discuss a selected and small range of issues. Effective groups usually begin with small and simple issues and move on to larger issues. Then, team members build task confidence as well as achieve valuable insights about working with others. Keeping the service projects simple, or at least progressing in an incrementalized fashion, tends to help groups achieve higher levels of success.

***The Nemesis of Groupthink.*** In the orientation phase of their development, zero-history groups are known for their lack of critical thinking. When personal relationships are "warm and fuzzy" and task expectations are high, the conditions for groupthink are also high (Janis 1982; 1985). Knowing how to identify and then curb or prevent a lack of critical thinking is a valuable skill for high-energy student groups. People who provide service to others, whether they are paid or unpaid, do not always have to face the consequences of their ineffective decision making. Students who have provided a service move on at the end of the semester. However, recipients may have to live with the consequences of the faulty decision making of student groups. Instructional materials that encourage critical thinking are very helpful in achieving satisfactory results for both group members and recipients.

## Guidelines for Course Instructors

***Waiver of Institutional Responsibility.*** No group member is permitted to engage in service-learning until he or she has signed a waiver. This signed agreement protects both the institution and instructor against any and all litigious claims.

***Instructor Contact With Community Members.*** Students are not expected to provide free labor or engage in non-problem-solving routine tasks. Providing service to the community, at least within the confines of a group problem-solving course, entails examining and researching the issues, engaging in critical thinking, identifying possible solutions, and selecting the best solution in each instance. Some community members who have an interest in hosting service-learning projects nonetheless want to maintain most of the decision-making authority for those projects. In these cases I have requested that the community members and students work with me to negotiate new project options. When possible, this negotiating is done on campus. Involving students fully in the decision-making process tends to decrease the likelihood of their being used as "constrained volunteers."

An example may clarify this point. Five students wanted to participate in a Habitat for Humanity project. The director greeted them warmly upon arrival at his office, but the only challenge he offered them was the challenge of moving a pile of dirt from one place to another. The project did not involve any meaningful problem-solving skills. After some guidance from the instructor and negotiations with the project designer, the students were given a new project — that of designing a "new" kitchen for an old home. They researched the limitations of the house, collected large amounts of data on costs and materials, and provided the project designer with three possible plans for the kitchen. At a meeting on campus, the project designer selected the plan he thought most fitting for the remodeling. Hence, this project went from simple labor to a relatively high level of critical thinking. Indeed, the kitchen was built according to the selected plans.

**Group-Instructor Liaison.** Individuals who function as communication links between one group and another can considerably reduce confusion among service-learning groups. Having one member of each group responsible for informing the professor of the group's progress is essential when groups are highly motivated, operating at a fast pace, and not always well-informed about what is happening elsewhere. Liaisons help keep everybody informed of organizational protocol, policies, and procedures.

**The Best Laid Plans of Successful Groups May Be Thwarted.** Occasionally, authority figures are reluctant to allow students to implement their plans for change within the community. On several occasions, groups from my classes have conceptually solved a problem, but could not implement their plan. Sometimes, solutions to university problems were blocked by administrative personnel who held higher decision-making authority. For example, upper-level undergraduate students identified a particular problem pertaining to the way freshmen were receiving information about the prevention of HIV and AIDS. After thorough preparation, these students took their plan of action to a high-level university administrator. The plan was blocked because the university administrator decided that students should not address issues pertaining to HIV and AIDS in a public forum. Although the academic portion of the project had been completed and credit for the course had been granted, students were restrained from implementing their proposal.

**Utilization of Class Members and Local Resources.** Highly effective teams utilize many of the resources within the class in general. Thus, about midway through the semester we have representatives from each group orally report on the nature and progress of their project. The networking that occurs often provides encouragement, support, and direction that may never have come from within the individual groups.

# Conclusion

When changing a traditional small group problem-solving course into a service-learning course, four major adjustments need to be made. First, both instructor and students need to acknowledge the challenges that exist between learning a concept or theory in the classroom and then applying those insights in their small groups while providing service to others. Second, the instructor should combine traditional academic learning with service-learning and pay attention to both the academic and the service components of the course. This is important because each form of learning facilitates learning within the other form. Third, some of the theoretical materials used in a traditional course may not be useful in helping students work effectively with others in service projects. Relatedly, some of the materials used in a traditional course may need to be removed to provide time and space for developing concepts fundamental to the working of service-learning task groups. For example, many pragmatic principles of group dynamics need to be examined. Fourth, I would recommend a waiver of institutional responsibility for all students working off campus.

Participating in a service-learning project has allowed students in the group problem-solving course to (1) receive academic credit for learning principles about small group problem solving, (2) apply their current academic learning toward solving real task and socioemotional problems experienced within a group, and (3) become more responsible citizens of their community by providing valuable service to persons in need.

## Note

1. For this work I received a 1993 Distinguished Faculty/Staff Community Service-Learning Award from Michigan Campus Compact.

## References

Davies, D., and A. Jacobs. (1985). "'Sandwiching' Complex Interpersonal Feedback." *Small Group Behavior* 16:387-396.

Ellis, D.G., and B.A. Fisher. (1994). *Small Group Decision Making.* New York, NY: McGraw-Hill.

Fox, H. (1994). "Teaching Empowerment." *Michigan Journal of Community Service-Learning* 1:55-61.

Hammond, C. (1994). "Integrating Service and Academic Study: Faculty Motivation and Satisfaction in Michigan Higher Education." *Michigan Journal of Community Service-Learning* 1:21-28.

Haslett, B., and J.R. Oglive. (1988). "Feedback Processes in Task Groups." In *Small Group Communication*. 7th ed. Edited by Robert Cathcart, Larry Samovar, and Linda Henman, pp. 254-267. Dubuque, IA: Brown.

Hedin, D., and D. Conrad. (1990). "Learning From Service Experience: Experience Is the Best Teacher — Or Is It?" In *Combining Service and Learning: A Resource Book for Community and Public Service, Vol. 1*. Edited by Jane Kendall and Associates, pp. 87-98. Raleigh, NC: National Society for Experiential Education.

Howard, J. (1993). *Praxis I: A Faculty Casebook on Community Service-Learning*. Edited by Jeffrey Howard, pp. 3-12. Ann Arbor, MI: OCSL Press, University of Michigan.

Jackson, J.M., and K.D. Williams. (1989). *Social Loafing: A Review and Theoretical Analysis*. Unpublished manuscript.

Janis, I. (1982). *Groupthink*. 2nd ed. Boston, MA: Houghton Mifflin.

Larson, C.E., and F.M.J. Lafasto. (1989). *TeamWork: What Must Go Right/What Can Go Wrong*. Newbury Park, CA: Sage Publications.

Likert, R. (1961). *New Patterns of Management*. New York, NY: McGraw-Hill.

Lindbolm, C.E. (1959). "The Science of 'Muddling Through'." *Public Administration Review* 19:79-88.

Williams, K.D., and S. J. Karau. (1991). "Social Loafing and Social Compensation; The Effects of Expectations of Co-Workers' Performance." *Journal of Personality and Social Psychology* 61:570-581.

————— . (1994). "Combining Small Group Problem-Solving and Service-Learning." *Michigan Journal of Community Service-Learning* 1:62-69.

# Performance of Oral Traditions:
## A Service-Learning Approach

by Kristin Bervig Valentine

In May 1996, the front page of *Insight*, the faculty/staff newspaper at Arizona State University (ASU) reported on a service-learning course I now regularly teach. The first two paragraphs of the article read:

> For the first time, 21 members of the ASU classified staff taught an upper-division class in the Department of Communication last semester. JP, secretary in Intercollegiate Athletics, told the class about the time her husband delivered their second child because the town doctor had gone to vote. Painting supervisor DH spoke with pride of raising his 12-year-old son alone. And electrician AJ recalled the daughter he hadn't heard from in five years and a grandson he learned about in a late-night phone call that came out of the blue.
>
> The "teachers" didn't appear in person. Their stories came to the class through the voices of individual students. Each student chose one staff member to interview. They performed parts of the staffers' oral traditions before the class. But just as surely as if they had been there in the flesh, the 21 staffers "taught the undergraduates about their values, attitudes and beliefs," said Kristin Bervig Valentine, professor for a junior-level class titled Performance of Oral Traditions. (Auffret 1996: 1)

## Rationale

Service-learning is a form of experiential education that allows students to carry out carefully planned activities that integrate and enhance their academic curriculum by involving them and their academic studies directly with the communities around them.

The service-learning project described in this chapter seeks to enhance students' understanding of their own discipline through the service they provide to the community. An essential element imbedded in the students' active participation in the community is their reflection on how the theories and methods learned in class are integrated with their personal experiences as they carry out their service activities.

Situated within the communication curriculum at Arizona State University, the upper division course entitled Performance of Oral Traditions has as its goal to teach the communication dynamics of oral traditions. By conducting original fieldwork, students learn the functions of storytelling; the power of skillfully communicated oral personal narrative, and narrative strategies of oral traditions in everyday life. During the process, they also learn (1) how to build rapport, (2) how to interview and listen effectively, (3) how to take fieldnotes, and (4) how to work with recording technology. Students in this class are asked to present the results of their communication interactions in light of their reading of related academic research, and to consider carefully what they are learning about themselves as well as about the oral traditions they co-create with their chosen storytelling partners.

Of all the groups that make up employees of a state university, members of the classified staff are the most likely to remain anonymous and unheard from except when they are carrying out their assigned duties. In the service-learning course described here, students learn not only about the valuable contributions to the campus community made by classified staff but also about them as individual carriers of the oral traditions of the larger communities and cultures to which they belong.

Listening to and performing personal narratives give the students a sense of cultural diversity, values, cohesion, and empowerment. Personal narratives, as one of the class textbooks describes them, are "constituted in a communal process; they tell about personal, lived experience in a way that assists in the construction of identity, reinforces or challenges private and public belief systems and values, and either resists or reinforces the dominant cultural practices of the community in which the narrative event occurs" (Stern and Henderson 1993: 35). When, at the end of the semester, students perform stories (selected by both student and narrator), their bodies become sites of discovery as well as instruments of intellectual and emotional expression. Thus, performance becomes a way of knowing whereby the experiencing, performing body can discover knowledge about both the self and the "other."

The organization of this service-learning course allows students to advance their understanding of class, gender, and cultural diversity through listening to, and then performing, personal narratives from classified staff personnel. As they hear, study, and then perform staff narratives (staff at ASU is 61.6 percent women and 22.3 percent minority), students discover realities that slick video and print cultural diversity materials could never reveal.

With the express permission of their supervisors, those members of the classified staff at Arizona State University who chose to work with the students are allowed one hour of company time for this service-learning communication project. Without fail, each staff member gives additional time either during lunch breaks or outside of work hours.

Through this interaction, staff reveal themselves as tradition-bearers of their cultures, communities, families, and as authors of their personal identities. In the process, all of those involved discover more about each other's age, race, gender, sexuality, ethnic, and economic class differences and similarities. As Mechling (1989: 348) has observed, "another way of saying this is that folklore fieldwork in the university contributes to the sociological study of American beliefs and values as they are actually constructed, interpreted, and employed in social interaction." Staff members benefit by becoming directly involved in teaching the students they serve, and by being recognized for whom they *are,* and what beliefs and values they have, as well as for what they *do.*

## Discussion

At the end of this chapter is the syllabus for Communication 344. In this section I will discuss course outcomes, detail certain procedures, and address ethical issues by answering a series of questions. With permission I will quote from student papers although without any specific identifications. Students vary greatly from each other in age, race, gender, sexuality, ethnic, and/or economic class.

    *What Strategies for Reflection Are Used?* At each stage in the process, we talk in class about what is being learned through the students' immersion in fieldwork. In connection with that immersion they reflect on the results of their interviews along with their reading of academic research so as to consider what they are learning about their own and the tradition-bearer's cultural beliefs and values. As part of her reflection, for example, RK wrote:

> After my tradition-bearer told me about how his ancestor escaped slavery by walking to Texas he said, "It is easy to forget that we are not the first to suffer, rebel, and fight. The grace with which we embrace life, in spite of the pain and the sorrows, makes life easier."

To understand this man's individual narrative as part of a cultural pattern, the student analyzed his narrative in the context of scholarly works concerned with the function of oral traditions in African-American culture as well as narratives of social control and racism.

    *What Is the Discernible Effect on Students?* Among the positive effects on students of participation in this course are increased understanding of the nature and function of personal narratives; increased understanding and appreciation of class, gender, and culture; improved communication skills; acknowledgment of limitations posed by trying to put the body's sensory experiences into the linear form of a term paper; and awareness of the power and importance of personal narratives. The people they interview are, generally, not individuals with whom they would have socialized before this project, even though students and staff are present together nearly every day in the same campus environment. As one student wrote in her introduction:

SL: It is a rare opportunity for a college student to experience a personal relationship with a classified staff member at ASU. Each one of us goes about our busy days never stopping for a moment to look around at the thousands of people on this campus who make our lives a little, sometimes a lot, easier. I have the rare opportunity to explore the life of one person who helped me with one of my own life stories.

Another student wrote in her term paper's introduction:

CL: My background and my tradition-bearer are both Mexican American. We both eat tamales, celebrate Christmas the same way, and have great respect for the older women in the family. These women are at the heart and soul of the Mexican-American cultures.

And a third student observed:

RK: Even though W was only able to tell me bits and pieces of his great-grandfather's story . . . he knew his family history which connects him with his African heritage. That a valuable story can often be told, but never written down, reiterates our discussion in class on the value of recording family stories.

Thus, within a structured academic framework, students learn about the diversity of their larger community. Championing the concept of field-work within the university setting, Mechling wrote:

In essence, the university really may be the laboratory for democratic pluralism that its rhetoric sometimes asserts, and students doing fieldwork projects in the university, rather than merely studying convenient folk groups, are actually in an excellent position to contribute to an understanding of modernity and pluralism. (Mechling 1989: 344)

As students' communication skills in interviewing and critical listening improve, they learn how to interact sensitively and compassionately with others as they reflect on the role of communication in building trust.

Evidence of trust building is clear in what these students have had to say about their research:

CT: I enjoyed the experience of collecting another person's oral traditions. I also enjoyed interviewing XY who did not hold back — when I asked him a question, he replied with detailed answers. We have a lot in common. When I have kids, I am going to bring them up the same way.

AM-C: *I admire her values about families and family relationships, her thoughtfulness of others and her determination to carve out a place for herself in the world. I am grateful that this ethnographic research project allowed our paths to cross and travel in the same direction for awhile.*

Along the way they also learn limitations in the conduct of their fieldwork projects. From their papers, I have culled typical examples of shortcomings they have recognized:

CT: *My first interview was a bust because I didn't realize that my cassette radio didn't have a mike. I should have taken the advice from Jackson's* Fieldwork *and at least have made a running log.*

AM-C: *I learned that cassette tapes are not infallible and need to be checked often.*

KM: *I made him feel nervous because I was nervous.*

AB: *I didn't understand until the third interview that when I headed in one direction with the questions she wanted to go in another. I also could have asked more in-depth questions.*

DS: *One of my shortcomings was my overconfidence as an interviewer. I was confident that I could probe and have the tradition-bearer elaborate on the questions but this rarely occurred. Another shortcoming was the noise. I shouldn't have interviewed him in a restaurant over dinner. A final shortcoming was that I did not do enough research on the background of his culture.*

Despite the limitations and shortcomings recognized by this particular class, motivation stayed high; no one dropped the course, and the following year when I offered it again, the number of students doubled.

*Of What Benefit Is the Course to the Members of the Classified Staff?* Participating staff members have demonstrated their enthusiasm for the project by their willingness to be interviewed for more than the minimum time originally scheduled, and by their enthusiastic oral comments to me and to the students. The project made them visible as people, not just as cogs in the task-wheel of the university. They were recognized for who they *are* as well as for what they *do.* They tell me they work for the university, in part, because they like being around students. With this project, staff members become *directly,* and not just peripherally, involved in the students' academic learning.

Another benefit for the staff is recognition of the value of bearing witness to one's life. Student JZ told me her tradition-bearer had told her she didn't have any good stories to tell. Yet, when I read JZ's paper, I came across this passage:

> She said I had license to use any of her stories. I explained why I wanted to use six particular stories to show that her life was full and interesting although when we started she said she didn't have an interesting life. She said "that participating in this project reminded her that her life has been full." We agree that this experience has been a blessing for both of us.

An unexpected benefit was that several of the staff told students they had been inspired by this project to start to interview tradition-bearers in their own families.

**How Do Classified Staff Feel About Having Their Stories Publicly Told (and Told by Students)?** Those classified staff who agreed to be interviewed understood the uses that would be made of their narrations because the students read a prepared statement to them, and gave each narrator agreement forms to sign. Those statements and agreements stated that, with their permission, some of the stories would be performed publicly, that those interviewed could choose to use a pseudonym, and that anyone could withdraw from the project at any time. The written agreement gives space for any emendation or restriction the narrator might wish to place on the material or its uses.

Given these conditions, all the classified staff people we contacted agreed to participate, and each of their supervisors agreed to their use of one hour of company time. Only one classified staff member added a limiting condition that was, as she wrote on the form, "If used for commercial endeavor, would want to be notified. Please notify me if any performance is to be done."

**How Could the Benefits Be Expanded to Include the Larger Community?** One benefit was almost immediate when the first course was described in a front-page story in the ASU faculty/staff newspaper (Auffret 1996). Supervisors, coworkers, faculty members, and other readers learned about their colleagues' contributions through this widely distributed house organ. I received calls from classified staff who wanted to be part of the project the next time I taught the class.

I plan, therefore, an expansion of the collaborative dialogue of students and classified staff in future communication classes and performances. The course, as it is described here, was taught again in the fall semester of 1997, with a full-scale public performance of selected stories from the classified staff. Entitled *Highly Classified: Narratives of ASU's Classified Staff,* this public performance was held in the Memorial Union, the central building on campus that serves the entire campus community. Students, staff, faculty, administrators, regents, and the general public were invited to the performances. Our goal was to demonstrate the power of personal narratives from the often-unsung heroes of the university — its classified staff.

**What Pedagogical and Ethical Issues Arise During the Process?** The principal and fundamentally unresolvable pedagogical issue is time. Each student's "limitation" section in the term paper has emphasized the issue of insufficient time:

> KF: *I felt guilty in robbing her of the time she had free and never felt comfortable in asking for more of her time.*

> AW: *There just aren't enough hours to devote to hearing all that I wanted to know.*

> JZ: *I know that if time allowed, she would be able to share so many more stories with me.*

> KM: *Creating a sense of rapport with any tradition-bearer takes some time and we had only three interviews.*

As an active ethnographer myself, I know that there is never, *ever* enough time. To help the students plan their time, I divide the term research paper into segments, due on different, successive weeks during the semester. Each of the readings and tests helps them learn ethnographic fieldwork techniques. Of course, they need more time and that, in itself, is part of the lesson of doing fieldwork as they deal with both accomplishment and frustration.

Ethical issues are also present. One of the older men was so taken with a younger woman spending time asking him questions that she felt uncomfortable with the flirtation. We solved this immediate problem by arranging for her to talk with him where other people were present.

From conversations with students and from reading their papers, it is apparent that some of the classified staff trust the students enough to share close personal information. Some of these disclosures could be problematic, and I urge students to be cautious and to talk through the ethical issues with me if personal information becomes problematic. On the other hand, in at least one of the situations, both participants may have been too cautious. Aware of their mutual circumspection, MJ wrote:

> *I think my tradition-bearer was not really sure what was safe to say and what was not so safe. She was being careful in what information she disclosed to me and I was being careful to be ethical and not overstep any boundaries in asking questions.*

Given the short time they had together and their identities, my evaluation is that the two made the best decision they could have at that point in time.

Another ethical question is raised by the instructions I was given before getting permission from the human relations office. I was told not to allow interviews "to end up as gripe sessions." Telling a tradition-bearer what NOT to say becomes a dilemma for the student interviewer — and for me as an ethical teacher — yet for the sake of being able to continue the course with classified staff we will obey this mandated restriction.

After each interview, the tradition-bearer has the right to amend, delete, or add information. Each student reads aloud his/her narrative and then signs and has the interviewee sign a narrative agreement form. This form helps make clear to the student both legal and ethical responsibilities.

One final ethical issue concerns interpersonal relationships. Early in the semester, I make a point of saying that both pleasures and problems arise with establishing an interpersonal relationship. If it has been beneficial to both student and interviewee, then both may feel an obligation not to drop the relationship once the project has been turned in. One of the students showed her concern with this issue by commenting on her imminent move to a different state:

> *I wish the information was just offered out of friendliness and not because I had requirement to fulfill. I probably won't speak to him again since I am moving to a different state. I feel as if I may have used his stories just to receive a grade in a class and to graduate from college.*

Her reflections on the ethics involved in this kind of class project show us that she was sensitive to the issues of student and interviewee responsibilities in a relationship born out of a class project but still entailing mutual trust and disclosure. I suggested she and her tradition-bearer send postcards to each other from time to time. Issues about interpersonal responsibilities cannot always be resolved, but they *can* always form part of the heightened awareness necessary when linking classroom to experiential learning.

## Conclusion

The first time I arranged the classified staff project as the basis of an oral traditions class, I had been teaching for 20 years, and it was even more successful than I had anticipated because of the willingness of classified staff to give so much of their free time for interviews with my students. To a person, students began to realize the enormous contribution the classified staff made to the university. Students developed friendly relationships with staff members whose lives they found amazing, exciting, and inspiring. They learned egalitarian behavior, collaborative and original research methods, and analytical reflection. This is the kind of research that Novek (1996) would like to see more of in the university:

These emergent views of an interdependent social world demand personal and reflexive levels of engagement from communication scholars. As a means of making scholarly study less hierarchical, many communication researchers now engage in collaborative dialogue with their subjects that draws on the life experiences and analytical abilities of all participants. (79)

This course experience confirmed my belief that, through service-learning, we individually and collectively take more responsibility for helping to make everyday existence more fulfilling for everyone we live and work with.

## References

Auffret, S. (May 24, 1996). "Oral Traditions: Students Focus on Life Experiences of Staff." ASU Insight: Arizona State University Faculty/Staff Publication: 1.

Mechling, J. (1989). "Mediating Structures and the Significance of University Folk." In Folk Groups and Folklore Genres: A Reader. Edited by E. Oring, pp. 339-349. Logan, UT: Utah State University Press.

Novek, E.M. (1996). "Observation Is Only the Beginning: A Case Study of Committed Communication Intervention." Women's Studies in Communication 19(1): 77-92.

Stern, C.S., and B. Henderson. (1993). Performance: Texts and Contexts. New York, NY: Longman.

Stucky, N. (1995). "Performing Oral History: Storytelling and Pedagogy." Communication Education 44: 1-14.

Toelken, B. (1996). The Dynamics of Folklore. Logan, UT: Utah State University Press.

# Communication 344: Performance of Oral Traditions
## SYLLABUS

---

## 1. Course Description

In Communication 344, which satisfies the university's cultural diversity requirement, we will study the collection, analysis, and performance of oral traditions. Oral traditions are, simultaneously, a mirror of culture, a direction for behavior, a response to individual needs and desires, raw material for written literature, and artistic expressions with their own structures and aesthetics. The study of oral traditions reveals how individuals communicate, reflect on, and even change their culture by means of the myths (sacred stories), tall tales, legends, humorous stories, proverbs, speech play, personal narrations, family history, and urban folklore which, in part, make up the oral traditions of a culture.

As Dwight Conquergood (1986) once said, "interpretive performance and participant-observer research share common goals and techniques. Both seek the liberalizing benefits and emancipating knowledge that come from imaginatively entering another world."

## 2. Required Reading (in Chicago Style Format)

Jackson, Bruce. Fieldwork. Urbana and Chicago: University of Illinois Press, 1987.

Stern, Carol Simpson, and Bruce Henderson. Performance: Texts and Contexts. New York: Longman, 1993.

Stucky, Nathan. "Performing Oral History: Storytelling and Pedagogy." Communication Education 44 (1995): 1-14.

Toelken, Barre. The Dynamics of Folklore. Rev. ed. Logan: Utah State UP, 1996.

## 3. Who and What to Research in Oral Traditions

**3.1** Our project is to co-create personal narratives from ASU's Classified Staff. Classified Staff people at ASU include secretaries, administrative assistants, custodians, groundskeepers, power plant operators, registrar's office staff, physical plant personnel (carpenters, electricians, plumbers, painters), media specialists, galleries and museum staff, human resources staff, campus police, purchasing staff, ASU Foundation staff, scholarship office staff, and student health staff.

**3.2** Locate a tradition bearer whom you believe you can interview successfully in the time available and who is willing to be interviewed on audio tape. Tell me the person's name and work site and I will seek permission from that person's supervisor.

**3.3** Here are some topics to talk with your tradition bearer about: tall tales; legends about people, places, and events; humorous stories; personal experience stories; proverbs, riddles; jokes, children's folklore; family histories; medical beliefs and practices; plant and animal lore; religious observations; ethnic traditions; rites of passage (birth, baptism, marriage,

funeral); saints and nameday celebrations; feast days; planting and harvest
festivals; civic celebrations; homecomings.

**3.4** Go to the library to review scholarly ethnographic, oral tradition, or
oral history journal articles and books related to the personal narration,
and oral traditions. Consult general sources (e.g., occupational folklore or
family folklore) and, if possible, specific sources (e.g., if the person is
from a Norwegian-American family, check Norwegian folklore).

**3.5** Conduct at least three personal (not phone) interviews with the
tradition bearer(s) designed to elicit stories about their lives. Audio-tape
at least one of the interviews. Eliminate background noise as much as
possible. The words on the tape must be intelligible when played back. HINT:
Avoid scheduling an interview during a meal.

## 4. Research Term Paper Instructions

For your term research paper, please use the following structure.

### 4.1 Introduction -- WHO

Describe the tradition bearer. Introduce us to her or his culture.
Review general and specific academic literature written on the topic
of personal narration and the tradition bearer's occupational,
religious, or ethnic culture.

Demonstrate the connection between these academic research reports and
your project. Note the similarities and differences between your
fieldwork and the information gained from your background reading of
previously published research in the library.

Quote from a minimum of three relevant academic oral tradition or
ethnographic research (chapters, articles, and/or books).

### 4.2. Method -- HOW, WHERE, and WHEN

First, read the "student narrative" to the tradition bearer and then
both you and your tradition bearer must sign the official "Narrator
Agreement" form. This "narrator agreement" is signed at the beginning
of the interview cycle and can be amended by either of you at any
point.

Describe how you interacted with the tradition bearer and how the oral
traditions were communicated (e.g., by long stories, jokes, short
anecdotes, tall tales, folktales, songs, demonstrations, or some
combination? other means?)

Describe the ambiance and context of the oral tradition communication.
Include sights, smells, tastes, touch, and auditory sensory images .
Describe what people are present, the physical setting, time of day,
atmosphere, and any other factors you think significant.

---

### 4.3. Results -- WHAT

In this section you will be presenting information from the interviews including a short transcription. Include here your record of the narratives and conversation (your data).

State the criteria you used to select which of the data to present in the paper.

From the interviews, choose one of the stories or conversations significant enough to transcribe. Provide a typed transcription of an appropriate 2-3 minute section from your interviews. Type the exact vocalizations you hear on your tape along with their paralinguistics (rate, pitch, volume, quality). Note significant nonverbal behavior (gestures and other movements) of the tradition bearer. Using the method and model handed out in class, type up the words and actions somewhat like a printed playscript might look on the page. You may use a pen to indicate paralinguistics and nonverbals on your transcript.

### 4.4. Discussion -- The WHY

Note the shortcomings of your project as you now understand them.

The most important part of the paper is to evaluate and interpret the implications of your project. Use the information in the syllabus' course description to help you reflect your understandings of the functions of oral traditions you have learned. Study the results of the interview and your reading of academic research. Consider carefully what you are learning about this person's cultural beliefs and values from the oral traditions.

Quote from the oral traditions you and your tradition bearer created together as you evaluate and interpret your data. That is, back up your assertions with specific, concrete detailed examples from your fieldwork. At appropriate points, refer back to the scholarly works you used and cited in your Introduction.

Within this discussion section, answer these questions:

1. What you have learned about the person and his or her culture from a study of the oral traditions you have co-created?
2. How are the values and beliefs of the tradition bearer demonstrated in the oral traditions?
3. What does the tradition bearer think is important for us to know?
4. What have you learned about yourself during this process?

----------------------------------------------------------------------------

### 4.5. Works Cited

All scholarly references should be in consistent Chicago Style Guide format.

### 4.6. Appendix: Running Log

Provide a running log of major topics in the order in which they occurred in each of the dated interviews. The running log is a short form record of what your tradition bearer said somewhat like a table of contents or an index of a book.

## 5. Final Oral Presentation

Prepare, rehearse and perform featured oral traditions research results from your project to the class.

The effectiveness of your presentation of the oral traditions you studied depends on the extent to which you:
- communicate sufficient information about the background of your featured culture;
- present a sense of the context in which the oral tradition was originally communicated;
- skillfully communicate the verbal and nonverbal content of those oral traditions that best represent the featured culture;
- communicate the reasons why the information presented to the class was considered important to the tradition bearer;
- present sufficient information and insight about this culture's attitudes, beliefs, and values gained from a study of this culture's oral traditions.

## 6. Point System for Final Grades

**Total accumulated points:**
900-1000 = A; 800-899 = B; 700-799 = C; 600-699 = D; 0-599 = E

**Point values:**

| | |
|---|---|
| Class attendance and participation | 40 |
| First oral performance | 50 |
| Oral ethnographic report on | |
|     a public or private ritual event | 50 |
| Tests (3 @ 100 points each) | 300 |
| Term Research Paper | |
|     Tradition Bearer and topic due week 4 | 10 |
|     Introduction due week 6 | 50 |
|     Method section due week 10 | 100 |
|     Results section due week 12 | 100 |
|     Full report due week 14 | 200 |
| Oral tradition performance due week 15 | 100 |
| | ---- |
| Total possible points | 1000 |

# Advocacy in Service of Others:
## Service-Learning in Argumentation Courses

by Mark A. Pollock

Hatcher and Bringle define service-learning as a means of experiential learning "in which students participate in service in the community and reflect on their involvement in such a way as to gain further understanding of course content and of the discipline and its relationship to social needs and an enhanced sense of civic responsibility" (1997: 153). In "Creating the New American College," Boyer argues that service "means far more than simply doing good. . . . It means . . . [we should] apply knowledge to real-life problems, use that experience to revise [our] theories, and become . . . 'reflective practitioners'" (Boyer 1994). In my efforts to implement these ideas in the Argumentation and Advocacy course that I teach at Loyola University Chicago I have encountered not only practical challenges, but also conceptual tensions within these understandings of service-learning. What I propose to do here is to discuss some of my reasons for trying to incorporate service-learning into this particular course; provide examples of service-learning assignments I have employed; and identify the tensions I have encountered in these efforts.

## The Course

An argumentation course seems a particularly appropriate site for integrating service-learning. One course objective is to improve students' ability to identify processes of argumentation in their daily lives: in the classroom, in their interactions with family and friends, at their jobs, and in the mass media. Since argumentation can be found virtually anywhere, service sites provide numerous concrete examples of arguments from which students can draw in applying course concepts. Even more important is the fact that service-learning and the argumentation course share a concern with developing in students an enhanced sense of civic responsibility. Indeed, the rise of argumentation instruction was spurred by John Dewey (1984), who saw education in argumentation as crucial in overcoming the difficulties of technocracy: "The essential need, in other words, is the improvement of the methods and conditions of debate, discussion, and persuasion. That is *the* problem of the public" (1984: 365).

Several years ago, Loyola University Chicago's Department of Communication developed an emphasis in communication and social justice. Skills in argumentation were seen as crucial to a program that aims to prepare students not only to identify communicative dimensions of social injustice but also to take action to rectify such injustice. This prompted a renaming of the course I am discussing here from Argumentation to Argumentation & Advocacy, with a corresponding revision of the course description to reflect an increased emphasis on developing advocacy skills. In an argumentation course that has a particular emphasis on advocacy, the mesh between more general notions of civic responsibility and the more particular concerns expressed by Boyer with acting to change social conditions that produce ills such as poverty, unemployment, poor housing, and pollution is even more clearly consonant with pedagogical objectives. Service sites typically serve populations in need of both advocates and improved opportunities to be their own advocates.

Another consideration led to my efforts to incorporate service-learning into this course. Although I have consistently tried to draw upon contemporary arguments and controversies to illustrate and test student mastery of course concepts, those arguments can become every bit as isolated from students' lives as those found in a symbolic logic text. Arguments about affirmative action, race relations, foreign policy, and even university policies, though lively and engaging for me, are often distant and lifeless for students. In the context of a classroom debate or an exercise in argument analysis, even students who are concerned with and engaged by those "real world" issues may view this activity as just another means of evaluation, detached from their "real" lives. This should be no surprise, considering that rhetorical approaches to argumentation and advocacy emphasize the centrality of audience and context to our understanding and evaluation of the reasonableness and meaning of appeals. Rejecting the applied formalism that viewed argument-in-use as if it were formal logic, argumentation theories and texts have grappled with ways to account for the specificity and contingency of everyday human arguments (e.g., Cox and Willard 1982; Inch and Warnick 1998; Perelman and Olbrechts-Tyteca 1969; Toulmin 1958). A pedagogical challenge has been to devise ways to incorporate an emphasis on situated argumentation into the class.

## Assignments

Service-learning seems an ideal means for meeting this challenge by providing opportunities for students to fulfill assignments by applying what they learn to their experiences outside of the classroom. I hope that my account of how I have tried to incorporate, first, experiential learning, and later, service-learning, along with some specific service-learning projects, may prove useful to others.

My earliest efforts took the form of in-class debates on a range of topics that seemed pertinent to my students' lives. I selected some topics, others by the students. They included controversies such as whether affirmative action in higher education should be banned, whether women should be ordained as Catholic priests, and whether United States policy after the invasion of Kuwait was justified. I also have required that my students write argument logs in which they analyze arguments from their personal interactions, their other classes, and public disputes. Like the debates, this assignment has encouraged students to think about the connections between what they are learning about argumentation and a wide range of practical issues they confront in their lives. But these and similar assignments often remained mere intellectual exercises. Students had no audience to engage and no audience to evaluate their arguments other than their classmates and me. No matter what the content of the arguments analyzed and debated, they often functioned in a manner analogous to readings from Cicero in a course on Latin grammar: to students, the point seemed to be the formal principles more than the substance of what was read.

What I noticed, though, was that the students who seemed most enthusiastic about their argument logs were those who took what they wrote in their logs, or what I wrote in response to them, and used this in resolving disputes or engaging in advocacy in their own lives. In some instances those disputes were personal (e.g., a grade dispute with another teacher, a conflict with parents over moving out of the dorms and into an apartment, a fight with a roommate over household chores). But in others, the disputes involved larger concerns (e.g., the fairness of procedures at the university's financial aid office, the allocation of student fees, the exclusion of students from eligibility for scholarships at their child's daycare facility). When students made these practical connections between the course material and their lives, the depth of their understanding of argumentation increased, as did their sense of efficacy. They realized, with excitement, that what they were learning was helping them to change things that mattered to them.

This experience prompted a move from more general experiential learning assignments to service-learning. I retained the argument logs, but with the additional suggestion that students who were engaged in service use their logs as a tool for reflecting upon the issues raised at their service site; different styles of argument that were employed (e.g., reliance on narrative as a mode of argumentation vs. more rationalistic modes); and conflicts tied to differences in the argument fields arguers operated within (e.g., legal vs. faith-based). While this change offered a more specific suggestion as to how they might use the course to reflect upon the service in which they were engaged, it still tended to emphasize the use of service as a vehicle for improving students' understanding of argumentation.

I also sought to devise assignments that provided opportunities for students to apply more directly what they were learning in their service. For example, in a semester during which the university was debating the strategic plan proposed by its president, students were given the option (in lieu of a final examination) of producing a series of programs on the controversy for the campus radio station. Those students selecting this option used their argument logs as a vehicle for analyzing the arguments about different aspects of the plan. The final result was three 30-minute radio programs consisting of taped interviews with students, analysis of issues by students in the course, and interviews of the president of the faculty council and of the university's executive vice president. To the extent that various members of the university community learned more about the strategic plan and those with questions about it had them aired, the student-produced programs provided a service to the university community.

Another service-learning assignment grew out of an experience that several students in the class had had the previous semester. They and I had participated in a seminar on the controversy over the burning of black churches. Some participants in the seminar went South to help rebuild a burned-out church, but others (including my students) were unable to make the trip. Looking for an outlet for concerns about racism — concerns heightened in the seminar — a number of students decided to develop and host a conference about the status of African Americans in higher education in the United States. Their hope was to bring together students and faculty from around the city not only to talk about issues such as affirmative action policies, standardized testing, and minority recruitment, but also to formulate concrete plans for action. One outcome of the conference was the development of a student working group at Loyola University Chicago to encourage more aggressive recruitment of African-American students and to make concrete proposals to the university.

The assignments given to students in the class varied according to their interests and their role in the development of the conference. For example, one student presented a paper at the conference in which he argued for the significance and value of affirmative action policies in higher education, offering rebuttals to common arguments for its abolition. Another student, who was involved in soliciting participation in the conference, analyzed the possible audiences for the conference and wrote a paper discussing lines of argument that might convince some of the less sympathetic ones that the presence of African Americans in higher education was of direct concern and benefit to them. That paper served as a guide for thinking about how to recruit a wide range of participation in the conference.

Most recently I have begun assigning a case construction that counts for

35 percent of the grade in the course. While it does not require a service-learning component, I have encouraged students to link the assignment to particular service projects with some success. The assignment calls for students to construct a case advocating a proposition of value or of policy. The case consists of an issues brief, a visual representation of pro and con arguments along the lines of stock issues for value or policy, and a case outline — a detailed, full-sentence outline of the case the student will present. I work with students to refine not only the proposition for their case, but also the audience to whom their arguments will be addressed. I insist that students select an audience that is not only capable of effecting some change, but also one that is accessible to them. As with other assignments, I do not require that people engage in service, but I encourage it and offer suggestions as to how they might connect service to the course.

The majority of students will not actually present their case to the audience they have selected, but some have and others will. One student used the assignment to help her organization develop a case for expanding the Women's Studies Program from a minor to a major. Another student has been doing volunteer work with an agency that provides assistance to Chinese immigrants, ranging from job placement to English classes. While the ESL classes have been quite effective for many immigrants, the agency believed that time and location were significant obstacles to many workers' taking advantage of the program. The student in my class researched the efficacy of conducting courses in factories after working hours and developed an issues brief detailing both the benefits of the program and the likely objections of factory owners. She then selected a particular factory with which the agency has placed workers and developed a case outline in support of the program that not only helped her to better understand the complexities of policy arguments, but also will provide a basis for her supervisor's arguments when she speaks to the owner of the factory. It is uncertain at this time whether this project will be successful in persuading the owner, but I believe that it does point to the great potential of such an assignment for enhancing student learning and for effecting social change.

## Tensions

There is, though, a potential problem that points to a conceptual tension in service-learning. One way to conceive of service-learning, consistent with the definition offered by Hatcher and Bringle (1997), emphasizes students' reflection on the connection between the service that they do with what they learn in the classroom. The service they provide does not require that they know course concepts nor that they be able to apply course materials in their service. For example, a student may work three hours each week in a soup kitchen, preparing meals, dispensing them, and cleaning up. This experience may lead the student, upon reflection, to better understand theoretical conceptions of power, social norms, and poverty. But the service that facilitates this does not require that the student grasp course concepts. From this perspective, service is of benefit to learning, but learning does not necessarily benefit service. Assignments such as argument logs clearly fit with this conception of service-learning. Boyer's (1994) definition seems to suggest a somewhat different understanding of the relationship between service and learning — one that emphasizes learning in the service of others. We might think of service-learning in reciprocal terms, as students doing service that is informed by their learning, and the enhancement and refinement of that learning via reflection on their service. Assignments such as the radio documentary series and those case constructions that are put into action are informed by this reciprocal understanding of service-learning.

There is ample material here for philosophical debate, but my pragmatic concern is that the latter form of service-learning becomes problematic if students do not grasp course materials. It is inevitable that some student learning comes through making mistakes, but when those mistakes are made outside the classroom in a presentation to a factory owner or a proposal to a funding agency, the stakes of failure escalate and expand beyond the grade of an individual student. The ethical obligation of instructors is far greater where we ask our students to take their knowledge and skills out into the world to do service for and with others. Although I have considered pulling back, being less ambitious in my goals for service-learning and settling for the real good done by encouraging students to engage in service to others and reflect on what that service teaches them about the role of argumentation in the world, the second vision of service-learning has greater allure for me. I hold out the hope that responsible ways may be found for the course in argumentation and advocacy to make more direct contributions to serving others while answering Boyer's (1994) call "to connect thought and action" in redressing the "violence, unemployment, poverty, poor housing, and pollution [that] often occur at the very doorsteps of our . . . colleges and universities."

### References

Boyer, E. (March 9, 1994). "Creating the New American College." *Chronicle of Higher Education*: A48.

Cox, J.R., and C.A. Willard. (1982). *Advances in Argumentation Theory and Research*. Carbondale, IL: Southern Illinois University Press.

Dewey, J. (1984). *The Later Works, 1925-1953, Vol. 2: 1925-1927; Essays, Miscellany, and The Public and Its Problems*. Edited by. J. A. Boydston. Carbondale, IL: Southern Illinois University Press.

Hatcher, J.A., and R.G. Bringle. (1997). "Reflection: Bridging the Gap Between Service and Learning." *College Teaching* 45(4): 153-58.

Inch, E.S., and B. Warnick. (1998). *Critical Thinking and Communication*. 3rd ed. Boston, MA: Allyn & Bacon.

Perelman, C., and L. Olbrechts-Tyteca. (1969). *The New Rhetoric: A Treatise on Argumentation*. Translated by J. Wilkinson and P. Weaver. Notre Dame, IN: University of Notre Dame Press.

Toulmin, S. (1958). *The Uses of Argument*. Cambridge: Cambridge University Press.

# Giving Students "All of the Above": Combining Service-Learning With the Public Speaking Course

by Sara Weintraub

As educators look for teaching strategies that allow students to gain real-life experiences and connect theory with practice, as they struggle to find ways to invigorate the curriculum and perhaps their own teaching, and as they search for methods that will prepare their students to be responsible, concerned, and conscientious members of society, many have found service-learning an effective way to structure and inform their teaching. Service-learning provides " . . . active educational experiences for students, experiences which enable and require students to reflect critically on the world around them, to link theory to practice and vice versa, and to induce, synthesize, and experiment with new knowledge" (Stanton 1990: 183).

This essay will highlight some of the programs that have been implemented by my students and me in basic communication courses with a public speaking focus. Three types of projects are involved. In the first, students utilized what they learned about public speaking and applied their skills to reach community organizations beyond the campus. In the second, students worked with other students on campus. The third project brought the college students together with elementary through high school student audiences.

In each case, students were given additional opportunities to enhance their public speaking skills, since they were asked to research, organize, develop, and deliver speeches to audiences beyond the classroom. The learning goals of the projects were compatible with the learning goals of the course. In addition, service-learning projects were presented as an option rather than a requirement. Some projects were student-driven, while others came about after specific requests were made by public school teachers with whom the institution has an alliance.

The first project integrated the principles of public speaking with service-learning through a speaker's bureau staffed by students from present and past public speaking classes. Through this experience students went beyond their immediate environment and spoke to community organizations. For example, there was a need to inform community organizations about a specific service-learning project that the school was sponsoring. Students were asked to develop speeches on various aspects of the project for a symposium presentation. This presentation fulfilled one of the standard requirements for the public speaking course and was also presented to the class. What was different about this assignment was that the topic was preselected rather than chosen by group members.

Once a speech had been formulated and presented in class, students were available to speak when needed to a variety of organizations. The benefits of this project included increased public speaking experience, the ability to adapt one's message to a variety of audiences, a better understanding of the project by the students as well as their audiences, and, I would like to think, more support for the project. Although students were given the particular program about which they would inform the public, they still had the option of discussing other programs sponsored by the college or by the community groups themselves. Likewise, individual students could represent any community-related project they chose.

In the second type of assignment, students spoke to their peers. Two different projects were organized in two different semesters by different groups of students while studying small group communication in the public speaking course. In the first case, students helped inform other college students about "Rape and Rape Prevention." They researched, organized, and presented to first-year students a symposium on this topic in one of the dormitories. The students worked with resident assistants to schedule and promote the talk. In the second case they helped others learn more about "Issues Facing College Students." Each student selected an issue to research and then discuss with his/her peers. The issues selected included gambling, alcohol, drugs, stress, and time management.

In both cases students first presented their symposium to the class and were given feedback. From the suggestions they received and as a result of their own review, they made changes before they made their presentations in the dormitories. Students could choose any topic that would help educate their classroom peers and could then be developed into a dormitory program and/or on-campus workshop.

The third type of project connected the students with local schools. Last year the acting director of service-learning was approached by a local high school business teacher concerned that, although his college-bound juniors and seniors would tell him they were planning to select particular majors, when questioned further, they seemed to know very little about what those majors entailed or would mean for their future. Students from two sections of the course were given an option of developing four-to-five minute speeches on their majors and then delivering these to the high school students. Most of the public speaking students were so enthusiastic that they went to the high school on two different days, and each student spoke to at least two and as many as four classes. Students spent time in each classroom informally discussing their majors and college in general, and fielding questions from the high school students. The program was so well-received last year that it was repeated this year with a different group of students from the same course.

In another project, a teacher from a different school in the area called the service-learning office to ask if there were any students who could come to speak to her eighth through 11th graders about college. I discussed the teacher's interests and concerns more fully with her and approached my students, who then began to construct a symposium that would help address the teacher's as well as her students' interests and needs. The students entitled their presentation "Getting to and Getting Through College." Topic areas such as selecting a college, applying for financial aid, accessing academic resources, getting involved in cocurricular sports and activities, and recognizing the responsibilities associated with being a college student were chosen by the group. The students first researched, organized, and presented the symposium to their classmates, who provided feedback on content, appropriate word choice for a school-aged audience, use of visual aids, and organization. The symposium designers also reflected on the presentation themselves and incorporated needed changes into their presentation.

This experience was also valuable for the nonsymposium members of the class. Although they did not go out into the field for this particular project, they were able to utilize what they had learned about audience analysis and other elements of speech preparation to assist their classmates.

The idea for still another project was generated by one of the students in the group who had served at a local elementary school in the past. Having enjoyed her time at this particular school and knowing the students in the school, she thought a presentation on health issues that affect fifth and sixth graders would be a worthwhile undertaking. She and other members of her group divided this issue into nutrition, smoking, alcohol, exercise, and self-esteem, and planned to call their presentation "The Healthier You." In a letter to the classroom teacher with whom the student had previously worked, the students sketched out the details and strategies for their symposium. In addition, they wrote a letter to the children's parents notifying them of the presentation. Using the same feedback procedure described above, the students reexamined the amount of interaction they would need with the elementary students. As a result, they developed a more interactive delivery style for their speeches.

These are only a few examples of the ease with which students can apply the skills learned in such a course to help a particular segment of the community. Very simple projects can be extremely beneficial for the students as well as their audience. Naturally, after the students complete their presentations, I ask them to reflect on their experience and to focus on considerations like the types of changes they made between the time they presented to their classmates and the time they presented in the schools; what they liked about their presentation and what they might still change; how they felt the audience responded to the individual speeches as well as to the presentation as a whole; how they felt about doing a presentation outside the classroom; how they themselves changed as a result of their involvement in a service-learning activity; and what they thought about service-learning projects in general.

As with any other instructional strategy, once service-learning is employed, it is the instructor's responsibility to assess its effectiveness. One of the limitations of the service-learning projects offered through my public speaking classes is their one-time nature. For example, students prepare a symposium on a subject chosen by the public school teacher or created by themselves, but once it is done, the project is over. They do not establish any ongoing relationships with the public school students. On the other hand, the college students have increased their public speaking experience, and the public school students do seem to enjoy and respond positively to the college students' visit. Still, it would seem that more of an ongoing connection between the two groups would be valuable.

Another issue worth considering is the coordination and time needed to establish such projects. Although the students handle most of the details, the instructor still must serve as a liaison linking the college, the students, and the public schools. He/She must make phone calls, hold additional meetings with the students doing the service projects, and coordinate when the students will make their presentations. In addition, it seems advantageous for the instructor to accompany the students when they make their presentations. Managing all of this during the course of a semester can become difficult.

With regard to programs working with elementary and secondary students, I hope future projects will be more long-term so that my students can build a stronger relationship with the elementary and/or high school youth. More firsthand knowledge of the latter could assist the college students in generating issues to be researched, organized, and delivered. Perhaps the formal speeches could serve as a vehicle for more informal dialogue between the two groups, and that in turn would serve to enrich the learning experience for both groups.

Other general issues to consider include carefully linking projects with course goals, grading, the need for reflection, and assessing community needs. Service-learning projects should be based on the educational objectives of the course. These objectives must be clearly articulated to the students and employed in the design of any project. When service-learning is not based on the goals of the course, " . . . service is a peripheral activity and the curriculum remains insular" (Perrone 1993: 7). In these projects it was clear to students how each project related to the course goals, since their focus was on audience analysis, organization, development, and the presentation of public speeches.

Grading is another concern educators need to consider carefully with regard to service-learning. As Cohen and Kinsey (1994) remark, service-learning projects may be "pedagogical tools inherently ill-suited to traditional grading" (8). The classes in which I have incorporated service-learning have used the initial speech to the class, the changes and improvements from the in-class presentation to the out-of-class presentation, as well as student reflections on their own presentations to measure student learning outcomes.

For service-learning to be pedagogically sound, reflection must also be a key element in the service-learning process. Service-learning must be " . . . accompanied by conscious and thoughtfully designed occasions for reflecting on the service experience" (Alliance for Service-Learning in Education Reform 1993: 71). Reflection allows students to carefully analyze, synthesize, and evaluate what they have observed through their service-learning experience and connect that reflection with the content of the course. In this way, they can also better sort out their reactions and evaluate their own performance against course goals. Berson (1993) indicates that reflection "differentiates service-learning from traditional classroom education" (35) while Buchen (1995) calls reflection structures "the passage from the experiential to the academic" (68). Again, in the projects undertaken by my students, reflection at each stage of the project was encouraged and expected.

One final recommendation to help ensure the development of a constructive service-learning project is to assess carefully community needs. This can be accomplished through surveys, meetings with school and community leaders as well as with students, teachers and administrators. "Assessing community needs is where service-learning begins. Many programs flounder because they fail to find out what the service needs truly are. They may assume that certain needs exist, but they may overlook less obvious needs" (National Center for Service-Learning 1990: 19). Once community needs have been assessed, they should be prioritized and reassessed periodically.

Service-learning works because it bridges theory and practice and allows students to meet the goals of any given course while accomplishing something worthwhile. Despite the additional effort, time, and coordination it takes, service-learning can invigorate the curriculum and those who teach it. There is currently a great deal of discussion about "building community" as academia moves into the 21st century. Linking what is done in the classroom with work that serves the community is one of the most effective methods by which educators and institutions can accomplish this goal.

Finally, as educators, it is important for us to move beyond the notion of education as solely acquiring the knowledge and skills of a discipline. Educators must also instill in their students a sense of responsibility toward others. Service-learning gives them the chance to give their students "all of the above."

## References

Alliance for Service Learning in Education Reform. (1993). "Standards of Quality for School-Based Service-Learning." *Equity and Excellence in Education* 26(2): 65-70.

Berson, J.S. (May 1993). "Win/Win/Win With a Service-Learning Program." *Journal of Career Planning and Employment* 53(4): 30-35.

Buchen, I.H. (1995). "Service Learning and Curriculum Transfusion." *NASSP Bulletin* 79(567): 66-70.

Cohen, J., and D.F. Kinsey (Winter 1994). "'Doing Good' and Scholarship: A Service-Learning Study." *Journalism Educator* 48(4): 4-14.

National Center for Service-Learning. (1990). "The Service-Learning Educator: A Guide to Program Management." In *Combining Service and Learning: A Resource Book for Community and Public Service. Vol. I.* Edited by J.C. Kendall and Associates, pp. 17-38. Raleigh, NC: National Society for Experiential Education.

Perrone, V. (1993). "Learning for Life: When Do We Begin?" *Equity and Excellence in Education* 26(2): 5-8.

Stanton, T. (1990). "Service Learning: Groping Toward a Definition." In *Combining Service and Learning: A Resource Book for Community and Public Service. Vol. II.* Edited by J.C. Kendall and Associates, pp. 65-84. Raleigh, NC: National Society for Experiential Education.

# Communication and Social Change:
## Applied Communication Theory in Service-Learning

by Robbin D. Crabtree

In the *Western Journal of Communication,* Nakayama (1995) argues for relevancy in the discipline of communication studies when he says, "[c]ommunication scholarship can (and should) make a difference in the everyday lives of people" (174). The same argument can be made for our teaching as an extension of our scholarship. Through service-learning in communication-related endeavors, our students will learn to do relevant research while also providing related and needed service to local communities. Service-learning courses also challenge faculty to unite the too-often disparate duties of teaching, research, and service. One master's-level course I teach at New Mexico State University serves as a case in point, using a service-learning model informed by Participatory Action Research (PAR) philosophy and methods.

This essay provides a rationale for service-learning in communication studies, delineates the features of this course and its major assignment, and explores some of the issues and dilemmas that faculty must consider when teaching a service-learning course.

## Service-Learning and Communication

Service-learning has gained popularity in recent years, despite concurrent trends reflecting an increasing emphasis on individualism, decreasing sense of civic responsibility, and general alienation from community (Barber 1992; Kraft 1996). While service should not be seen as a panacea for deeply rooted social problems, it does fulfill a number of educational objectives including active learning, *praxis* (Freire 1970), collaborative learning, application, intercultural communication/perspective-taking, and critical reflection (CNCS 1993; Gamson 1997), along with providing needed service to local communities and opportunities for university-community collaboration. Related to the goals of participatory grass-roots community development, service-learning creates opportunities for collaboration among various communities, both in the solution of problems and in the generation of knowledge (Ansley and Gaventa 1997; Sirianni and Friedland 1997). The development of communication skills is central — by design and/or by outcome — to service-learning projects (e.g., Nelms 1991) as well as community development projects (e.g., Moemeka 1994). The terms "leadership," "participation," and "empowerment" are peppered throughout the literature on service-learning and community development; *the* critical component of each is communication (Windahl and Signitzer 1992).

## Communication and Social Change: A Case Study

During the spring semester of 1995, I taught a master's-level seminar called Communication and Social Change. Having a background in development communication but teaching students mainly interested in organizational communication, I decided to build the class around a collaboration with a local nonprofit agency. The executive director of La Piñon Sexual Trauma Recovery and Crisis Center (heretofore referred to as the rape crisis center or RCC) agreed to a collaboration to be centered around their spring fundraising event, Take Back the Night. This agreement was somewhat difficult to arrange since the executive director had had disappointing experiences with university faculty in the past. The students' agreement was unanimous when I presented the idea.

The course was based in two essential areas of communication theory. First, the literature on development communication, focused primarily around so-called "third world" community development issues, provided the foundation and rationale for our project (Hornik 1988; Moemeka 1994; National Academy of Sciences 1972). Second, the literature on communication campaigns served as the empirical and practical guide for our endeavors (Jones 1982; Kotler and Roberto 1989; Rice and Paisley 1981; Rogers 1995; Rogers and Storey 1987). Together these literatures provide a strong theoretical and empirical basis for communication-for-change projects within a service-learning framework. Finally, the Participatory Action Research literature added some specific methodological and ethical guidelines that informed the project (Brown and Tandon 1983; Fals-Borda and Rahman 1991; Hall 1981; Tandon 1981). The attached syllabus summarizes the general framework for the course.

The primary course assignment was a group project around the Take Back the Night (TBTN) event. While TBTN varies from place to place, it is a world-wide event protesting the prevalence of sexual violence. In Las Cruces, New Mexico, it entails an afternoon 5K walk/10K run, then a public gathering with awards and a raffle followed by a candlelight vigil at sunset where some participants may tell their stories while others simply speak the names of people they know who have been sexually assaulted. It is a powerful example of collective action with the potential of raising both awareness and funds for the local rape crisis center. Unfortunately, the agency did not have the personnel or expertise to plan the event for maximum effect. For the previous two years the event had had a disappointing turnout and had resulted in almost no media attention or public awareness.

Working in collaboration with agency staff and volunteers, the 12 students enrolled in the course formed the following committee structure. One group did fundraising. The previous year, TBTN had broken even. The event made back only what it had put out to fund the event itself. The fundraising committee raised approximately $2,500 to fully underwrite that year's event. Another $2,500 was earned by the event itself, all of which went toward the provision of agency services. This was the agency's single most successful fundraising event in its three-year history.

A second group did media relations. It used guerrilla journalism (Gallion 1993) and public relations strategies to get the issue of sexual assault more coverage in local media. It arranged for the executive director and various class members to serve as panelists on local radio and television talk shows. It created public service announcements for print and broadcast media. When an eight-month pregnant woman was raped by an English Department teaching assistant during the semester, the committee was in the position to bring the rape crisis center to the public's attention as never before.

A third group handled campus relations. Given the prevalence of sexual assault on college campuses, this committee attempted to raise campus awareness through holding teach-ins, making class presentations, setting up tables in the student union, recruiting volunteers for the agency, and orchestrating campus organizations' participation in the TBTN event (fraternities, sororities, athletic teams, clubs).

A fourth group handled promotions throughout the community and outlying areas. Through the use of posters, stickers, buttons, and fliers that they created, this committee promoted awareness of the issue as well as the event itself. Participation in Take Back the Night quadrupled from the previous year, and was double the participation of the Albuquerque event despite the fact that Las Cruces has only about one-fifth of Albuquerque's population.

Together the students in the class represented more than 50 years of related education and/or experience. Breaking down the hierarchical structure of the traditional classroom where the teacher is the expert, they were able to identify and use the education, work, and life experience they already had as undergraduates; community volunteers; political activists; P.R. and marketing personnel; along with their newly-acquired theoretical and empirical knowledge in communication for change. In course evaluations, they acknowledged the opportunity to apply both their education and their experience as the single-most important feature of the course (also see Kraft 1996).

The impact on the agency was also powerful. As the executive director of the rape crisis center stated in her letter of appreciation, "This is the first time that a professor has reached out to my agency for the purpose of a project with such long-term and long-reaching effects. To give a class the 'real life' experience as a group, as opposed to independent studies, allows the cohesiveness and team building so desperately needed in this community." The fact that some of the students have continued their association with the agency as volunteers, contributors, and event participants further attests to the project's meaningfulness.

## Logistical, Ethical, and Professional Considerations

Service-learning is not without its problems, despite its being exciting and effective. The following brief discussion pinpoints some of the dilemmas faculty tend to confront when they do service-learning courses or class projects.

*Logistical Problems.* The first issue I confronted concerned the negotiation of compatible goals between the agency and the students. While we usually encountered success in this arena, coordinating a class project with the daily functioning of a nonprofit agency can be difficult. Since discourse between the service partners should take place throughout the project (Freire 1970), creating time and opportunities for this exchange can be disruptive to both agency functioning and student and faculty schedules. I personally underwent the RCC 40-hour training during spring break and by becoming a crisis advocate achieved a dual membership that allowed me to serve as the bridge person. In addition, at least one student attended every event planning meeting for agency staff and volunteers so we could coordinate our efforts. Becoming familiar with each other, building mutual trust, and learning to respect each other's distinctive roles took time and effort.

Further, there exist barriers between the town and the university. As in most college towns, our two communities often coexist with little interaction. Of specific concern here was the fact that all but one of the students spoke no language other than English, whereas much of the community is Spanish-speaking. In the future, this barrier will need to be addressed more effectively by both the agency and any service-learning projects sponsored by the university.

In addition to communication knowledge and skills, the students need creative talents. In order to complete many of the tasks outlined by the group, specific skills that are not part of our curriculum need to be accessed. We, ourselves, for example, were fortunate to have a team member who had experience as a graphic artist. Also, some students have a tendency to be passive learners. While excited about the applied nature of the course, those without activist inclinations needed to be prodded into action.

Finally, campus authorities may dislike collective action on the part of students. For instance, when this group staged a leafletting before a major public lecture at the student union, administrators were displeased and called the Communication Studies Department in protest. The students had done nothing illegal, but their visibility had repercussions for the department.

There are logistical issues related to identifying and developing a functional relationship with an agency, creating contacts with local media, and the sorts of difficulties students face in most group projects they do for courses (finding times to meet, etc.). However, with advance work by the instructor, above-average students, and a supportive department, most of these obstacles can be overcome.

*Ethical Concerns.* The ethical issues that need to be dealt with in the course of a service-learning project cannot be overemphasized. One early dilemma came after students did their first paper assessing various issues related to sexual assault (date rape, serial sex criminology, the legal system, counseling and recovery, etc.). The students' consciousness was raised. However, as a result, they became more afraid of sexual assault. They reported unusually heightened sensitivity to the issue, and their peace-of-mind was alarmingly disrupted. One solution was to schedule a self-defense workshop for the class, which we held one week in place of our conventional seminar. I felt it was my responsibility to respond to this unforeseen consequence produced by my course.

An important consideration any instructor must make concerns the long-term effects of one semester's service-learning project on an agency. I knew that the agency we worked with would be left without a comparable infrastructure or people-power the following year; no long-term commitment had been made. One way in which we addressed this situation was through my becoming cochair of the event on an ongoing basis as part of my responsibilities as an RCC volunteer. In this way I could maintain some of the infrastructure designed by my students. Individual students also remained committed to the organization in various ways.

Another ethical concern revolves around the implicit competition between an instructor's teaching goals and social change objectives. For instance, even if parts of the project fail, the project as a whole can still serve as a great learning opportunity for students. Also, while truly participatory projects have more integrity, the semester system is too short to allow achieving bona fide participation at the community level. This long-term issue needs to be confronted by faculty as well as by the institution if service-learning programs are to be implemented ethically, using the most responsible and effective (i.e., participatory) methods (see Ansley and Gaventa 1997).

Perhaps the most important ethical issue is exploitation. As Gamson

(1997) states, "We must recognize that communities are not voids to be organized and filled by the more knowledgeable; they are well-developed, complex, and sophisticated organisms that demand to be understood on their own terms — or they will not cooperate" (13). Neither communities nor individual agencies within communities should be exploited for the learning opportunities of (sometimes) elite college students. Assuring that genuine service to communities is taking place — on their own terms — must be paramount. University-community collaboration requires "moving over, making space, and in some instances sharing or giving up certain kinds of power" (Ansley and Gaventa 1997: 53).

These issues should be the subject of advanced soul-searching on the part of the instructor, should be brought to the attention of department heads and administrators in a forthright manner, and should serve as subjects for class discussion and reflection. In fact, critical reflection has been identified as the key component to successful service-learning projects (e.g., Kraft 1996; Rutter and Newman 1989).

**Professional Considerations.** One of the most significant barriers to the implementation of service-learning is motivating faculty to participate (Bringle and Hatcher 1996). Service-learning is often incompatible with current professional pressures on faculty, which place emphasis on publishing *über alles*. The faculty should carefully weigh the following considerations.

Service-learning courses take more time and more energy than does regular classroom teaching. For example, in addition to my own training, I met with student committees outside of class, participated in student-organized actions, put in many hours related directly to the event itself, and spent several hours in the hospital emergency room with recent victims/survivors of sexual assault. For me, service is critical to my own sense of community. Nevertheless, teaching responsibilities and tenure worries are legitimate priorities that can be overwhelming. When compared with publications, neither teaching innovations nor community service is particularly valued in most tenure reviews (Bringle and Hatcher 1996; Gabelnick 1997).

Teaching a service-learning course may also mean a public profile for the instructor. The class and the instructor can become newsworthy. Such visibility, in turn, can bring criticism as often as acclaim — depending on the values of one's department head, deans, and other administrators. For instance, I appeared on television and radio, besides being interviewed for several newspaper articles. During these media appearances, I did not hide my radical feminism beneath a veil of "professionalism," and my department head expressed his concern.

While potentially risky, service-learning is a "practice-what-you-preach" opportunity for faculty. Service-learning demands that faculty practice the active learning strategies they purport to value, respect the diversity of student learning styles, and work to overcome the disconnection between our work as teachers and our profession as researchers (Gamson 1997). In order to do service-learning, faculty need to be personally committed. Ironically, like my department head, some of the students in my course were uncomfortable with my intense personal commitment. In course evaluations, a couple of students noted that they found my involvement "subjective" and "unprofessional." This points to a broader concern about what it means to be a professional academic. Ansley and Gaventa (1997) explore this problem eloquently when they note:

> A young, untenured professor does not have to be a heartless or craven careerist to find herself cut off from the very social problems and people that initially drew her to her discipline. She finds in her everyday academic life no existing conduits through which to receive information about or build relationships with those people and those problems. (52)

Service-learning can be one of these conduits and make a professional academic feel more alive, more connected, and more empowered as she passes the same feelings on to her students and, through them, to the community. As with most social action, service-learning encompasses the often dangerous practice of democracy (Ansley and Gaventa 1997).

## References

Ansley, F., and J. Gaventa. (January/February 1997). "Researching for Democracy and Democratizing Research." *Change* 29(1): 46-53.

Barber, B. (1992). *An Aristocracy of Everyone*. New York, NY: Ballantine.

Bringle, R., and J. Hatcher. (1996). "Implementing Service-Learning in Higher Education." *Journal of Higher Education* 67(2): 221-239.

Brown, L., and R. Tandon. (1978). "Interviews as Catalysts in a Community Setting." *Journal of Applied Psychology* 63(2): 197-205.

Commission on National Community Service. (1993). *What You Can Do for Your Country*. Washington, DC: Government Printing Office.

Fals-Borda, O., and M.A. Rahman, eds. (1991). *Action and Knowledge: Breaking the Monopoly With Participatory Action Research*. London: Intermediate Technology.

Freire, P. (1970). *Pedagogy of the Oppressed*. New York, NY: Continuum.

Gabelnick, F. (January/February 1997). "Educating a Committed Citizenry." *Change* 29(1): 30-35.

Gallion, K. (1993). "Guerrilla Journalism and Health Promotion: De-Marketing Negative Behavior Through Media Advocacy." Paper presented at the International Communication Association annual meeting, Washington, DC.

Gamson, Z.F. (January/February 1997). "Higher Education and Rebuilding Civic Life." *Change* 29(1): 10-13.

Hall, B. (1981). "Participatory Research, Popular Knowledge, and Power: A Personal Reflection." *Convergence* 14(3): 6-17.

Hornik, R. (1988). "The Roles of Communication in Education/Information Projects." In *Communication and Development: Information, Agriculture, and Nutrition in the Third World.* New York, NY: Longman.

Jones, S. (1982). "Social Marketing: Dimensions of Power and Politics." *European Journal of Marketing* 16:46-53.

Kotler, P., and E. Roberto. (1989). *Social Marketing: Strategies for Changing Public Behavior.* New York, NY: The Free Press.

Kraft, R. (1996). "Service-Learning: An Introduction to Theory, Practice, and Effects." *Education and Urban Society* 28(2): 131-59.

Moemeka, A. (1994). *Communicating for Development.* New York, NY: SUNY.

Nakayama, T. (1995). "Disciplining Evidence." *Western Journal of Communication* 59(2): 171-75.

National Academy of Sciences. (1972). *Communication for Change With the Rural Disadvantaged: A Workshop.* Washington, DC: National Academy of Sciences.

Nelms, E. (1991). "Community Service Projects and Communication Skills." *English Journal* 80(6): 89-91.

Rice, R., and W. Paisley, eds. (1981). *Public Communication Campaigns.* Beverly Hills, CA: Sage.

Rogers, E. (1995). *Diffusion of Innovations.* New York, NY: Free Press.

Rogers, E., and J. Storey. (1987). "Communication Campaigns." In *Handbook of Communication Science.* Edited by C. Berger and S. Chaffee. Beverly Hills, CA: Sage.

Rutter, R., and F. Newman. (1989). "The Potential of Community Service to Enhance Civic Responsibility." *Social Education* 53(6): 371-374.

Sirianni, C., and L. Friedland. (January/February 1997). "Civic Innovation and American Democracy." *Change* 29(1): 14-23.

Tandon, R. (1981). "Participatory Research in the Empowerment of People." *Convergence* 14(3): 20-29.

Windahl, S., and B. Signitzer. (1992). *Using Communication Theory.* London: Sage.

# Supplemental Reading List

Adler, P. (1975). "The Transitional Experience: An Alternative View of Culture Shock." Journal of Humanistic Psychology 15(4):13-23.

Amir, Y., and C. Garti. (1977). "Situational and Personal Influence on Attitude Change Following Ethnic Contact." International Journal of Intercultural Relations 1(2):58-75.

Brager, G. and S. Holloway. (1983). "A Process Model for Changing Organizations From Within." In Readings in Community Organization Practice. 3rd Edition. Edited by R. Kramer and H. Specht. Englewood Cliffs, NJ: Prentice Hall.

Brown, L. and R. Tandon. (1983). "Ideology and Political Economy in Inquiry: Action Research and Participatory Research." Journal of Applied Behavioral Science 19(3):277-94.

Gudykunst, W. (1979). "Intercultural Contact and Attitude Change: A Review of Literature and Suggestions for Future Research." International and Intercultural Communication Annual, Vol. 4:1-16.

Heller, K. (1990). "Social and Community Intervention." In Annual Review of Psychology, Vol. 41. Edited by M. Rosenzweig and L. Porter. Palo Alto, CA: Annual Reviews, Inc.

Hornik, R.; J. McDivitt; S. Zimicki; S.Yoder; E.Contreras-Budge; J.McDowell; and M Rasmuson,. (1993). "Communication for Child Survival: Evaluation of 'Healthcom' Projects in Eight Countries." Paper presented at the International Communication Association annual meeting, Washington, DC.

Hovland, C.; I. Janis; and H. Kelley. (1963). Communication and Persuasion. New Haven, CT: Yale University Press.

Huijing, S., and Z. Yonghua. (1991). "Communication and Development in China." In Communication in Development.Edited by F. Casmir. Norwood, NJ: Ablex.

Laughrin, A. (1993). "Addressing Date Rape on the College Campus: An Evaluation of U.S.C.'s CARE Program." Paper presented at the International Communication Association annual meeting, Washington, DC.

Maruyama, M. (1983). "Cross-Cultural Perspectives on Social and Community Change." In Handbook of Social Intervention. Edited by E. Seigman. Beverly Hills: Sage.

Paisley, W. (1981). "Public Communication Campaigns: The American Experience." In Public Communication Campaigns. Edited by R. Rice and W. Paisley. Beverly Hills: Sage.

Shefner, C., and T. Valente. (1993). "Fakube Jarra Says Entertainment-Education Works: Using Radio Drama To Promote Family Planning in The Gambia." Paper presented to the International Communication Association annual meeting, Washington, DC.

Steinkalk, E., and R. Taft. (1979). "The Effect of Planned Intercultural Experience on the Attitudes and Behavior of the Participants." International Journal of Intercultural Relations 3:187-97.

Sypher, B. (1990). Case Studies in Organizational Communication. New York: Guilford Press.

Taplin, S. (1981). "Family Planning Communication Campaigns." In Public Communication Campaigns. Edited by R. Rice and W. Paisley. Beverly Hills: Sage.

Triandis, H. (1983). "Essentials of Studying Cultures." In Handbook of Intercultural Training, Volume 1: Issues in Theory and Design. Edited by D. Landis and R. Brislin. New York: Oxford.

Voth, D. (1979). "Social Action Research in Community Development." In Community Development Research: Concepts, Issues, Strategies. Edited by E. Blakely. New York: Human Sciences Press.

# COMM 560:
## Communication & Social Change

### REQUIRED TEXTS:

Moemeka, A. A. (Ed.). (1994). Communicating for Development: A New Pan-Disciplinary Perspective. Albany, NY: SUNY Press.

Windahl, S. & Signitzer, B. (with J. T. Olson). (1992). Using Communication Theory: An Introduction to Planned Communication. London: Sage.

### SUPPLEMENTARY READING AND RESEARCH: (On Reserve)

Many of the items on the attached bibliography are on reserve. Others are available in the library's regular collection. These are made available as supplementary reading (some of them will be referred to in lecture) and for your individual research. This list is by no means exhaustive (either in terms of available materials on the subjects or in terms of NMSU library holdings on these subjects).

### COURSE DESCRIPTION:

This course marries theory and practice towards the objective of social change. We begin from the perspective that there are serious social issues before us, and that communication is central to addressing those issues. In this course, we continue with the perspective that we have the social responsibility to apply our knowledge and skills to the betterment of society, and to commit ourselves to the service of those most disadvantaged by the structures and norms of our society. Further, this course brings the academic out to the community as we undertake an actual communication campaign around a serious issue facing this community. The course will entail a single group project which allows students to apply communication theory in a social change effort. (If you have interests or research needs which don't fit with the group project, an individual project may be proposed as an alternative.)

### COURSE OBJECTIVES:

- To build understanding of the key issues related to communication and social change;
- To explore various theories of and approaches to communicating for change;
- To identify and analyze a social problem relevant to our community;
- To develop, plan, and undertake a communication campaign to address the specific problem;
- To consider ethical and methodological issues related to the study and practice of communication for social change.

## EXPECTATIONS:

- Attendance and thoughtful, informed participation in class are critical to the development of a stimulating and collaborative learning environment.
- All reading assignments should be done prior to the class period when they will be discussed.
- All writing assignments must be APA style with appropriate and thorough notations and citations.
- All oral presentations should be done in a scholarly fashion.
- All assignments will be turned in on time.
- Communication is a two-way and transactional process. Every effort should be made to practice effective interpersonal, group, and public communication skills in and out of the classroom.

## ASSIGNMENTS:

| | | | |
|---|---|---|---|
| 5 Microtheme Exams | 25% | Group/Campaign Contribution | 20% |
| Problem Assessment | 15% | Campaign Evaluation | 15% |
| Literature Review | 20% | Attendance/Participation | 5% |

## MICROTHEME EXAMS:

Rather than formal examinations on the course readings, a series of essay exams will be given randomly throughout the semester. These questions require that you have done the reading and are able to thoughtfully reflect on those readings in relation to ongoing class content discussions. Responses should be well-reasoned and well-written. Generally you will have 30-45 minutes to consider the question and write your response. Sometimes these exams may be given as take-home essays to complete as you do the reading. Microthemes allow you to demonstrate familiarity with the literature, synthesize your ideas, and make connections between various perspectives. An analytical approach is more useful than the ability to regurgitate specific details from the readings; although, details help you to support your answer.

## GROUP/CAMPAIGN CONTRIBUTION:

This course will require a great deal of group cooperation, both within the class and between the class and a community agency. Therefore, you will be expected to attend meetings, generate ideas for the campaign, and accomplish tasks assigned by the group. In order to measure your contribution, I will consider: the grade assigned to you by your fellow group members, a grade I assign you as an observer (and frequent participant) of the group, and a journal of your campaign activities. Journals will include a log of phone calls, meetings, and so forth; samples of your ideas (whether or not the group adopted them); reflections on the group process and the readings when appropriate; and an assessment of your own performance as a team member.

## PROBLEM ASSESSMENT PAPER: (6-8 pgs)

Based on your specific area of interest, you will explore an aspect of the social problem which could be addressed through communication. Your assessment of this problem should include a thorough description of the problem as discovered in previous writing on the subject (think about using both scholarly publications as well as other sources of information), and a description of the specific population affected by this problem. Your paper should address the following questions:

- What is the specific problem and how does it relate to the state of social well-being and the notion of social justice? (this will be the main part of the paper)
- Why is this problem/situation important to study? To change?
- What specific attitudinal, behavioral, and/or structural changes need to be made in order to address this problem?
- Who are the populations most affected by this problem? (demographic characteristics, geographic locations, etc.)
- What are the cultural factors which will influence the ways this population should be approached about the problem?
- What are the communication norms of this population and how might they influence project design?
- At what level (individual, organizational, community, mass public, etc.) is the solution to this problem best sought?

## LITERATURE REVIEW: (8-10 pgs)

Find three articles which report on communication for social change projects. These can be in the so called "first" or "third" worlds; they can be related to health, agriculture, political consciousness, education, etc. They can be campaigns that sought to change attitudes or behaviors. Review and assess these projects according to what you have learned through course readings and lectures. Be sure to set up your evaluative criteria (and cite your sources). Remember, you can't discuss everything, so focus on what you think are the most significant strengths and weaknesses of the projects. This paper will help you apply what you have read and heard in class, and assist you in planning our communication-for-change project.

## CAMPAIGN EVALUATION: (5-7 pgs)

After the campaign is completed, we will need to evaluate its effectiveness. It will be impossible to do this using systematic research of the target population, but you will be able to assess our campaign according to all you have learned in class. This paper should be both academic and reflective; in other words, there should be citations from class and other readings, as well as personal insights and anecdotes. The format can be similar to your literature review, but should include readings and class discussions completed since the literature review.

# Community Media as a Pedagogical Laboratory

by Virginia Keller, Jeff Harder, and Craig Kois

*In an electric information environment, minority groups can no longer be contained — ignored. Too many people know too much about each other. Our new environment compels commitment and participation. We have become irrevocably involved with, and responsible for, each other.*

— McLuhan and Fiore 1967

George Stoney is well-known to independent film and video-makers as someone who has devoted his life to making documentary films, promoting public access to cable television, working for social change, and helping to empower people through community use of media. A recent profile (Boyle 1997) of the activist octogenarian emphasizes Stoney's philosophy of using public access television for social good. Boyle explains:

> This notion of being of service to the community, of exercising one's right to freedom of expression by serving an audience beyond oneself, was planted in Stoney early in life and remains a sustaining directive. . . . Asked once how he wanted to be remembered, he replied, 'As a very happy collaborator.' (31)

It is this same notion that we hope to plant through service-learning.

When students begin working with video, audio, or film production they experience the excitement of finding a new mode of expression. They can express their creativity in the new-found medium in endless ways, and typically the urge comes from the personal realm of their experience. Too often it takes the form of parodying the plethora of media genres around them, but the purposes of production can change when students discover the potential of visual and aural media to reach people, to connect them, to help them see and hear in new ways, and to reveal the extraordinary in the ordinary world. Putting audio and video media to work in the community can be a tremendous learning opportunity and a "sustaining directive."

This chapter traces recent efforts at Loyola University Chicago to use community radio and video production as pedagogical laboratories. The development of the Lake Shore Community Media Project and a shift to community programming at the Loyola radio station provide case studies for how community service can provide opportunities for student learning and vice versa. For the purposes of these courses and the radio station, community is defined in two ways — geographically and socially — and generally refers to groups that are underrepresented in the dominant culture.

We follow a brief description of the restructuring of the radio station with a discussion of the philosophical and practical traditions informing these changes. We then discuss the pedagogical design of service-learning in relation to the Lake Shore Community Media Project and two production courses.

## WLUW and Community Radio

WLUW 88.7 FM is a 100-watt radio station located at Loyola University Chicago (with studios at both the Water Tower and Lake Shore Campuses and a broadcast antenna on the latter). The Department of Communication oversees the station, which is run by a professional station manager and assistant with a staff consisting primarily of students and community volunteers. Students may also earn course credit for supervised work at the station.

After its establishment in the late 1970s, the station moved through brief periods of block and all-news formats, and then implemented a dance music format modeled after commercial radio and aimed at a teen/young adult audience. Any community programming included was relegated to the Sunday morning public affairs ghetto. In 1993, following a recommendation by the Social Justice Task Force within the Department of Communication and a university-wide service-learning initiative, the communication faculty voted to shift some of the station's programming to a university/community model. That model would share air time with large blocks of contemporary music. As a result, the current weekday broadcast schedule now is split between blocks of community and educational programming and progressive popular music played by student DJs. The weekends have larger blocks of community programming produced primarily by local volunteers and students.

## Philosophical and Practical Traditions

The conversion of WLUW to a community-oriented, service-learning and social justice project was informed by several philosophical and practical traditions, some of which evolve from Loyola University's Jesuit roots: social justice, ethics, service-learning, community development and empowerment, and *praxis*.

**Social Justice.** WLUW's community programming shift accompanied the development of a social justice concentration within the communication major. Social justice is a long-standing component of a Jesuit education. Its role in applied communication is explained in a paper authored by several Loyola Communication faculty:

> Social justice weaves together several strands of intellectual, moral, and social traditions. At a minimum, a social justice sensibility: (1) foregrounds ethical concerns; (2) commits to structural analyses of ethical problems; (3) adopts an activist orientation; and (4) seeks identification with others.
>
> First, a social justice sensibility foregrounds ethical concerns in what scholars do. It demands that scholars not be content to limit ourselves to the discourse of epistemology or relegate the discourse of ethics to the last place in our considerations. Questions such as "Whose interests are being served by our research?" are foregrounded.
>
> Second . . . . Without denying the importance of individual virtue (in fact, while insisting on it), a sensibility toward social justice focuses on the ways that dominant discourses, social structures, patterns of interactions, and the like produce and reproduce injustice.
>
> Third . . . it is not enough merely to demonstrate or bemoan the fact that some people lack the minimal necessities of life, that others are used regularly against their will and against their interests by others for their pleasure or profit, and that some are defined as "outside" the economic, political, or social system because of race, creed, lifestyle, or medical condition, or simply because they are in the way of someone else's project. A social justice sensibility entails a moral imperative to act as effectively as we can to do something about structurally sustained inequalities. . . .
>
> Fourth, a social justice sensibility is one of identification with others. Such identification is not to be confused with the practice of "identity politics." . . . This critical perspective is grounded in the fundamental realization that we share a world with others, and thus ethical conduct requires consideration of the stories of others. (Frey et al. 1996: 111)

**Ethics.** As a Jesuit institution, Loyola University Chicago emphasizes the study of ethics. There is a university-wide effort to train faculty via ethics workshops and to provide faculty fellowships for focused study on ethical concerns within all disciplines. Faculty are encouraged to address ethics in their coursework.

**Service-Learning.** Loyola University Chicago has developed a service-learning component within the university and encourages faculty to incorporate service-learning techniques into appropriate classes.

**Community Development and Empowerment.** A radio station licensed as a noncommercial/educational (NCE) station has a responsibility to focus on the needs of communities not met by commercial stations. Every licensed radio station is mandated by the FCC to serve the "public interest" of its community; therefore, WLUW is charged with addressing the needs of the communities that geographically surround the campus. This is one way that the Department of Communication can directly serve the community, as do the departments of social work and education.

**Praxis.** The Communication faculty desires to link critical theory with practical applications. The department has made a commitment to expand the application of critical approaches to communication into practical, problem-solving areas. This approach holds that the applied production courses of the department should function as a response to the issues explicated in the theoretical courses and that such production courses in themselves constitute a theoretical approach to communication issues that may be achieved in a social justice context.

# The Lake Shore Community Media Project

Along with the development of a social justice concentration within the major and the move to community programming at WLUW, the Department of Communication established the Lake Shore Community Media Project (LSCMP) as a service-learning component within the media production program. This project was designed to: (1) integrate theoretical and applied coursework; (2) develop service-learning within the media production courses; (3) incorporate the production area into the newly created social justice curriculum of the department; (4) develop a bridge to the communities geographically surrounding the Lake Shore campus of the University; (5) facilitate the development of community-based, street-level media productions; and (6) constitute an ongoing, interdisciplinary research project focusing on the role of media in community building.

The Lake Shore location of the Community Media Project on the north side of Chicago situates it in one of the most ethnically diverse neighborhoods in the country. This allows students, faculty, staff, and volunteers to work with a culturally diverse population. For many students this interaction is an end in and of itself.

## Pedagogical Design

The pedagogy of the LSCMP synthesizes philosophical and practical traditions — social justice, ethics, service-learning, community development and empowerment, and praxis — to provide a framework for the organization of classroom and fieldwork. It is a goal of the project to be reflexive in its approach to the issues related to teaching community media production and working with the community. Mindful of the harmful tendency to allow interactions between institutions and communities to assume a dynamic of charity or of experts helping "the needy," the pedagogical design of LSCMP addresses the following concerns.

1. The issue of how to "work with" community members is part of the process of preparing the students for fieldwork. The project seeks to work with community members as true collaborators and not as research subjects or simply receivers of technical assistance. It is our hope that the boundary between classroom and community can be breached so that these "academic" events will take place with community members in the classroom and students and faculty in the community.

2. To avoid hierarchical arrangements of inequitable power, students strive to function as facilitators for the community. This takes place on two levels — inviting community members to set the agenda for news and cultural programs and training community members in the technology to produce their own programming. This second level provides opportunities for the project learners to become its teachers and for the particular programs to become sustainable by the communities themselves.

3. The pedagogical philosophy of colearning, a process that acknowledges that students and faculty have as much to learn from community members as the community members have to learn from the students and faculty, is integral to the project.

Community media production may take various forms; two courses that integrate service-learning with radio and video production are described below. The first, Community Radio Production, uses the "laboratory" to produce community and alternative programming for WLUW. The second, Introduction to Video Production, provides a framework for students to produce video "tools" with and for community groups.

## Community Radio Production

> *The radio would be the finest possible communication apparatus in public life. . . . That is to say, it would be if it knew how to receive as well as to transmit, how to let the listener speak as well as hear, how to bring him into a relationship instead of isolating him.*
>
> — *Bertolt Brecht 1932*

Students may participate in the Community Radio Production course without any previous radio or audio production experience. The learning objectives for the course include the following specific skills: audio production (both field recording and studio editing), alternative journalism, community-based news gathering, interviewing, writing for radio, and understanding the theoretical basis for all of the above. The Community Radio Production course is not organized around the traditional lecture/lab format, but rather uses group discussions to explicate the issues and processes associated with community media production in an ongoing reflexive process.

Students organize and produce the Community News Hour for WLUW by gathering news and stories from the local neighborhoods. In the process, they sometimes develop an idea into an on-going program and collaboration with community members. The ideal model for this can be seen in a recent example. A student produced several segments on Native American cultural news and events for the Community News Hour. In the process, the student began participating in local activities of the Native American community, and its members began to help her produce the radio segments. They recorded pow-wows and other events of great importance to the local Native American community, which were not being broadcast on any other Chicago area channel. Eventually the interest was strong enough to spin off a weekly 30-minute program called "Coming of Thunder," which the student continued to coproduce with a staff member of the NAES (Native American Educational Service) College in Chicago.

In the process of gathering and reporting on community news, students gain a new understanding of newsworthiness. Localization returns to journalism. They become aware of what is not being covered by the mainstream broadcast journalists, and they realize the importance of alternative journalism. Through working with a broad spectrum of community members, the students make possible an on-going presence of diverse voices on the radio.

## Community Video Production

The course Introduction to Video Production is an option within the undergraduate core curriculum at Loyola University Chicago. In this course, students participate directly in producing videos with and for nonprofit community agencies. In the electronic media age, video can be a valuable medium for organizations to promote their services (in the form of public service announcements on television or as directly-distributed video "leaflets"), train or instruct their constituent audiences (particularly helpful for multilingual or non-English-speaking audiences and youth), and organize social reform or change through educating viewers. For students, this kind of community involvement accomplishes a number of goals. In addition to providing a practical training ground for learning technical and aesthetic skills, the act of producing socially engaged media introduces students to a potential use of video beyond commercial television.

The course is taught as an applied introduction to video field production. The general objectives for student learning are to:

1. Learn the basic principles of video production;

2. Understand the formal elements of visual media and learn to analyze their use;

3. Become competent in basic stages of production (planning, shooting and editing);

4. Gain an understanding of general video practices and theory, across various contexts (broadcast TV, educational, community media);

5. Learn to work collaboratively;

6. Apply and test theories of visual media through creating them.

Students learn specific techniques of video-making and put them into practice. They also engage in analysis and critique and consider the potential purposes and use of video beyond broadcast television programming or corporate video production.

Working in teams (of two or three students) with a selected community organization, the students participate in the entire process, from helping to conceptualize the form of the video project, to writing the script, shooting the video, and editing the final program. During every stage of this process students work directly with members of their partner agencies to create a program that will be most useful to the group. The projects might be informational tapes to educate the public about an issue or to promote the agency's services (e.g., a public school program for pregnant and parenting teens producing a short video it can use to recruit students; or a community center making a video to promote its youth programs); or it might be a video to be used as an advocacy or organizing tool by a particular community group.

Through readings and discussion, participants wrestle with issues of theory and *praxis* related to video-making, questions of form and content, and how they can focus their creativity on the various applications that extend video beyond an entertainment medium. Throughout the production process the class meets and discusses each group's progress — ideas, techniques, problems, solutions, etc. At each stage the student producers prepare written materials that plan that particular stage; e.g., they write a treatment to describe the proposed project, a shooting script, and an edit decision list. These standard production components provide ongoing means for the "client" agency to collaborate on the project design and participate in its realization. The completed projects are critiqued by the instructor, the students, and community agency representatives according to criteria established within the course. When time allows, there are opportunities for the videos to be distributed and/or screened more widely, providing a test of their effectiveness for the targeted audience.

Such a project is not without its problems. When asking students to produce a video for actual use outside the classroom, there is the potential risk of failing to meet the community collaborator's quality standards for a usable video. From the start, partner groups have to recognize that the project is somewhat experimental and the more collaboration on both sides — the greater the investment of time and creative energy — the better the outcome. Also, advance work done between the instructor or community liaison and community group representatives can clearly establish needs, objectives, criteria, and cooperative working methods. For all participants, the *process* of making television and using it as a method of organizing and teaching should become as important as the final product.

Many benefits come from community media production for all participants. In both radio and video production, students learn much about the technical process by doing, but they also learn about the community in new, often unexpected ways. They discover the power of media and how it can be used for meaningful communication within and between communities. The service projects provide them a vital opportunity to get real-life experience and to produce media that have usefulness beyond a formal classroom exercise — a situation that is relatively nonthreatening but still has the pressures and realities of professional work: deadlines, collaborators, clients, outside audience, etc. In addition to bringing the students into an engaged relationship with the community and service, such projects increase student accountability. Finally, both students and communities learn that there are practical applications of media that can be used for prosocial purposes at a time when commercial radio and television are under attack for contributing to social decay.

### References

Boyle, D. (October 1997). "Oh, Lucky Man: George Stoney." *The Independent* 20(8): 28-31.

Brecht, B. (1932, 1964). *Brecht on Theatre.* New York, NY: Hill and Wang.

Frey, L.R., W.B. Pearce, M. Pollock, L. Artz, and B.A.O. Murphy. (1996). "Looking for Justice in All the Wrong Places: On a Communication Approach to Social Justice." *Communication Studies* 47:110-127.

McLuhan, M., and Quentin Fiore. (1967). *The Medium Is the Massage: An Inventory of Effects.* New York, NY: Bantam Books.

# Read All About It! Using Civic Journalism as a Service-Learning Strategy

by Eleanor Novek

The concept of civic journalism is enjoying new prominence in the commercial news media. Broadly defined as newsmaking that creates a "support system for public life" by generating public dialogue (Rosen 1993), civic journalism may offer a partial solution to the lack of civic engagement affecting the country at the local and national levels. In the field of education, civic journalism may also be used as a learning strategy that combines teaching communication skills with community service.

Unlike traditional forms of journalism, publicly oriented newsmaking explicitly encourages young people to participate in community life. Supported by a directed curriculum and reflection, student journalists go out into their neighborhoods and talk to people actively engaged in social and political networks. Then the students construct a problem-solving dialogue with readers, writing stories that focus on issues that affect people's daily lives. A key benefit of this work lies in the exchange between the young writers and their audiences. Though only some civic journalism students may pursue careers in the news media or community development, all are exposed to relational and communicative skills that help prepare them for civic participation as adults.

As a part of my own communication research, I have implemented two civic journalism service-learning projects. In the first, I designed and implemented a youth-produced community newspaper at an urban high school, creating a curriculum model designed to encourage community responsibility, intergroup connectedness, and problem-solving dialogue. In the second, I conducted a college-level news editing class that published the writings of rural high school students and mentored high school students in the classroom. Both projects engaged students in writing about their communities, and both offered evidence that the practice of civic journalism can be used to encourage civic participation in the young.

This essay has three parts. First, it sets forth a rationale for using civic journalism as a service-learning strategy, including a consideration of some of the ethical and pedagogical issues involved. Second, it offers case histories of two civic journalism learning projects conducted by the author with high school and college students. Finally, it describes a new three-credit undergraduate course in civic journalism developed by the author, including assessment measures and strategies for student reflection.

# The Rationale for Service-Learning in Journalism

Service-learning is a combination of directed study and community service; educators often use this approach to bring their students into direct contact with various types of contemporary social problems and the people who work to solve them. Stanton (1990) asserts that community service broadens the educational experience of students, "potentially stimulating in them passionate reactions to social injustice and a commitment to work for change" (344). Parker Palmer (1990) argues that service privileges "those ways of knowing that form an inward capacity for relatedness" (111). Because consideration of social change and community connectedness is an integral part of civic journalism courses, such courses are well-suited to the service-learning approach.

Civic journalism is broadly defined as a branch of newsmaking devoted to the stimulation of public discourse and problem-solving dialogue on local issues. Theorists from John Dewey (1927) onward have placed great faith in the democratizing potential of public conversation and the gathering of voices and viewpoints affected by news. Contemporary views of journalism often make explicit reference to community building.

News is a social construct — each news story involves the subjective rendering of events into knowable and discussible accounts that are embedded in social relations (Tuchman 1978). Claims about what constitutes the "real world" are offered, tested and shared. Journalists trying to make sense out of key public events form an interpretive community with a common history and a shared set of values (Zelizer 1993).

Outside the newsroom, Eliasoph (1988) asserts, journalism can also stimulate public discussion across social divides. "As a shared cultural form, news can bring people together, potentially giving strangers a common ground of conversation" (331). Glasser (1991) calls newsmaking a "'storytelling dialogue' which allows people to recognize their connectedness to others. An individual's knowledge of experience is not only confirmed and validated but affirmed as something shared and therefore common. Stories, in short, build community" (236). Dykers (1995) maintains that this sharing of experience plays a vital role in helping groups bridge their differences and reach practical goals.

The concepts of public discourse and community participation resonate in the realm of journalism education as well. *Captive Voices* (Nelson 1974), the ground-breaking report of the Robert F. Kennedy Memorial Commission's investigation of high school journalism, may have been the first study to identify newsmaking as an important tool for teaching adolescents about community involvement. The commission asserted that newsmaking could play a role in "inducting youth into the true meaning of democratic citizenship" (xx-xxi). Certainly, not every journalism class or course explicitly promotes civic involvement, but many of the practices of newsmaking also teach young people skills or attitudes that support engaged social interaction (Novek 1995).

Any course in media production — whether print journalism, radio, television broadcast, or multimedia — offers students a chance to interact with strangers and explore local issues. In and of themselves, these basic information gathering efforts may not be "public service," but they do meet the goals of service-learning when used to strengthen community ties and provide missing perspectives (Bachen 1994). Newsmaking can motivate young people to take active roles in their communities if it is used to identify and help solve local problems by supporting dialogue among many voices (Novek 1995).

Courses that frame the practice of journalism as an enabler of public dialogue allow students to meet three objectives: (1) to see themselves as agents of change in their communities; (2) to enhance their interpersonal skills in dealing with people unlike themselves; and (3) to reflect on the ways in which scholastic learning is preparing them to take on active adult roles in their communities. When taught through service-learning, civic journalism can bring new relevance to commonly taught skills and contemporary news theory by illustrating the real-world value of communication.

## "Not All Teenagers Are Bad": Service-Learning in an Urban Setting

Many educators have become advocates of service-learning after seeing its practical effects firsthand, and the author, a former journalist turned professor of communication, is no exception. Two modest service-learning projects based on civic journalism have persuaded me that this teaching approach holds real value.

From 1991 to 1993, I produced a community newspaper with African-American high school students in Philadelphia. In collaboration with an English teacher and other educators, I developed and team-taught a curriculum model based on civic involvement. Students used their communities as resources for learning, wrote news stories about issues important to their neighbors, and looked for solutions to the difficulties they saw around them. Lesson plans were designed to enhance verbal skills, develop practical knowledge, offer an experience of group connectedness, and stimulate analytical abilities.

The high school was well-situated for this service-learning approach. Its surrounding neighborhoods had well-established roots and a strong sense of local identity, but also suffered from high rates of drug use, street crime, and teen pregnancy. Many of the students came from low-income households and had to work after school or care for siblings while a parent worked. Some were raising children of their own. These conditions were reflected in the school's performance levels; attrition was extremely high (60 percent or more), and failure rates for English, mathematics, science, and social studies ranged from 45 to 60 percent. When the class began, many adult observers at the school doubted that students would be at all interested in community involvement.

However, over an 18-month period some 97 high school sophomores and juniors did participate, producing five newspaper issues and distributing them in the surrounding community. In planning their publication, the young people were encouraged to see their surroundings as sites of learning. Assignments included trips into the field to do background research, conduct interviews, and take photographs. Students interviewed neighbors, relatives, entrepreneurs, law enforcement officers, ministers, elected officials, professional journalists, community organizers, and others. A group of 18 to 20 deeply engaged students served as standing members of the paper's editorial board. This crew shaped the class's collective voice, reading the rough drafts of all the stories, critiquing and editing them, and deciding how they should be illustrated and displayed in the paper.

In support of their fieldwork, the students studied African-American social life and experience, including works by Maya Angelou, James Comer, Henry Louis Gates Jr., Langston Hughes, Malcolm X, Alice Walker, Ida B. Wells, and Richard Wright; current news coverage; and videos such as "Eyes on the Prize" and "Color Adjustment." Lessons in journalism theory included basic elements of news, the concept of objectivity, inverted pyramid style, interviewing, and editorials. Students also conducted a comparison of commercial newspapers, community-focused papers, and youth newspapers from around the country to recognize differences in content and focus. They discovered the history of African-American newspapers, considered a social responsibility model of the press, and explored the role of the mass media in perpetuating ethnic stereotypes.

Other journalism concepts or theories field-tested by students in this project included the value of multiple viewpoints for accuracy, credibility, and balance; recognition of the need to communicate simply and clearly to the largest number of readers; awareness that a source's relationship to events influences the depth and credibility of his or her information; and hands-on experience of the power of language.

To create their stories, participants traversed the community for information, visiting museums, offices, schools, businesses, and many social spaces that were new to them. A shy young woman who never spoke up in class obtained an interview with a nationally known political activist. A taciturn young man with an abiding love of hip-hop music visited one of city's radio stations to interview a popular disc jockey on the air. Another, after writing about an AIDS peer-counseling group, became a counselor himself. The young writers focused on local issues, including teen pregnancy, family violence, crime, intergenerational conflict, AIDS, drug abuse, and peer pressure. They objected to the racial discrimination they perceived in the school system and the mass media. They challenged the low expectations of teachers, parents, and other adults. They also wrote profiles of local businesses, arts organizations and civic groups, and discussed African-American identity and pride. In sum, the young people wrote about experiences they shared, and used their stories to explore ways of working together as a community.

Students were also asked to keep journals about their experiences, and these writings showed that they valued the civic journalism experience. Some, especially those who served on the editorial board, wrote that they felt a bonding sense of "groupness." Students said their newspaper had given them a chance to reframe prevailing public views of themselves in their own neighborhoods. "There are so many negative things said about [the high school's] students that people are shocked to see us come together and do something positive," a young woman wrote. Said a young man, "The paper shows that not all teenagers are bad. There are some who want to really better the community."

A number of students, excited by the paper's positive reception in their community, wrote that they viewed their efforts as a genuine public service. "Some people applaud the story writers for helping the community and having solutions to some of these problems," a young woman said. "They also see that the young generation isn't falling apart everywhere so they don't give up hope." Another wrote, "Issues and problems in the community have been discussed in these articles. From these articles, changes can start to be made. Also, by us as youth addressing and recognizing the problems, adults can see that we want a change for the better and that we are willing to work at it." "Solving problems within our community is going to be long and hard, but I really think that we are approaching it the right way," said a young man.

Despite the project's lack of a formal mechanism for assessing the degree of service the young people offered the community, many of the families, neighbors, and local business owners who responded to the paper said they found the young people's writings significant and important to the area. Teachers and administrators at the school noted that they had seen significant progress in the communication skills of students taking part in the project. The research period was too brief to demonstrate whether the skills and attitudes stimulated by the civic journalism experience would eventually contribute to long-term community involvement, but the project supported promising opportunities for cooperation between the young people and their community, both in the classroom and in the neighborhoods outside the school.

## "Little Farmer Kids": Service-Learning in a Rural Setting

In a shorter, second project, conducted in 1995-96, my undergraduate class in news editing published the writings of high school youth in rural upstate New York. The high school students lived in an impoverished county where for several decades light manufacturing had propped up a sagging agricultural economy, and then had also failed. Now, while closed-down warehouses and deserted dairy farms characterized the physical landscape, the young people's sociocultural environment was marked by high rates of poverty, unemployment, school dropout, teen pregnancy, and alcoholism.

In the fall of 1995, I began collaborating with a high school teacher who agreed to assign his three sections of freshmen English to write news stories about the conditions they witnessed in their communities. During this period I also recruited undergraduates to work alongside the high school teacher as writing coaches. When the semester ended, the high school students deemed 19 of their stories worthy of publication. The youths also selected a title for their publication: "The Students Speak."

In the spring of 1996, I took these writings to my college-level course in editing and newspaper design. Several students in this group had tutored the high school students the previous semester, and they now joined the rest in editing the stories of the young writers, composing headlines, taking photos, finding graphics, and laying out the publication in tabloid newspaper format. Students in this class studied the basic principles of newspaper design and developed editing expertise by correcting spelling and grammar and utilizing Associated Press style. Then they applied these skills to creating a publication. I encouraged the class to embrace service-learning by continuing to tutor in the high school, and about half did work with the younger writers, discussing the problems of the surrounding community, consulting them about editing changes and illustrations for their stories, and sharing the final publication. Some 100 copies of the paper were produced at the college and donated to the high school.

Written reflections from this class demonstrate that undergraduates' short-term learning discoveries included increased sensitivity to children at risk and the beginnings of a sense of commitment to the welfare of youth (journals from student reflections, News Editing and Design class, May 1996):

*I never would have thought that they would be so hip with the times. I thought they would be little farmer kids with no sense of what is cool. But they certainly proved me wrong. It was fun to get to know a little bit about people who I thought would be from another world.*

*I was quite skeptical about working with high school freshmen and sopho-mores. I thought they would never have anything important to say, or know how to write it very well. Boy was I surprised. They have a lot of tough things facing them like peer pressure, sex, drugs and just trying to grow up.*

*When I was in high school, all I wanted to do was get out. When I visited this high school, I noticed the same thing about these kids. It was in their mannerisms. It was in the way they spoke to me. It was in their essays. I learned that kids learn to be individuals and form their opinions at that age.*

This effort, though of shorter duration than the first project, was well-received by some of the high school students and all of the college students who participated. Community service was measured only by the number of mentoring hours the college students spent, a strictly optional effort chosen by only half of the undergraduates in this small class. Still, students who took part said the experience had made them want to do more community service in the future, especially involving underprivileged youth.

Although the two service-learning projects discussed here were conduct-ed with different populations, both involved collaboration with high school teachers and community groups outside the schools. Both engaged students in writing, discussion, and reflection about concerns of their communities. Students in both efforts expressed interest in serving their communities in the future, a commonly recognized by-product of the service-learning expe-rience. An upcoming third project will involve some of the strategies identi-fied here and some new ones, including assessment measures.

## Design for a Service-Learning Course in Civic Journalism

In 1998 I taught an undergraduate course in civic journalism with a service-learning component. Students began by exploring the theory, history, and contemporary practices of civic journalism to gain an understanding of the potentially enabling and democratizing role of the press in public life. Then, shifting their focus to communities outside the university, the students undertook background research on a number of problems affecting cities and towns surrounding the university — problems such as environmental pollution, domestic violence, the need for youth mentoring, alcohol and drug abuse, unemployment, disability and access issues, racial discrimination, and AIDS awareness. This research was informed by class visits by community advocates well-versed in specific local concerns.

Next, students went into local neighborhoods to observe how the problems they were studying manifested themselves amid the socioeconomic and political realities of these communities, interviewing residents, entrepreneurs, local officials and community groups. In talking to different types of people, student journalists learned not only to recognize issues that can unite communities but also how to share information about these concerns with diverse audiences. Finally, students wrote news reports that made sense of their semester-long inquiries, framing the issues they had studied in terms of potential solutions. They shared these reports with their community contacts to solicit feedback and generate more discussion about solutions. Comments from these sessions will be incorporated into the reports before publication.

The main goal of the course is to use the practice of civic journalism to teach students to recognize, value, and serve the information needs of their community. By studying local concerns and reporting on them to a committed local audience, students will gain new perspectives on civic responsibility, and engage in dialogue about remedies or solutions that may actually improve the quality of local life. This approach departs from traditional models of journalism that stress the value of detached observation and official sources, in favor of an advocacy model that values the expertise of local residents. It also differs from many forms of service-learning, where students are "placed" to work in service organizations. Students in this class contribute to the common good by gathering information about local concerns and seeking their solutions.

The course will include two areas of assessment. All semester, students will reflect in group discussion and individual journals on the experiences they are having and the contradictions they encounter while researching and reporting about community issues. These expressions will offer one form of qualitative assessment. A second measure will come in the form of feedback from the news audiences — that is, the community residents and agencies who read and hear the students' news reports. Students will be considered to have performed community service if these involved audiences say they consider the news reports helpful in generating public problem-solving dialogue over local concerns.

## Conclusion

My preliminary experiences with service-learning and journalism have encouraged me to think that they may be an excellent match. Watching young people observing and discussing community life, exploring their neighborhoods, and talking to people actively engaged in social and political networks, one cannot help but feel a sense of encouragement. Civic journalism gives young people an "excuse" to learn about their surroundings and to care about a common future, and many respond with enthusiasm.

The learning approaches described in this essay can be replicated in other settings and in other types of communication courses. The efforts described here are grounded in journalism-based skills, but also emphasize interdependence and community responsibility. Activities for similar courses should be structured to include ongoing opportunities for reflection about the nature of community and the need for service. Because community needs and social networks will vary according to location and population, service-learning curriculum designs should always be generated, tested and adapted through ongoing dialogue among educators, community residents, and students.

It may be useful to remember that, as students respond well to service-learning, so do many of us older adults. The pairing of traditional communication courses with service brings educators into increased contact with the community as well. To create successful service-learning programs, we must engage in ongoing dialogue with our neighbors and constituents. We must join the parents of our students, the leaders of our communities, and organizers, activists, and critics in a dialogue about learning and serving. Ultimately, the service-learning approach allows communication educators to broaden the relevance of our subject matter and our pedagogy by building "real-world" concerns and connections into academic work through strong partnerships with community residents and groups.

## References

Bachen, C. (November 1994). "Integrating Communication Theory and Practice Into the Community." Paper presented at the annual conference of the Speech Communication Association, New Orleans, LA.

Dewey, J. (1927). *The Public and Its Problems*. New York, NY: Henry Holt.

Dykers, C. (August 1995). "A Critical Review: Re-Conceptualizing the Relation of 'Democracy' to 'News.'" Paper presented to the Association for Education in Journalism and Mass Communication, Washington, DC.

Eliasoph, N. (1988). "Routines and the Making of Oppositional News." *Critical Studies in Mass Communication* 5:313-334.

Glasser, T.L. (1991). "Communication and the Cultivation of Citizenship." *Communication* 12: 235-248.

Nelson, J., ed. (1974). *Captive Voices. The Report of the Commission of Inquiry Into High School Journalism.* New York, NY: Schocken Books.

Novek, E. (October 1995). "Buried Treasure: The Community Newspaper as an Empowerment Strategy for African American High School Students." *The Howard Journal of Communications* 6(1-2): 69-88.

Palmer, P. (1990). "Community, Conflict, and Ways of Knowing: Ways to Deepen Our Educational Agenda." In *Combining Service and Learning: A Resource Book for Community and Public Service.* Edited by J. Kendall and Associates, pp. 105-113. Raleigh, NC: National Society for Experiential Education.

Rosen, J. (1993). *Community Connectedness: Passwords for Public Journalism.* St. Petersburg, FL: Poynter Institute for Media Studies.

Stanton, T.K. (1990). "Service-Learning and Leadership Development: Learning to Be Effective While Learning What to Be Effective About." In *Combining Service and Learning: A Resource Book for Community and Public Service.* Edited by J. Kendall and Associates, pp. 336-352. Raleigh, NC: National Society for Experiential Education.

Tuchman, G. (1978). *Making News, A Study in the Construction of Reality.* New York, NY: Free Press.

Zelizer, B. (1993). "Journalists as Interpretive Communities." *Critical Studies in Mass Communication* 10:219-237.

# The Communication Campaigns Course as a Model for Incorporating Service-Learning Into the Curriculum

by Katherine N. Kinnick

Mass communication programs traditionally have emphasized the need for students to gain preemployment skills through internships, practica, work for campus publications, and other forms of experiential learning. As public relations and advertising became more popular as majors during the 1970s and their curricula expanded to include more upper-level classes, campaigns courses were added as capstone experiences in many college and university communication programs. Many of these courses were the first in their departments to adopt a service-learning emphasis that linked them with worthy community organizations. Today, two generations of graduates are alumni of service-learning classes, and new variations of campaigns courses — from health communication campaigns to fundraising campaigns and integrated marketing campaigns classes — are expanding the opportunities for service-learning to specialized arenas.

While service-learning has only recently gained recognition as an effective pedagogical approach in many fields, its comparatively long connection with the communication campaigns course offers some lessons for new adoptees — regardless of discipline — who don't wish to reinvent the wheel. This chapter provides guidelines drawn from the pedagogical literature, case studies of service-learning in others' campaigns courses, and my experience in developing and teaching such a course.

## Benefits to Students, the Institution, and Campaign "Clients"

The campaigns course aids students in making the transition from college to work by giving them realistic expectations about what their day-to-day job assignments will entail. In addition, it provides career-related experience that may be listed on their resumes, valuable networking contacts, and artifacts (i.e., campaign plans, newsletters, news releases) that become part of the professional portfolios they will bring to job interviews. Somewhat analogously, Feldman (1995) has found that early experiential learning activities such as working on one's school newspaper or yearbook, or taking journalism or writing classes in high school, significantly increase the likelihood that an individual will choose a career in print journalism and acquire a job immediately after college graduation. The institution may benefit from the campaigns course both indirectly — through enhanced visibility and community goodwill — and directly as a "client." Instructors might consider partnering with on-campus programs related to wellness, voluntarism, continuing education, summer camps, recycling, crime prevention, small business or agricultural extension services, or recruitment programs for academically talented high school students or other special populations.

Benefits for clients are typically measured in terms of saved expenditures and staff time. Service activities involve planning and/or implementing a campaign the client wants but lacks personnel or expertise to develop.

## Selecting a Course to Adapt to Service-Learning

In every discipline there are courses that emphasize applied skills — for instance, speaking, researching, writing, planning, and designing — and these are usually a more obvious fit than those focusing on more abstract concerns. For this reason, the communication campaigns courses provide a natural entry point for introducing service-learning into communication studies. While the focus of the campaigns course varies among institutions, domains such as health communication or political campaigns are easily adapted to emphasize service-learning.

The pedagogical literature includes a number of case studies that provide good examples of service-learning. These include traditional public relations campaigns courses (Carlist 1987; Refiled and Incus 1987; Slater 1991); students managing other students in implementing a campaign for the American Red Cross and state blood services (Hunt 1991); a student-run anti-shoplifting campaign for public school students (Boyd and Harrell 1975); and a student research and fundraising initiative on behalf of college development offices (Sallow 1996). The common thread shared by these and all service-learning courses is that service activities are used as a means of fostering understanding of course concepts.

## Developing the Course

The National Community Service Act of 1990 identifies three critical elements of academic service-learning (Stacey and Larger 1996):

1. Meaningful service to the community;

2. A clearly conceptualized connection between course objectives and service activities;

3. Structured opportunities for students to reflect upon and derive new meaning from their experiences as they relate those experiences to course goals and objectives (1).

All decisions related to course format and course assignments should be predicated on these criteria. Primary decisions relate to selection of a community partner, course structure, and integration of theory into assignments.

*Considerations in Choosing a Community Partner.* Criteria that should be taken into consideration in the selection of a class "client" include the relative need of the organization, the organization's appeal to students, and its willingness to make personnel accessible to them. The old marketing adage "find a need and fill it" applies here. Stacey and Larger (1996) stress that in order to qualify as meaningful service, the projects students undertake should meet a need identified by the community agency, not one created by the instructor or the students.

It is important to find a client that students can rally around. In teaching the campaigns class, I have found that students are most motivated by clients addressing compelling human needs, such as the national shortage of bone marrow donors or homelessness. It is helpful if target audiences are groups that students can identify with and meet; thus, a community organization trying to reach local high school students would be a more appealing client than one whose target audience is out-of-state business leaders. Similarly, service projects that allow students to see firsthand the fruits of their labors are preferable. For example, students who had promoted a campus bone marrow registry drive were gratified to see the campus turn out for blood typing. By contrast, students who developed longer term plans to offset negative perceptions of a suburban community were unable to enjoy the satisfaction of seeing their plans implemented during the same term.

A deciding factor in selecting a service-learning partner may simply be how well one relates to the organizational contact person — particularly, his or her level of cooperativeness and interest in working with students. One person from the client organization must be willing to serve as the key contact person for the class. In addition to collaborating with the instructor on the focus of the service project, this contact person's role includes coming to class early in the term to present the organization's needs and provide background information and materials. In the campaigns course, the contact needs to be available to consult with students as they develop campaign plans, and then to attend a final class session in which projects are presented. If students' work will culminate in a proposal or recommendations, the client must be willing to assure students that their best ideas will be implemented.

The client also should be cognizant of the course goals and willing to work in partnership to achieve them. It is essential that the client be given realistic expectations about what he/she will receive from the class, including the capabilities and limitations of the students and any constraints on what the students can and cannot do.

**Structuring the Course.** A variety of formats for student-client relationships have been used in communication campaigns courses and illustrate the options available to instructors. Frequently, service projects take a team approach that allows for collaborative learning. In small classes, the entire class might work together on the same service project. For instance, the entire class might function as an agency developing a campaign for a non-profit client, and each student be assigned a role and title: media buyer, copywriter, designer, researcher, CEO. In larger classes, students may be divided into several teams, each of which takes on a specific component of the project. Another option is to divide the class into several teams that compete against each other to develop the plan that will be chosen by the class client. Finally, instructors may decide to allow students to work individually, choosing their own clients and developing campaigns with those clients in mind. Instructors should be warned that this approach not only multiplies the grading task but also denies students the opportunity to practice effective team-building and group communication skills.

With any of the above scenarios, decisions need to be made about the amount of client contact. Students working independently have greater flexibility to go regularly to their clients' offices to work on-site; a group approach usually means it will be logistically easier for the client to come to campus for a limited number of visits.

**Activities and Assignments.** The primary consideration in choosing service-learning activities is that they relate to key course concepts. According to Ernest Boyer in *Scholarship Reconsidered: Priorities of the Professoriate* (1990), "to be considered scholarship, service activities must be tied directly to one's special field of knowledge and relate to, and flow directly out of this professional activity" (22). Otherwise, in Stacey and Larger's words (1996: 2), "students are performing volunteerism and not academic service-learning."

While other courses may have weekly service-learning assignments or one time-limited service component, the campaigns course generally involves service-learning from beginning to end. Assignments relate to all components of campaign planning suggested by the four-step model of public relations (e.g., RACE — Research, Adaptation, Communication, and Evaluation). This includes developing a situation analysis that summarizes the challenge at hand and identifies trends and issues that may impact the success of campaign; conducting research, including focus groups, surveys, and library research; establishing goals and objectives; formulating message strategy; developing an array of promotional tactics and an evaluation plan; and budgeting and scheduling the entire plan. Theoretical concepts with applications for campaigns are integrated into the course through reading assignments, lecture, and discussion as students work on related components of their campaigns. For instance, Grunig's (1982) situational theory of publics and the psychographic clustering models of VALS and PRIZM are introduced as students are working on audience segmentation strategies. The fear appeals literature (e.g., Sutton 1982) is introduced as students develop message strategies. Barriers to effective communication such as selective exposure and perception (Zillman and Bryant 1985) are presented as students develop campaign evaluation methods.

Structured opportunities for reflection are a critical element of service-learning. Assignments designed to prompt students to relate their service experience with class concepts, as well as their personal development, should be built into the course. These might include journals, "one-minute papers" written in class once a week, exam questions, and class discussion.

**Evaluating the Service-Learning Approach.** Campus Compact, a national organization promoting service on college campuses, suggests that evaluation of service-learning should identify its impact on students' grasp of course content, moral development, vocational decisions, and perceived relationship to the larger community (Campus Compact 1994: 2). Because standard course evaluations do not address these topics, a supplementary method of evaluation should be developed.

Several existing assessment tools may be adapted for the campaigns course or other service-learning classes. These include the Community Service Experience Evaluation developed by Augsberg College and reproduced in Stacey and Larger (1996), which includes questions pertaining to skills gained and course-relatedness. A Community Service Attitude Survey has been developed by Illinois Campus Compact to provide pre- and posttest measurements of the impact of service-learning on attitudes toward community service and gains in areas of personal growth, skills, and traits, including working well with others, openness to new experiences, and time-management skills. This assessment instrument, based on Mueller's procedures in *Measuring Social Attitudes: A Handbook for Researchers and Practitioners* (1986), includes suggestions for statistical analysis and is available through Campus Compact.

I have relied on less formal, more open-ended written evaluations. A frequent comment I receive from students is, "I've never worked so hard in my life — but I've learned a lot." It is also a good idea to administer an assessment of student and client attitudes and satisfaction midway through the term. In this way, one can identify and resolve potential problems early on.

Finally, part of the service-learning experience can be assessing the impact of the class's work on the client organization. This should be measured against goals previously established for the service project, and might include number of hours logged; products (newsletters, brochures, campaign plans, etc.) produced, and their quality and usefulness; publicity obtained and attendance at events; and client satisfaction with the experience. Although clients will not find every idea suggested by students feasible to implement, they should be impressed with the professionalism and quality of the campaign plans and be able to implement selected tactics.

## Keys to Successful Service-Learning

*Adequate Orientation.* Because the demands and expectations of the service-learning course are very different from those of traditional lecture courses, student orientation is critical. Professors who are accustomed to devoting only the first class meeting to orientation may find that they need several class meetings to make students fully aware of these differences. Two aspects of the service-learning course that I find cannot be emphasized enough are the time commitment required outside of class, which can be substantial, and the responsibility that students will bear to the client and to each other. In addition, because students will be interacting with community clients and their constituencies, a discussion of client courtesy should be included to reinforce the idea that students will be acting as representatives of the college, and their behavior will reflect back on the institution.

If students will be working in teams, an additional orientation to group work is needed, such as assigning individual grades and dealing with team members who do not pull their weight. I have found it invaluable to devote one class period to effective teamwork. Topics during this session include characteristics of effective teams, roles of team members, common problems in teams, and strategies for effective meetings. At the end of this discussion students meet in groups to create their own group contract that lays out as specifically as possible the group's criteria for success, its expectations for attendance at meetings, quality of work, rewards for extra effort, and reprisals for failure to attend meetings or turn in work. Students often come up with creative ideas that go beyond positive or negative peer evaluations, such as requiring group members to pay $20 for every meeting missed, with funds to go toward an end-of-term party. This process helps to set the tone for the course and ensures that all team members understand what they expect from each other.

*Strong Course Policies.* Because one's course may well be many students' first experience with service-learning, course policies must be crystal clear and in writing. In particular, policies regarding grading (will grading be based to any extent on client evaluations, peer evaluations, time put in?) and consequences for nonproductive class members should be spelled out explicitly. In my campaigns course syllabus, I spell out provisions under which a student can be "fired" by his or her group, and that the fired student will then be responsible for completing all course requirements on his or her own. Similarly, because learning to work collaboratively and resolve differences is part of real-world training, I note on my syllabus that I do not permit a student to voluntarily resign from a team.

To avoid liability issues, if the course requires outside class meetings, the syllabus should instruct students to meet on campus and in public buildings rather than in students' apartments or dorm rooms.

**Motivating Students.** Maintaining students' motivation is another factor critical to the success of a service-learning course. Initially, the idea of helping a community organization may provide enough intrinsic motivation for students. But as the term wears on, and as work settles into a routine and pressures from other classes begin to mount, students may need to be re-energized. This may be a good time to invite constituencies who will benefit from student work to visit the class — for example, a person on a bone marrow waiting list — or to invite guest speakers with prestige appeal — a high-ranking business or community leader, for instance. Position the students as heroes: Without their efforts, a project would go unpromoted or otherwise be less than successful.

It also helps if the class is treated as an elite group. Class members should feel, within the limits of their background and training, that they are working professionals rather than students. Providing access to clients' and community leaders' phone numbers and to special campus resources and facilities helps to reinforce this message. Remind students that quality is important because their work will actually be used. Foster team spirit by having student groups create names for themselves. If groups are competing with each other, keep posted who is ahead in the "horse race."

Heighten the class's visibility on campus by seeking publicity that showcases its work in student, alumni, and community newspapers, or displaying photos documenting the service project on a hallway bulletin board. An end-of-course culmination celebration, such as a reception after a competitive pitch day, or a party at the client's offices also designates the class as something special.

# Conclusion

Realizing the full potential of service-learning means looking for ways to maximize and extend the impact of community involvement. The service-learning course can be the launching pad for additional academic and community collaborations that continue beyond the end of the academic term. Participation in the communication campaigns course has led clients to create internships for students and led students to pursue independent study projects related to a client's needs. Service-learning projects can also facilitate collaboration with other faculty, academic departments, and campus resources. Other obvious linkages for campaigns classes are with art and graphic design students or public speaking classes whose members could speak to campus organizations about related topics.

A recent survey of participants in summer institutes on service-learning found that service-learning is gaining legitimacy on college campuses as an alternative to traditional teaching pedagogies (Campus Compact 1994). Many campuses now have community service/voluntarism centers that can help faculty adapt a course to a service-learning approach and identify community partners. However, faculty have expressed a desire for more discipline-based case studies and conferences to discuss the integration of service with academic curricula. As an early adopter of the service-learning approach, the communication campaigns course provides the communication disciplines with a reservoir of experience that should not go untapped.

## References

Boyd, John A., and Jackson Horoll. (November 1975). "The Administration of Student-Run Public Persuasive Campaigns: The Experience of 'Shoplifting Hurts Everyone.'" *Communication Education* 24:341-347.

Boyer, Ernest L. (1990). *Scholarship Reconsidered: Priorities of the Professoriate.* Princeton, NJ: The Carnegie Foundation for the Advancement of Teaching.

Campus Compact. (1994). "Summary of Findings: Experiences of Teams Attending the 1991, 1992, and 1993 Summer Institutes on Integrating Service With Academic Study." Providence, RI: Campus Contact.

Carlist, J. (Winter 1987). "Experts and Novices Contribute, Learn in PR Case Course." *Journalism Educator* 41(4): 44.

Grunig, James E. (1982). "The Message-Attitude-Behavior Relationship: Communication Behaviors of Organizations." *Communication Research* 9:163-200.

Hunt, Todd. (February 1991). "Management Students Can Learn to Manage Others." *Teaching Public Relations:* 21.

Mueller, Daniel J. (1986). *Measuring Social Attitudes: A Handbook for Researchers and Practitioners.* New York, NY: Teachers College Press.

Refiled, R.E., and J.D. Incus. (Winter 1987). "Students Control In-Class PR Agency." *Journalism Educator* 41(4): 45-47.

Sallow, Lynne. (Spring 1996). "Using a Public Relations Course to Build University Relationships." *Journalism & Mass Communication Educator* 51(1): 51-60.

Slater, M. (October 1991). "Combining Cooperative Learning and Individual Client Work in the Public Relations Capstone Course." *Teaching Public Relations:* 22.

Stacey, Kathleen, and Georgea Larger. (1996). *Faculty Training Manual*. Ypsilanti, MI: Office of Academic Service-Learning, Eastern Michigan University.

Sutton, S.B. (1982). "Fear-Arousing Communications: A Critical Examination of Theory and Research." In *Social Psychology and Behavioral Medicine*, pp. 303-338. Chichester, England: John Wiley & Sons.

Zillman, Dolf, and J. Bryant. (1985). *Selective Exposure to Communication*. Hillsdale, NJ: Erlbaum.

# Public Relations and Public Service: Integrating Service-Learning Into the Public Relations Seminar

by Lynne A. Texter and Michael F. Smith

Public relations practitioners often are required to be both strategists who counsel organizations about their opportunities and challenges and technicians who produce communication messages distributed over a variety of channels. A comprehensive public relations curriculum should prepare students to assume both roles. Both professionals and scholars endorse a public relations curriculum in which students explore the public relations planning process and discover how to apply the process to actual communication situations in organizations (Ehling 1992). Service-learning offers public relations educators a means of integrating these goals.

This essay examines two distinct approaches to integrating service-learning into a single senior-level public relations seminar. We will outline the goals of the course; discuss the selection of community partners; describe the two approaches to the course; and examine outcomes and assessment.

## Goals of the Course

Designed to provide in-depth study of systematic and ethical public relations management, the public relations seminar focuses the process of making communication decisions by emphasizing systematic research, strategic planning, implementation, and evaluation. This capstone course is designed to allow senior-level students to extend and apply the knowledge acquired in previous communication courses, particularly in public relations courses, to communication case analysis and program/campaign design.

The goals of the course include:

1. To provide students with an opportunity to apply communication theory, research, and skills to a practical public relations problem or opportunity. Students learn to:

a) Assess organizational needs and relevant situational variables;
b) Establish communication goals and objectives;
c) Develop an appropriate communication course of action;
d) Implement a public relations program, if applicable;
e) Assess the results of the implementation.

2. To foster interpersonal and small-group communication skills as stu-

dents interact with clients and peers.

3. To provide students with an opportunity to partner with a nonprofit, community-based organization. (Ideally, students develop an ongoing relationship with the organization.)

4. To assist community organizations with public relations or other communication needs.

## Selection of Community Partners

Each semester, the class forms a community partnership with a local nonprofit organization to work toward course goals. The selection of an appropriate organization is critical to the success of the project and to the quality of the students' experience. A poorly organized group or unrealistic organizational expectations, for example, can severely undermine a project. Thus, the instructor must devote adequate time and attention to the selection process prior to the semester.

On occasion, the potential client organization may approach the instructor or the department seeking communication assistance, but more commonly the instructor must recruit and select organizations by culling potential nonprofit organizations from the phone book or by using campus community service resources. Phone calls, letters, and meetings with the organizational representatives are necessary to determine the viability of the student-client partnership.

The organizations are selected on the basis of the following criteria:

1. *Appropriate communication needs and expectations.* The organization's needs must call for ethical public relations or other communication services. Students should not, for example, be primarily expected to run fundraisers or stuff envelopes. Students may plan and publicize fundraisers but may not actually collect money on behalf of the organization.

2. *Interest and availability of organization representatives.* A contact person must be available throughout the semester to work with students and to address questions and concerns. Ideally, the contact person should be interested in working with college students and have the authority to approve projects. The person should be responsive to students and willing and able to provide constructive criticism from beginning to end.

3. *Viable project for senior-level undergraduates.* The project's difficulty and scope must be appropriate for senior-level communication students to complete on a part-time basis within the constraints of a 14-week semester. This project is one portion of but one of each student's five courses, and the project should be designed with this time frame firmly in mind.

4. *Organization size and proximity to campus.* The organization must have sufficient personnel and structure to develop a mutually beneficial partner-

ship. It is desirable that the organization be in the local campus community to allow frequent student contact with the organization and to enhance campus ties with the community.

5. *Sufficient organization budget and other resources.* One of the approaches to this project sometimes requires that potential clients possess the resources to complete a task. These include financial resources to pay for outside vendors such as printers. But they may also include things such as computers and staff able to continue to produce communication tools such as newsletters after the students leave.

## The Seminar Project

We outline two distinct approaches to incorporating service-learning into the public relations seminar. Each approach has the service-learning experience as a central portion of the course but varies in the focus of the work, one approach emphasizing the strategic planning process and the other more specific events or communication needs. The instructor would select one approach or the other for the entire semester.

Although the nature of the project varies, both approaches organize the class into groups or "account teams." Instructors may designate the teams or allow students to self-select, but whatever the selection method, four- to six-person teams function best to encourage participation and to keep everyone busy. The project is too daunting for smaller groups, and larger groups may allow people to become "lost." One student from each group is selected to become the "account executive," whose responsibilities include keeping the group on task and serving as a liaison among the group, client, and instructor.

Group projects, by their very nature, seem to generate an array of communication and relational issues and problems. Because one of the course goals is to foster interpersonal and small-group skills, learning to work together efficiently and effectively is another critical element of the project. The instructor should consider implementing methods of process and performance evaluation (e.g., journals and peer evaluations) throughout the semester to assess real and potential problems in the groups.

One effective method we have used to deter problems is to make it clear that team members who do not perform satisfactorily may be removed by unanimous action of the group and with consultation with the instructor (i.e., "fired"). A written warning must first be provided for the student, with a probation period to adjust his/her behavior. If this effort fails, the group may remove the member after consulting with the instructor. Again, written notification is required. The person who has been fired has three options: (1) formally seek to interview to join another group (no group is obligated to hire a fired worker); (2) negotiate with the instructor to complete the entire final project and presentation individually; or (3) withdraw from the course.

**The Strategic Plan Book Approach.** One approach to incorporating service-learning into the seminar focuses on the strategic planning process (see Hendrix 1995; McElreath 1993; and Nager and Allen 1984 for resource materials for either project). Student teams consult with the client and the instructor to develop a highly detailed campaign book that uses primary and secondary research on the organization (e.g., its purpose and relevant history, communication needs, available personnel and resources, and previous communication efforts), relevant situational factors, and the organization's internal and external stakeholders as a foundation for decisions about the communication problem or opportunity, the specific communication goals and objectives, the target audience, the communication channels and message strategies, the proposed budget, and evaluation methods. The teams design and produce some of the communication vehicles, although the focus is primarily upon research, planning, and general design rather than upon the actual production and implementation of brochures, videos, newsletters, events, and the like.

At the end of the semester each student team submits its campaign book to the instructor and the client. The campaign books are expected to be detailed in content and professional in appearance. Student teams also prepare and deliver 45-minute professional presentations of their campaign books for the client, followed by 15 minutes of questions and challenges by the client, instructor, and other student teams.

The client acquires detailed public relations plans from several teams to guide implementation and further development of communication programs. The organization may use or adapt portions of any or all of the proposals. The students gain intensive practical experience in the public relations management process as well as in the joys and frustrations of working with actual clients under strict time lines. They also have an impressive binder to take with them on job interviews.

Habitat for Humanity/Germantown is one example of a successful community partner in the strategic plan book approach to the course. Through interviews with organization members and original survey research in the community, student groups discovered that, while there was a fairly high level of awareness about the national organization, there was limited knowledge about the activities and needs of the local chapter of Habitat for Humanity. Students then incorporated this research into a situational analysis and developed a strategic plan that included communication goals, courses of action, a discussion of resources, and an implementation and evaluation plan. Student teams presented their plans to representatives from Habitat, and the organization made the decision to implement some of the proposed communication activities.

*The Project Implementation Approach.* The second approach to linking public relations and community learning requires the students to propose, execute, and evaluate a specific public relations project (Smith 1995). The project approach begins where the campaign book approach leaves off. Student groups meet with clients and conduct research to determine the organization's needs. Students then produce a proposal that identifies the client's needs, establishes the specific objectives the students hope to achieve, outlines the tasks the students will undertake to reach the objectives, and establishes a budget and schedule for completing the tasks. Once the client and students agree to the terms of the proposal, the students complete the work and write a final report.

Students have completed a variety of projects for clients, including establishing internal communication tools, such as newsletters; creating publicity pieces for particular services; and planning, publicizing, and executing special events. The key distinction between this approach and the planning approach is that students not only learn to analyze a situation and set goals but also negotiate with the community partner over the acceptability of the plan and experience the challenges that face practitioners attempting to complete tasks for a client. These challenges include revising pieces to meet the standards of both the instructor and the client, working with printers and other service providers, and meeting deadlines for submitting information to the media. At the end of the semester, students also must evaluate the success of their project and make recommendations to the clients for future public relations efforts. The students gain not only the strategic sense that comes from research and planning but also tangible public relations tools that might benefit the client and can become part of their portfolios.

The Clean Air Council of Philadelphia has been a community partner with several seminar groups using the project implementation approach. One group helped publicize the opening of a new recycling center, which entailed media relations, producing and distributing information to users of existing recycling facilities, and placing ads in local newspapers. The grand opening was successful and generated some media coverage in community and city-wide outlets. Other groups have helped publicize the annual Earth Day Run, targeting special-interest publications in addition to general media relations and event promotion. Each year the number of participants has increased.

## Outcomes and Assessment

Students require constant and consistent monitoring and feedback for projects that are so extensive. Methods of assessment might include commenting and grading student work, eliciting student feedback on the project and process, and distributing client surveys.

First, and seemingly of the most concern to the students, the projects represent a significant portion of the course grade. Typically, the final course grade reflects a balance between the grades on the seminar group project — which reflects the quality of the final project, peer evaluations, and contributions to the process — and grades on individual assignments and exams.

The second method of assessment is student feedback. Student feedback should ideally allow the students to reflect upon the experience as well as report what they have accomplished (Connolly 1989), and two methods might be combined to gather this information: journals and peer evaluations.

Students are required to submit journals at a number of points during the semester. They are asked to reflect on experiences, issues, and concerns. For example, students might detail perceptions of working with the client, areas of the project that are unclear or problematic, the difficulties of group work, and the challenges and benefits of community service.

Students also provide feedback on their group and on their own work. Their written peer evaluations detail every group member's specific contributions to the project, the quality of his/her participation, attendance at group meetings, and overall progress on the project. The students must also evaluate their own contributions as well as indicate the amount of time spent on the group project each week. This allows them to garner a bit of perspective about the demands of the project and how they use their time.

The final method of assessment is a survey of the clients at the end of the semester to determine their satisfaction with the groups and the projects. Most clients are assertive enough to indicate dissatisfaction and problems as they occur throughout the semester, but the survey formalizes their reactions and assesses the willingness of the organization to participate in future class-client partnerships.

The two approaches to service-learning projects outlined here help students explore the dual public relations roles of strategist and tactician. Although the projects require significant effort by students, clients, and the instructor, all parties can accrue significant benefits.

References

Connolly, K. (November/December 1989). "Think About It: Taking Time Out for Reflection." *Campus Outreach*: 1.

Ehling, W. (1992). "Public Relations Education and Professionalism." In *Excellence in Public Relations and Communication Management.* Edited by J. Grunig, pp. 439-464. Hillsdale, NJ: Erlbaum.

Hendrix, J. (1995) *Public Relations Case.* 3rd ed. Belmont, CA: Wadsworth.

McElreath, M. (1993). *Managing Systematic and Ethical Public Relations Campaigns.* 2nd ed. Madison, WI: Brown and Benchmark.

Nager, N., and T. Allen. (1984). *Public Relations Management by Objectives.* New York, NY: Longman.

Smith, M. (1995). "Communicating in the Community: Integrating Community Learning Into Communication Courses." In *Service-Learning: Linking Academics and the Community.* Edited by J. Eby, pp. 56-58. Harrisburg, PA: Pennsylvania Campus Compact.

# Sample Syllabus #1
## Strategic Plan Book Approach

## Course Requirements:

1) Team Contract
2) Journal/Peer Evaluations
3) Situational Analysis/Statement of P.R. Problem or Opportunity
4) Team Campaign Book & Presentation
5) Essay Exam

## Assignments and Papers:

### 1) Team Contract:

Groups must develop a written contract that will minimally include: a timeline for the project, individual assignments within the project, and what constitutes satisfactory and unsatisfactory performance by team members. The contract must detail the specific expectations and requirements for each team member as well as what specific actions will be taken for unsatisfactory performance. Additionally, each group must schedule formal meetings for discussing individual performance and airing concerns.

The team needs to devote sufficient time to discussion and negotiation of this contract. All must agree to the conditions and sign the document. Provide copies for each member, in addition to the copy submitted to the instructor.

### 2) Journal/Peer Evaluations:

At five points during the semester, you will need to submit a journal reflecting on your experiences with the course, in general, and with the group project, in particular. Your entry should be at least two pages in length, addressing reflections, issues, and concerns. You will also submit detailed written evaluations of each group member's contributions to the project, performance, attitude, attendance at group meetings, and the like. Be sure to provide a report on your own contributions, time commitment, and attendance.

### 3) Situation Analysis:

The public relations campaign begins with a clear understanding of the organization and the situation that prompts the campaign. Most campaigns are the result of a problem or opportunity that the management or the client wishes to address.

Each group member will individually research and write a situational analysis. Typically, the analyses run about 8-10 pages in length. These individual analyses may be refined and combined for incorporation into the final plan book.

The situational analysis should include:
    A) Your statement of the perceived public relations problem or opportunity;
    B) Relevant organizational history, industry trends, situational factors e.g., economic, social, political, or legal factors), previous campaigns, on-going communication efforts, and the like;
    C) The structure of the organization's decision-making process (i.e., who contributes to and who ultimately makes the final decision?);
    D) An outline of the categories and types of facts needed to confirm or refute the problem or opportunity as it is perceived.

**4) Team Campaign Book and Presentation:**

You will need to work on this project throughout the semester as each week's readings, discussions, and activities will focus on topics related to the campaign plan and book. Each team will submit three copies of a comprehensive and formal plan book and will make a formal presentation to the class at the end of the semester. Provide detailed explanation and solid support for your information and ideas throughout your plan book.

The plan book will include at least the following:
* Table of Contents (detailed and specific)
* Situational Analysis
* Statement of Perceived P.R. Problem or Opportunity
* Proposed and Actual Research to confirm or refute perceived problem
    or opportunity
* Communication Goals and Objectives
* Target Public(s) and Characteristics
* Campaign Strategies -- clearly explained and justified courses of
    action, implementation, etc.
* Media Characteristics
* Limitations in time, money, personnel, and the like
* Timeline/Calendar
* Narrative Budget
* Proposed Research to evaluate the campaign
* Summary Statement of Campaign Benefits and Strengths
* Creative Supplement with all creative/written work
* List of References

Plan books should conform to professional standards -- sloppy or substandard work is absolutely unacceptable. Team presentations of plan books should also conform with professional standards, with appropriate attire, audio-visual support, and the like expected. Demonstrate that you can communicate clearly and effectively in oral and written form.

**5) Essay Exam:**

The exam asks students to demonstrate their knowledge of the public relations management process by analyzing a case study. The exam is given before the last month of the semester so that students may give their full attention to the campaign book.

# Sample Syllabus #2
## Project Implementation Approach

## Course Requirements:

1) Project Proposal
2) Contract
3) Final Report
4) Group Grade
5) Individual Grade
6) Midterm and Final Exams
7) Class Discussion Leader

## Assignment Descriptions:

### Group Project:

The class will work in groups on public relations projects for local community organizations. The exact nature of these projects, and the work required, will be determined by you and the client. We are establishing a mini-agency through which we will assess the client's public relations needs, propose ways of meeting those needs, determine a plan, execute and evaluate that plan, and report the results. A more detailed description of the project is in the course packet.

You will be graded on the following components of the project:

### Proposal:

The written plan submitted to the client organization. It will be graded on the quality of writing, the soundness of the ideas, thoroughness of research, and clarity. You will have the opportunity to revise the proposal as needed to meet acceptable standards. However, only the first two drafts will be graded.

### Final Report:

The written summary and evaluation of your work for the client. Quality of writing, thoughtfulness of the evaluation, and soundness of the recommendations will be the criteria for grading the report.

### Group Grade:

This is the overall evaluation of the work for the client. I will grade both the process--the efficiency, skill, and professionalism your group displays in its relationships with the client, me, and each other--and the product, or the quality of the various components of the project as they are completed.

**Class Discussion Leaders:**

Working in teams, students will pick one of the areas indicated on the schedule, become thoroughly familiar with the readings for that area, and apply the principles to a current public relations case of their choosing. Discussion leaders will be graded on their preparation, quality of the questions raised, and application of case to principles discussed in class.

**Exams:**

You will be tested twice with two essay exams. They will cover material outlined on study guides to be distributed prior to the exams.

**Individual Grade:**

This will be based on a combination of your contributions to the group project and to the class overall. Part of this will be based on your performance of your role in the group project, cooperation with others, and the quality of the work you submit to the project. You will write a journal of your experience in order to help me keep track of your work. The other members of the group will be asked to complete a performance appraisal at the end of the project. Finally, your attendance and contributions to class will be evaluated.

# Critical Organizational Communication Theory, Feminist Research Methods, and Service-Learning: Praxis as Pedagogy

by Angela Trethewey

Our charge as educators is not simply to pass on knowledge to passive students, but to ask and demand of our students their active participation in constructing knowledge and social transformation. Communication scholars are well-positioned both to provide models for and to enact social transformation within our own classrooms and communities; however, our discipline has yet to fully explore and contribute to meaningful social change (Conquergood 1996; Deetz 1995). This essay provides a pedagogical framework that bridges the gap between communication theory and social action in the community by combining three mutually reinforcing elements: critical organizational communication theory, feminist qualitative methods, and service-learning.

## Critical Organizational Communication Theory

Recently, critical organizational communication scholars have articulated provocative theories for examining and critiquing contemporary organizational structures, practices, and consequences (Alvesson and Willmott 1992; Buzzanell 1994; Deetz 1992a, 1992b, 1995; Mumby 1987, 1988, 1993; Trethewey 1997). In this essay, I will draw primarily from the work of critical theorist Stan Deetz.

*Contemporary Organizations and the Threat to Democracy.* Deetz (1992, 1995) suggests that corporations are the primary site of political life in contemporary America. Decisions regarding the use of natural resources, the nature of work and leisure, the content and form of public knowledge, income distribution, and a host of other essential issues are being made in corporations. The health and well-being of democracy is threatened when "private" corporations begin making these "public" decisions. Increasingly, social direction and planning takes place in our corporations, yet many of those decisions are made by a privileged few (usually managers) under the veil of "privacy" and "economics." As critical communication scholars, we should be asking who *should* be planning, through what processes, toward what ends, and for whose benefit.

*A Stakeholder Model of Representation.* Deetz (1995) offers the stakeholder model of organizational representation to expand our conceptions of the democratic potential of corporations. This critical model asks us to view organizations as sites where a multiplicity of stakeholders are represented and where various stakeholder interests might be negotiated in more democratic ways. Stakeholders include consumers, workers, investors, suppliers, host communities, the general society, and the world ecological community. In this model, the function of management is to coordinate the conflicting interests of stakeholders rather than control them. If the full variety of stakeholder interests were represented in organizational decision making, each of the following would serve as a competitive measure of organizational effectiveness (Deetz 1995: 50): goods and services, income redistribution, use of resources, environmental effects, effects on local communities, life-styles and social values, and expanded organizational identities.

The stakeholder model suggests corporations are the site of a great deal of important potential, but unrealized, negotiation. Such negotiation, in the context of the corporation, can move us away from discursive closure and fixed corporate-driven meanings to creating talk that aids in building meanings no one has ever had before. "Such a discussion would aim at enrichment of concepts of self, other, and life in and through organizational decision making" (Deetz 1995: 171). Through politically sensitive dialogue we can recover the democratic potential of corporate organizations and reenvision the identities of members in ways that reflect the full range of their interests.

Our job as educators is to make a difference by preparing students for their democratic role in corporations. But first, we need to arm them with something other than a managerialist education. We can, for example, teach alternative organizational theories and provide our students with alternative organizational experiences, including appropriately politicized service-learning. To fully reap the benefits of service-learning, however, we must also arm students with an appropriate epistemology and methods for exploring and analyzing their service experiences.

# Feminist Epistemologies and Feminist Methods: Tools for Analyzing and Understanding Service Experiences

Feminist epistemologies and methods can augment students' understanding of critical organizational theory in a variety of ways. While I applaud critical organizational communication scholars, few of them provide models for "looking" or methods that allow students to observe and analyze their very real and lived experiences. Feminist scholars fill that sorely needed gap in critical organizational theory. Feminist theory reveals that gender, race, class, sexuality, and other categories that are used to exclude, are social constructions, not fixed or essential features of the lived world. It is in and through our communicative actions that gender, race, class, and sexuality are constructed and intersect in ways that have very real and material consequences for organizational actors, clients, and communities. Feminist methods offer students the tools to begin to understand the politics of everyday life and the ways in which they might contribute to social changes to enhance the lives of those who have been marginalized inside and outside the walls of contemporary organizations.

**Traditional Approaches to Service-Learning.** There is no reason to assume that simply because students are actively engaged in community-based organizations or providing services they will conduct political analyses of representation and/or identity construction, including gender (or race or class) issues. Like Herzberg (1994), "I don't believe that questions about social structures, ideology, and social justice are automatically raised by community service" (309). Even when students are deeply moved by their service-learning experience, there is "little evidence that students spontaneously gain critical self-consciousness — an awareness of the ways their own lives have been shaped by [gender, race, and class]" or social consciousness — an awareness of the ways others' lives have been shaped by such forces (Herzberg:309).

Traditional service-learning rarely strives for such critical awareness and even less frequently addresses the issue of social change (Moore 1990). Much of the literature on service-learning assumes a positivist epistemology. As a case in point, Kolb's experiential learning cycle provides the conceptual framework and epistemological assumptions for a great deal of adult education and training (Coghlan 1993). In this model, learning is constituted by the following four related processes or abilities: concrete experience abilities (CE), reflective observation abilities (RO), abstract conceptualization abilities (AC), and active experimentation abilities (AE). Kolb (1984) contends that:

> *[Learners] must be able to involve themselves fully, openly, and without bias in new experiences (CE). They must be able to reflect on and observe their experience from many perspectives (RO). They must be able to create concepts that integrate their observations into logically sound theories (AC), and they must be able to use these theories to make decisions and solve problems (AE). (30)*

Here service-learning is designed to help students learn "through experience in 'real-world' settings" via "learning activities that engage the learner directly in the phenomena being studied" (Moore 1990: 275). Kolb (1984) further argues that:

> One's job as an educator is not only to implant new ideas but also to dispose of or modify old ones. In many cases, resistance to new ideas stems from their conflict with old beliefs that are inconsistent with them. If the education process begins by bringing out the learner's beliefs and theories, examining and testing them, and then integrating the new more refined ideas into the person's belief system, the learning process will be facilitated. (28)

Thus, in this model the student either applies course concepts to his or her placement site or compares course theories and methods with their application in the organizational setting, thus facilitating the learning process. This positivist epistemology can effectively situate or contextualize knowledge.

Many positivist service-learning projects also include one particularly important feature, namely a focus on personal development and affective growth (Moore 1990). In my own experience, I have heard many students tell animated and sincere stories of personal growth as a result of their service-learning activities. These students emerge from the experience more compassionate and more committed to further community-based service. Service-learning experts also speak of the increased self-esteem that often accompanies students' site-based learning. Coleman (1976) argues that one of the important characteristics of service-learning is "the self-assurance and sense of accomplishment that successful action provides . . . this intrinsic reward of accomplishment is even stronger in the context of other persons: either actions toward the other persons or in some other direct relation to them, in a realistic setting" (60).

## Feminist Approaches to Service-Learning

While there is much to be gained from service-learning projects that help students apply conceptual knowledge to "real world" experiences and better understand themselves, feminist theory, research, and pedagogy can further enhance their experiential education. Feminism provides students with an appropriate conceptual frame for understanding, critically interrogating, and ultimately transforming their experiential learning sites in particular and their experiential worlds in general. The five following themes derived from feminist research are particularly useful pedagogical tools for making service-learning experiences meaningful: (1) analysis of the social construction of identity; (2) reflexivity; (3) attention to the affective components of human interaction; (4) collaboration; and (5) an action orientation.

*Analyses of the Social Construction of Identity.* Feminists have argued forcefully that gender is a social construction rather than a fixed, essential aspect of an individual's identity (Butler 1990; Harding 1987; Houston and Wood 1996; Sawicki 1991; Weedon 1987). Gender is acquired and learned through interaction with others in the social world. As a society, we inscribe biological sex with social meanings through communication and attendant practices. In like fashion, racial and class distinctions are constructed in and through discourse.

This being the case, students may begin to explore how certain tasks at their service-learning sites come to be constituted as "gendered," "raced," or "classed." They may ask why it is, for example, that victims of domestic abuse are often "feminine?" By doing so, students can discover how gender and other differences are created in everyday interactions. Additionally, students can explore how their own and others' lives are shaped by communication that defines what is normal and superior, as well as abnormal and inferior. When students understand that previous "taken-for-granteds" such as race, class, sexuality, gender, and even organizational forms are social constructions, they can examine the ways those constructions inscribe and imbue privilege in very different and often inequitable ways.

*Reflexivity.* Reflexivity is a notion that is most clearly articulated in feminists' accounts of the research process, but it can be appropriated by students in their own knowledge-construction processes. In the context of the research process, reflexivity, for Harding (1987), means that "the class, race, culture, and gender assumptions, beliefs, and behaviors of the researcher her/himself must be placed within the frame of the picture that she/he paints" (29). Here the researcher makes herself — her political position, her interests, her goals — available to the reader. In the context of service-learning, reflexivity means that students must begin to examine their own political positions. More specifically, students must reflect upon how their own gender, class, race, and age have shaped the way they view and experience the world and their community service organization. In addition, students may analyze reflexively how the individuals they encounter in the course of community service have been positioned by larger, inequitable social discourses. In short, students should be led to reflect upon and examine critically the nature of communication processes, the provision of services, social definitions of problems and solutions, and a host of related issues that make service-learning particularly meaningful (Harding 1987:29).

One danger of nonreflexive service-learning is that students will view social, systemic problems as individual problems or shortcomings. Students typically have little trouble putting a "human face" on issues of poverty, homelessness, domestic violence, or racism after they see, some for the first time, these injustices up close and personal. Students also begin to see how something like homelessness can happen to them. Reflexive service-learning education takes this consciousness-raising process one step further by making the personal political. As feminist educators, we can encourage students to explore the links between individual problems and the larger political and social context. For example, we might discuss and read about how contemporary social/political constructions of masculinity and femininity support and maintain domestic violence, rape, and the economic hardships of mother-headed households — phenomena that have traditionally been considered private, personal, and individualized problems. If our community service practice is not reflexive, then we run the danger of performing charity rather than moving toward social change. Reflexivity enables us to "make connections between the adverse conditions in the fabric of society and the problems experienced by [individuals] in everyday life, and through action, to overcome these conditions" (Longress and McLeod 1980: 268).

**Attention to the *Affective Components of Human Interaction*.** Feminist theorists and researchers have long recognized the value that comes from attending to the affective components of human interaction (Gilligan 1982; Oakley 1981). This aspect of epistemology involves not only acknowledgment of the affective dimension of research, but also the recognition that emotions serve as a source of insight and a foundation for knowledge building. Feminist researchers frequently attempt to develop special relations with the people studied (Reinharz 1992). As a case in point, Oakley's (1981) friendship model of feminist interviewing is potentially quite liberating and empowering for both researchers and the researched, and contributes to the production of a different, and some would argue, more powerful sort of knowledge than might be produced if emotion or affect were "controlled" during the research process.

Similarly, students in communication courses with service-learning components should be encouraged to develop interpersonal relationships with those who are being served and to examine their own emotional responses to their experiences. Traditional approaches to service-learning do not always provide the space for addressing and learning from students' emotional reactions (Coghlan 1993). Feminist educators can validate those emotional or affective responses and use them as learning tools. Indeed, several students in my service-learning courses have used their own emotional responses as starting points for further analysis and understanding. For example, when students become outraged that a local after-school program for urban youth has so few resources, they often begin their discussions by blaming the employees at the site. During in-class debriefing, however, the conversation quickly turns to the larger structural barriers that prevent children from having the resources they need and ways the students might affect those barriers. The starting point for such analyses is the students' very real, visceral, emotional responses. Communication students are particularly well-positioned to practice and understand how emotional responses enter into their own communicative behaviors and to learn from those responses, especially those who have been encouraged to be reflexive about the learning process.

**Collaboration.** Another strategy that is often practiced by feminist theorists, researchers, and practitioners is collaboration. Feminist researchers, for example, often collaborate with their "subjects" regarding the nature of the research problem, process, and final product(s). In Meis's (1991) participatory study, the rural women of Nalgonda, along with the researcher, jointly created a regional conference where they discussed and developed collective solutions to the problem of domestic violence. Likewise, feminist social work practitioners argue that direct service providers and their clients can collaborate to advocate policy changes, including the enforcement of child-support payments and gender wage-equality (Bricker-Jenkins, Hooyman, and Gottlieb 1992; Gottlieb 1992).

Following feminist researchers and practitioners, students should be encouraged to develop (small-scale) or participate in collaborative projects with service providers and clients at their service-learning sites. Students in a course I recently taught planned in conjunction with service providers *and* service recipients a breakfast at a homeless youth shelter. These collaborative endeavors serve a variety of purposes: They enable students to be active participants rather than detached observers; encourage interaction; provide a context for students to observe the hurdles, barriers, and opportunities involved in participatory projects; actively contribute to worthy social programs; and highlight the fact that our "responsibility for social justice includes, but also carries beyond personal acts of charity" (Herzberg 1994:317). Ideally, service-learning should be conceived as collaborative or reciprocal learning where all parties — those serving and those being served — have a voice in determining what is to be learned and/or transformed. Certainly, a collaborative approach to service-learning would enhance and make particularly meaningful Deetz's (1992, 1995) call for more participatory and more democratic organizational processes.

**Action Orientation.** From its inception, feminism has been committed to meaningful social action and transformation. The broadly conceived goal of feminist research remains the liberation and emancipation of women and other historically marginalized and oppressed groups (Fonow and Cook 1991; Meis 1991; Reinharz 1992). Patricia Hill Collins (1991) argues that women's everyday behavior can be a source of resistance and a form of activism; she claims, "People who view themselves as fully human, as subjects, become activists no matter how limited the sphere of their activism may be" (46). I argue that we can best infuse this spirit of activism in our communication courses by incorporating service-learning components in conjunction with feminist principles. The transformations that students pursue on interpersonal, organizational, and community levels should be grounded in a firm understanding of the relationships among communication, democracy, and gender, race, and class.

As Deetz (1995) suggests, the problem today is not knowing what to do; "it is wanting to do it, seeing the necessity of change, and taking the risks" (172). Service-learning grounded in an action orientation offers students the chance to move beyond imagining transformation to participating in that transformation, even of their very selves. Astin (1994) contends, and I concur, that community service projects demonstrate "to each participant how he or she can become personally engaged in *changing* a small-scale system" [original emphasis] (22). Indeed, many students have already begun to make positive changes in their own communities through service-learning.

## Transformations

When critical organizational communication theory and feminism are used to frame students' service experiences, service-learning can be understood as an "approach to experiential learning, an expression of values — service to others, community development and empowerment, reciprocal learning — that determines the purpose, nature, and process of social and educational exchange between experiential education programs and the community organization with which they work" (Stanton 1990: 67). As educators, we have a responsibility to ask our students to critique and ultimately transform oppressive practices in a wide variety of organizational contexts. That transformation can be most powerfully achieved in communication courses that incorporate a community-based service-learning component framed by critical organizational communication theory and feminist epistemologies and methods. When students are armed with these conceptual and methodological tools, they are better able to empower others, to create social change, and to grow as thoughtful and active citizens are. When our communication courses are appropriately politicized through the meaningful combination of critical organizational communication theory, feminism, and service-learning, students may begin to see that opportunities for meaningful and important action are everywhere "since the stuff of social transformation is identical with the stuff from which our daily lives is made" (Astin 1994:26).

# References

Alvesson, M., and H. Willmott, eds. (1992). *Critical Management Studies.* London: Sage.

Astin, A.W. (October 1994). "Higher Education and the Future of Democracy." Allan Murry Carter Chair Inaugural Lecture. University of California, Los Angeles.

Bricker-Jenkins, M., N.R. Hooyman, and N. Gottlieb, eds. (1992). *Feminist Social Work Practice in Clinical Settings.* Newbury Park, CA: Sage.

Butler, J. (1990). *Gender Trouble: Feminism and the Subversion of Identity.* New York, NY: Routledge.

Buzzanell, P. (1994). "Gaining a Voice: Feminist Organizational Communication Theorizing." *Management Communication Quarterly* 7:339-383.

Coghlan, D. (1993). "Learning Through Emotions Through Journaling." *Journal of Management Education* 17:90-94.

Coleman, J.S. (1976). "Differences Between Experiential and Classroom Learning." In *Experiential Learning: Rationale, Characteristics, and Assessment.* Edited by M. Keeton & Associates, pp. 49-61. San Francisco, CA: Jossey-Bass.

Collins, P.H. (1991). "Learning From the Outsider Within: The Sociological Significance of Black Feminist Thought." In *Beyond Methodology: Feminist Scholarship as Lived Research.* Edited by M.M. Fonow and J.A. Cook, pp. 35-59. Bloomington, IN: Indiana University Press.

Conquergood, D. (February 1996). "Making a Difference in the Lives of Those We Study." Paper presented at the annual convention of the Western States Speech Communication Association, Pasadena, CA.

Deetz, S. (1995). *Transforming Communication, Transforming Business: Building Responsive and Responsible Workplaces.* Cresskill, NJ: Hampton Press.

———. (1992a). *Democracy in an Age of Corporate Colonization.* Albany, NY: State University of New York Press.

———. (1992b). "Disciplinary Power in the Modern Corporation." In *Critical Management Studies.* Edited by M. Alvesson and H. Willmott, pp. 21-45. London: Sage.

Fonow, M.M., and J.A. Cook. (1991). "Back to the Future: A Look at the Second Wave of Feminist Epistemology and Methodology." In *Beyond Methodology: Feminist Scholarship as Lived Research.* Edited by M.M. Fonow and J.A. Cook, pp. 1-15. Bloomington, IN: Indiana University Press.

Gilligan, C. (1982). *In a Different Voice.* Cambridge, MA: Harvard University Press.

Gottlieb, N. (1992). "Empowerment, Political Analyses, and Services for Women." In *Human Services as Complex Organizations.* Edited by Y. Hansenfeld, pp. 301-319. Newbury Park, CA: Sage.

Harding, S. (1987). "Is There a Feminist Method?" *Hypatia* 2:17-32.

Herzberg, B. (1994). "Community Service and Critical Teaching." *College Composition and Communication* 45:307-319.

Houston, M., and J.T. Wood. (1996). "Difficult Dialogues, Expanded Horizons: Communicating Across Race and Class." In *Gendered Relationships*. Edited by J.T. Wood, pp. 39-56. Mountain View, CA: Mayfield.

Kolb, D.A. (1984). *Experiential Learning: Experience as the Source of Learning and Development*. Englewood Cliffs, NJ: Prentice-Hall.

Longress, J.F., and E. McLeod. (1980). "Consciousness Raising and Social Work Practice." *Social Casework* 61:267-276.

Meis, M. (1991). "Women's Research or Feminist Research: The Debate Surrounding Feminist Science and Methodology." In *Beyond Methodology: Feminist Scholarship as Lived Research*. Edited by M.M. Fonow and J.A. Cook, pp. 60-84. Bloomington, IN: Indiana University Press.

Moore, D.T. (1990). "Experiential Education as Critical Discourse." In *Combining Service and Learning: A Resource Book for Community and Public Service. Vol. 1*. Edited by J.C. Kendall and Associates, pp. 273-283. Raleigh, NC: National Society for Experiential Education.

Mumby, D.K. (1993). "Critical Organizational Communication Studies: The Next Ten Years." *Communication Monographs* 60:18-25

———. (1988). *Communication and Power in Organizations: Discourse, Ideology, and Domination*. Norwood, NJ: Ablex.

———. (1987). "The Political Function of Narrative in Organizations." *Communication Monographs* 54:113-127.

Oakley, A. (1981). "Interviewing Women: A Contradiction in Terms." In *Doing Feminist Research*. Edited by H. Roberts, pp. 30-61. London: Routledge & Kegan Paul.

Reinharz, S. (1992). *Feminist Methods in Social Research*. New York, NY: Oxford University Press.

Sawicki, J. (1991). *Disciplining Foucault: Feminism, Power, and the Body*. New York, NY: Routledge.

Stanton, T. (1990). "Service-Learning: Groping Toward a Definition." In *Combining Service and Learning: A Resource Book for Community and Public Service, Vol. 1*. Edited by J.C. Kendall and Associates, pp. 65-67. Raleigh, NC: National Society for Experiential Education.

Trethewey, A. (1997). "Resistance, Identity and Empowerment: A Postmodern Feminist Analysis of Clients in a Human Service Organization." *Communication Monographs* 64:281-301.

Weedon, C. (1987). *Feminist Practice and Poststructuralist Theory*. Oxford: Basil Blackwell.

# COM 407

## ADVANCED CRITICAL METHODS IN COMMUNICATION STUDIES: COMMUNICATION, IDENTITY, AND SOCIAL CHANGE

Dr. Angela Trethewey

### Course Objectives:

- To explore a variety of types of interpretive and critical research in communication studies.
- To understand and practice qualitative research methods used in interpretive and critical communication studies.
- To connect course concepts/issues with your lived experience at a community based organization. You will spend at least 30 hours this semester in a community based organization providing needed services.
- To articulate a (political) position as a communication researcher. What does it mean to 'represent' others as a manager, volunteer, community member, or organizational actor?
- To explore organizations as sites where various stakeholders are (or are not) represented.
- To understand how communication creates social identities that are enabling and/or constraining.
- To understand how communication creates and recreates structures and cultures that are variably empowering or transformative.
- To examine the relationship between communication and democracy in the context of everyday life.
- To practice communication skills (presentational, analysis, writing, research).

### Course Assignments:

| | |
|---|---|
| Journals | 50 points |
| Practicum Assignments (2 @ 75 points each) | 150 points |
| Quizzes (3 @ 100 points each) | 300 points |
| Final Project | 300 points |
| Final Project Presentation | 50 points |
| Site Hours | 50 points |
| Participation | 100 points |
| | ---------------- |
| Total | 1000 points |

### Journals:

You will be assigned a journal question about every third week. Your journals are designed to help you explore connections between course reading/discussion and your own experience at your service-learning sites. Your journals will be a forum for you to analyze your organization, to develop ideas for your final project, and to critically reflect upon your experiences. Use one to two full pages to share your perspective on, understanding of, and experiences with the topics assigned. As most of the issues we will be exploring are personal, I can assure you that I consider your journals confidential. At the same time, I do not want to force you to share experiences you would rather not disclose. The journals will be evaluated based on the depth and understanding you display of course concepts. Include <u>analysis</u> of the topic/issue assigned, not just a description. Don't be afraid to examine what you believe and why you believe it. Most importantly, remember that these journals are for your benefit, not mine.

## Practicum Assignments:

You will be assigned two small-scale field research projects. These assignments are designed to enable you to practice two different qualitative research methods – interviewing and participant observation. Details will be provided later.

## Quizzes:

There will be three quizzes covering the readings over the course of the semester. The quizzes will include multiple choice questions, true/false questions, and short essays.

## Final Project:

The final project is designed to provide you an opportunity to use your communication skills and research expertise to create  something useful for your organization or for the community. This project will enable you to use what you know about communication, your service-learning site, and research methods to create a meaningful product. That final product may take a variety of forms including, but not limited to, the following: an advocacy speech, a grant proposal, a feature story for the newspaper, and editorial, a public service 'spot', a research report, or a training seminar. The final project should be developed with the stakeholders' needs in mind. In addition to the final product, you will be asked to write a short conceptual paper (4-6 pages) that provides the "theoretical" or conceptual grounding for your project.

## Final Project Presentation:

You will present your final project to the class in a 10 minute presentation/demonstration. Use this presentation as an opportunity to practice preparing and delivering a professional, public presentation.

## Site Hours:

You will be asked to spend a total of at least 30 hours at your site, providing volunteer service, over the course of the semester. Your activities or duties at your service-learning site will be negotiated by you and your site supervisor and will respond to the needs of the organization's stakeholders. Your site supervisor or contact person will "sign off" on your hours and provide you with feedback regarding your performance.

## Participation:

Your attendance is expected. It is vital that you substantively participate in class discussion, as well as keep current in the reading assignments. Participation is especially important in this class as it is designed to become a dialogue between all of us as we reflect upon the material and its relevance to our lives. Such a dialogue requires we assume several responsibilities. First, being prepared for class is a commitment that is necessary from each of us. Second, we must be willing to be open to and consider the thoughts and ideas of others in the classroom. No one experience or viewpoint is more important or valuable than any other. You may not agree with the views expressed by others, but we must all agree to respect each other's right to voice their own experiences and beliefs. Third, ask questions in class and respond to the questions raised in class. Fourth, come see me to discuss ideas and problems. Finally, continually look for ways to apply course material to your own communication, and talk about what you discover. If you participate in these five ways, and perhaps others, your own learning and the learning of others will be enhanced.

**Course Readings:**

Deetz, S. (1995). Transforming communication: Transforming business: Building responsive and responsible workplaces. Cresskill, NJ: Hampton Press.

**Additional Readings:**

Moore, D. T. (1990). Experiential education as critical discourse. In J. C. Kendall & Associates (Eds.), Combining service and learning: A resource book for community and public service (pp. 273-282). Raleigh, NC: National Society for Internships and Experiential Education.

Liu, G. (1995). Knowledge, foundations, and discourse: Philosophical support for service-learning. Michigan Journal of Community Service-learning, 2, 5-18.

Putnam, L. L. (1983). The interpretive perspective: An alternative to functionalism. In L. L. Putnam & M. Pacanowsky (Eds.), Communication and organizations: An interpretive approach (pp. 31-54). Beverly Hills, CA: Sage.

Van Maanen, J. (1991). The smile factory: Work at Disneyland. In P. J. Frost, L. F. Moore, M. R. Louis, C. C. Lundberg, & J. Martin (Eds.), Reframing organizational culture (pp. 58-76).

Tompkins, P. K. (1994). Principles of rigor for assessing evidence in 'qualitative' communication research. Western Journal of Communication, 58, 44-50.

Trujillo, N. (1992). Interpreting (the work and the talk of) baseball: Perspectives on ballpark culture. Western Journal of Communication, 56, 350-371.

Lofland, J., & Lofland, L. H. (1995). Analyzing social settings: A guide to qualitative observation and analysis, 3$^{rd}$ ed. (pp. 66-98). Belmont, CA: Wadsworth.

Harding, S. (1987). Is there a feminist method? Hypatia, 2, 17-32.

Allen, M. (1993). Critical and traditional science: Implications for communication research. Western Journal of Communication, 57, 200-208.

van Dijk, T. A. (1993). Stories and racism. In D. K. Mumby (Ed.), Narrative and social control: Critical perspectives (pp. 121-142). Newbury Park, CA: Sage.

Corey, F. C. (1996). Personal narratives and young men in prison: Labeling the outside inside. Western Journal of Communication, 60, 57-75.

Trujillo, N. (1993). Interpreting November 22: A critical ethnography of an assassination site. Quarterly Journal of Speech, 79, 447-466.

Oakley, A. (1981). Interviewing women: A contradiction in terms. In H. Roberts (Ed.), Doing feminist research (pp. 30-61). London: Routledge & Keegan Paul.

Houston, M., & Wood, J. (1996). Difficult dialogues, expanded horizons: Communicating across race and class. In J. T. Wood (Ed.), Gendered relationships (pp. 39-56). Mountain View, CA: Mayfield.

Sarri, R. C., & Sarri, C. M. (1992). Organizational and community change through participatory action research. Administration in Social Work, 16, 99-122.

Park, P. (1993). What is participatory research? A theoretical and methodological perspective. In P. Peter,

Adelman, M. B., & Frey, L. R. (1994). The pilgrim must embark: Creating and sustaining community in a residential facility for people with AIDS. In L. R. Frey (Ed.), Group communication in context: Studies of natural groups (pp. 3-21). Hillsdale, NJ: Lawrence Earlbaum Associates.

# Communication and Service-Learning: Bridging the Gap

by April R. Kendall

Although service-learning has earned national attention in the past two decades, its roots are often traced to John Dewey, who advocated the link between academic learning and community (Giles and Eyler 1994; Kunin 1997). Indeed that link remains at the heart of the service-learning movement today. Defining service-learning is no simple task, considering the number of practitioners engaging in the process in diverse contexts. While there have been over 100 recorded definitions of service-learning (Olney and Grande 1995; Jacoby 1996), service-learning commonly involves two concepts that distinguish it from student volunteering or community service: "(1) students engage in active reflection on their community experience, and (2) community learning is linked to academic learning" (Olney and Grande 1995: 43).

Service-learning is rapidly being adopted across higher education and is gaining both momentum and popularity. As Wutzdorff and Giles remark: "Our optimism [regarding service-learning] is fueled by seeing so many solid programs grow from well-intentioned volunteerism to closely integrated components of institutional curricula" (1997: 115). This surge in national popularity has resulted in a proliferation of literature on service-learning.

One of the challenges of incorporating service-learning into a traditional class is making room for "new" material. In a service-learning course, citizenship — which has been defined in a multitude of ways, including awareness of social issues, commitment to democratic ideals, and development of a responsibility to community — has been identified as the major supplement to course content. Although the problems and benefits of introducing citizenship concerns into course structures and pedagogies have received considerable attention, a third essential topic area is being overlooked in many discussions of service-learning courses: communication skills. What communication skills do students learn in service-learning courses across the curriculum? If students do indeed learn communication skills, how can we, as communication scholars, contribute to the pedagogy and institutionalizing of service-learning?

Thus far, there has been a limited amount of literature linking communication to service-learning, though there exist both ample opportunity and a pronounced need. In an effort to provide background information as well as a starting point for future research, I will in this essay (1) briefly review the current literature on service-learning, grouping it into four thematic areas and (2) address significant gaps in the current literature, with a focus on bridging the gap between communication and service-learning.

# Literature Review

The literature regarding service-learning is diverse, ranging from the philosophical and theoretical to the pragmatic and prescriptive. However, these writings can be categorized into four prominent thematic areas: (1) philosophy and theory of service-learning; (2) value and benefits of service-learning; (3) institutionalizing service-learning; and (4) the pedagogy of service-learning in the classroom.

### Philosophy and Theory of Service-Learning

The first division of the service-learning literature includes philosophical, theoretical, and rhetorical essays that provide a rationale for service-learning in education. These arguments are minimally substantiated by research; instead, they make the argument for service-learning from a philosophical foundation. Essays within this area address issues of democracy, citizenship, and the need for students to develop civic responsibility and community involvement in society. Guarasci and Cornwell (1997) provide a viewpoint representative of this approach: "Clearly the development of a new educational vision and genuine experience with democracy, community, and difference must begin with changes in the administration of colleges and universities" (15). Madeleine Kunin (1997), former deputy secretary in the U.S. Department of Education, proposes an additional philosophical rationale for service-learning: "For learning to be truly worthwhile, it must develop values of right and wrong, foster the development of problem-solving skills, and provide hands-on learning experiences, as well as teaching the basics" (149). The debate over the appropriateness of teaching values and citizenship in schools is voiced in this kind of literature.

Issues of epistemology, theoretical underpinnings, and academic legitimacy are among the philosophical issues addressed in this first division (Liu 1995; Palmer 1987). What is the place of service-learning in the academy? What philosophical and theoretical foundations support arguments to include service-learning in the curriculum? These philosophical questions pave the way for the second thematic area in the literature: the value of service-learning in education.

### Value and Benefits of Service-Learning

The value and benefits of service-learning are discussed for four constituents: students, faculty, the academy, and the community. Much of the literature related to the value of service-learning explores the benefits for student participants. There is, however, limited research that links the service-learning experience to learning outcomes in students, in either the cognitive, affective, or behavioral domains. Lipka (1997) characterizes the research as "unconnected, [and] lacking a broad conceptual framework that explicates the theory, practice and current status of research of long term effects of service-learning" (56). The limited literature reveals that the primary student benefits include the development of social responsibility and values, a greater awareness of societal problems, and an ability to apply principles learned in class to new situations (Markus, Howard, and King 1993; McCarthy 1996; Olney and Grande 1995; Seigel 1997; Wade 1997).

Much of this research relies heavily on anecdotal evidence of students' positive experiences with service-learning assignments. Recently, efforts to provide quantitatively derived evidence to support claims that service-learning is correlated to student learning have been conducted by researchers associated with UCLA and the RAND Corporation. This comprehensive research involves a national, longitudinal study of nearly 3,500 students at 42 institutions. The major findings are related to three service-learning constituencies: the community, the academy, and student service-learners.

First, community organizations strongly valued the contributions of student volunteers and perceived the students as highly effective in meeting both organizational and client needs. Second, institutions were increasing their capacity and support for service-learning, particularly by developing new service-learning courses. Relations between higher education institutions and community organizations also improved during the year. Third, participation in service was associated with gains in student learning and development. Students participating in service showed greater increases in civic responsibility, academic achievement, and life skills than did nonparticipating students (Gray et al. 1996: 70).

Faculty members who integrate service-learning into the curriculum also receive benefits from the experience. Although Seigel (1997) refers to faculty instituting service-learning at the K-12 level, the findings here may be also true for higher education faculty. Benefits sited include "opportunities for creativity in developing curriculum [and] positive recognition from administrators, faculty, and parents. . . . [However,] most rewarding . . . is the changes teachers observe in their students . . . [including] . . . students' enthusiasm and motivation to learn (Seigel 1997: 210). Hesser (1995) further elaborates on faculty benefits when he notes that "by continuing to actively experiment with changes of sites, critical reflection tools, and other experiences that enhance the learning outcomes, we, as well as our students . . . become practitioners and beneficiaries of experiential education" (40).

Academies can also benefit from service-learning as a way of addressing increasing pressure for accountability to the public and to the communities that support and fund them. Reciprocity is, of course, a key principle of service-learning, and nowhere can this principle be more clearly witnessed than in the mutually beneficial relationships that can develop between the community and the university: "Service-learning is about more than students' learning: it is also about effectively meeting community needs and applying intellectual expertise in a way that adds value to service" (Enos and Troppe 1996: 157). Mechanisms are needed that ensure and provide for the continuation of this reciprocal relationship. Institutionalizing service-learning in the academy is evidence of a movement in that direction.

## Institutionalizing Service-Learning

The essays in this category focus primarily on how to incorporate service-learning into the curriculum (Bringle and Hatcher 1996; Jacoby 1996; Rubin 1996). Though there is still some discussion as to "why" service-learning should be incorporated in general, these articles differ from the philosophical essays in that they highlight the practical application of service-learning as it relates to at least one of the constituencies: students, faculty, academy, and community.

Bringle and Hatcher (1996) provide a complex model for incorporating service-learning into higher education through guidelines on establishing and organizing a service-learning center. They develop a "comprehensive action plan for service-learning, or CAPSL" that addresses steps in planning a program that accommodates each of the four constituencies. The CAPSL model provides practical activities to aid each group in the incorporation of service-learning into its experience. A particular strength of this model is its plan for assessing the developmental process for each constituency.

Jacoby (1996) integrates a rationale for service-learning with a practical model for its implementation, stating, "Service-learning must be fully integrated into the mission, policies, and practices of individual institutions of higher education if it is to remain viable" (328). She also explores factors relevant to implementation, including: securing funding, developing partnerships with community agencies, encouraging faculty leadership and participation through the "tenure, review, and promotion process" (329), and creating institutional resources that foster interdisciplinary outreach (330-331).

## Pedagogy of Service-Learning

The most pragmatic literature regarding service-learning is that related to it as pedagogical practice. These articles fall into two general categories: (1) how to integrate service-learning into the classroom; and (2) models of service-learning courses in a variety of disciplines.

## How to Integrate Service-Learning

The "how to" articles include practical models and tips for incorporating service-learning into the classroom. In this kind of literature the link between service-learning and experiential learning is most clearly made (Coleman 1976; Morton 1996; Svinicki and Dixon 1987). There are also established models of integration, offering guidelines for the integration process. Pardo (1997) delineates several considerations for successful integration, including time commitments, orientation of participants, evaluation, personnel involved, paperwork, and public relations. McCarthy (1996) offers suggestions for successful "one-time and short-term" projects that can ease students into the service-learning experience and capitalize on providing students with rewarding experiences (114).

Several articles and books refer to the process of reflection, which encourages students to actively make connections between service and learning (Enos and Troppe 1996; Eyler, Giles, and Schmiede 1996; Goldsmith 1995; Lipka 1997; Morton 1996). As I stated above, one of the generally agreed upon requirements for service-learning is a process by which "students engage in active reflection on their community experience" (Olney and Grande 1995: 43). Reflection can be a cooperative effort, such as class or small group discussion sessions, or an individual effort, taking, for example, the form of essay writing or journal keeping. Each of these approaches encourages critical thinking from the students. In the literature that links service-learning to learning outcomes, the reflection process is a key component (Lipka 1997; Markus, Howard, and King 1993; McCarthy 1996; Olney and Grande 1995; Seigel 1997; Wade 1997).

***Models of Service-Learning Courses.*** Service-learning is well-represented in a wide range of disciplines, from business to English, engineering to communication. Reporting on these courses are both individual articles (Krupar 1994; Markus, Howard, and King 1993; McCarthy 1996) and compilations such as *Snapshots of Service in the Disciplines* (Patton 1996) that provide descriptions of sample courses. This kind of literature provides feedback on incorporating service-learning into specific courses, often including information on syllabi, implementation, project models, and suggestions for practitioners (Patton 1996).

***Service-Learning and the Communication Discipline.*** It is within the pedagogy-oriented literature that the connections between communication and service-learning are most clearly explored; however, these connections need still further development on several levels. A limited number of articles provide examples of service-learning as it has been incorporated into communication courses: Communication and Aging (Krupar 1994), Small Group Problem Solving (Yelsma 1994), and Mass Communication and Society (Cohen and Kinsey 1994). In a compilation work (Patton 1996) five service-learning courses in communication are outlined: Leader-Communicator-

Mentor; Speech and Sociology Service-Learning; Finding Dialogue; Building Community Through Communication; and Organizational Communication. Service-learning has, of course, been incorporated into many more kinds of communication courses than these, as the variety of courses included in this monograph makes apparent.

In addition to underreporting successful course models, the literature up until now has also overlooked important theoretical links between communication studies and service-learning. This leads us directly to our next major section.

## Gaps in the Current Literature

The review undertaken for this essay reveals two noticeable gaps in the current literature on service-learning. The first relates to the research that supports the value of service-learning as linked to learning outcomes; the second concerns the limited amount of material linking service-learning to communication.

There is a pronounced lack of empirical research providing support for the correlation between engaging in service-learning and learning outcomes. Such support is needed to substantiate the claim that students learn more or differently when participating in service-learning experiences. The RAND and UCLA research serves as an excellent example of a recent comprehensive study, but the need exists for more research of this kind. Service-learning programs are seeking acceptance and funding in university settings. In competitive battles for funding, service-learning programs may fare better if a definitive link to learning outcomes can be established.

Most remarkable — at least from the perspective of a communication scholar — is the limited amount of literature linking communication studies with service-learning. While there exists literature that provides models of communication courses, additional examples would be helpful as more instructors attempt to incorporate service-learning into their classrooms. Furthermore, the "institutionalizing" literature discussed in this review should enable communication studies to create a framework or guide that could assist departments in including service-learning in their courses even in the absence of an established university-wide service-learning center.

In addition to these pragmatic concerns, the theoretical connection between communication and service-learning needs to be better addressed. This connection includes those communication skills fundamental to the very experience of service-learning. What can communication as a discipline contribute to service-learning as pedagogy? Relatedly, what communication skills do students learn when they participate in a service-learning course regardless of the discipline? By addressing these connections, communication scholars might get to the heart of issues central to the discipline and be able to provide evidence that supports an essential link between service-learning and communication. By establishing this relationship, communication could be instrumental in the further development of service-learning programs, or at least in assisting in the development of complex, critical, informed, and self-aware programs. Additionally, communication research could contribute to one of the primary goals of service-learning: increased student learning. As Jacoby has remarked: "Service-learning affords students opportunities to develop such skills as the ability to synthesize information, creative problem solving, constructive teamwork, effective communication, well-reasoned decision making, and negotiation and compromise" (1996: 21). Communication scholars could substantiate and document this claim.

Communication research, particularly instructional communication research, could prove to be especially useful in the development of service-learning in teacher training programs. For example, instructional communication research may provide guidance to questions such as: How can teachers facilitate active student reflection? Research regarding immediacy, classroom interaction, and power could inform this specific question. In addition, instructional communication could provide insights for service-learning practitioners as they design, redesign, or develop new courses and curricula and endeavor to link theory and practice.

## Conclusion

This essay has analyzed the current service-learning literature, identified gaps in the service-learning literature, and articulated connections between communication and service-learning. As a discipline, communication has a central role to play in the future of service-learning since that future may well depend on efforts to research and analyze it critically. One of the most important challenges facing us as communication scholars is the necessity of designing and conducting research that provides such critical analysis. In this way they can make a major contribution to both existing and developing service-learning programs.

### References

Bringle, R.G., and J.A. Hatcher. (1996). "Implementing Service-Learning in Higher Education." *Journal of Higher Education* 67:221-239.

Cohen, J., and D. Kinsey. (Winter 1994). "'Doing Good' and Scholarship: A Service-Learning Study." *Journalism Educator* 48(4): 4-14.

Coleman, J.S. (1976). "Differences Between Experiential and Classroom Learning." In *Experiential Learning: Rationale, Characteristics, and Assessment*. Edited by M.T. Keeton and Associates, pp. 49-61. San Francisco, CA: Jossey-Bass.

Enos, S.L., and M.L. Troppe. (1996). "Service-Learning in the Curriculum." In *Service-Learning in Higher Education: Concepts and Practices*. Edited by B. Jacoby and Associates, pp. 156-181. San Francisco, CA: Jossey-Bass.

Eyler, J., D. Giles, and A. Schmiede. (1996). *A Practitioner's Guide to Reflection in Service-Learning: Student Voices and Reflections*. Nashville, TN: Vanderbilt University.

Giles, D.E., and J. Eyler. (1994). "The Theoretical Roots of Service-Learning in John Dewey: Toward a Theory of Service-Learning." *Michigan Journal of Community Service-Learning* 1:77-85.

Goldsmith, S. (1995). *Journal Reflection: A Resource Guide for Community Service Leaders and Educators Engaged in Service-Learning*. Washington, DC: The American Alliance for Rights and Responsibilities.

Gray, M., S. Geschwind, E. Ondaatje, A. Robyn, S. Klein, L. Sax, A. Astin, and H. Astin. (1996). *Evaluation of Learn and Serve America, Higher Education: The First Year Report, Vol. I*. Los Angeles, CA: UCLA Higher Education Research Institute.

Guarasci, R., and G.H. Cornwell. (1997). "Democracy and Difference: Emerging Concepts of Identity, Diversity, and Community." In *Democratic Education in an Age of Difference: Redefining Citizenship in Higher Education*. Edited by R. Guarasci, G.H. Cornwell, and Associates, pp. 1-16. San Francisco, CA: Jossey-Bass.

Hesser, G. (1995). "Faculty Assessment of Student Learning: Outcomes Attributed to Service-Learning and Evidence of Changes in Faculty Attitudes About Experiential Education." *Michigan Journal of Community Service-Learning* 2:33-42.

Jacoby, B. (1996). "Securing the Future of Service-Learning in Higher Education. In *Service-Learning in Higher Education: Concepts and Practices*. Edited by B. Jacoby and Associates, pp. 317-335. San Francisco, CA: Jossey-Bass.

Krupar, K. (1994). "Service-Learning in Speech Communication." In *Building Community: Service-Learning in the Academic Disciplines*. Edited by R.J. Kraft and M. Swadener, pp. 105-115. Denver, CO: Colorado Campus Compact.

Kunin, M.M. (1997). "Service Learning and Improved Academic Achievement." In *Service-Learning: Ninety-Sixth Yearbook of the National Society for the Study of Education: Part I*. Edited by J. Schine, pp. 149-160. Chicago, IL: University of Chicago Press.

Lipka, R.P. (1997). "Research and Evaluation in Service-Learning: What Do We Need to Know? In *Service-Learning: Ninety-Sixth Yearbook of the National Society for the Study of Education: Part I*. Edited by J. Schine, pp. 56-68. Chicago, IL: University of Chicago Press.

Liu, G. (1995). "Knowledge, Foundations, and Discourse: Philosophical Support for Service-Learning." *Michigan Journal of Community Service-Learning* 2:5-18.

Markus, G.B., J.P.F. Howard, and D.C. King. (1993). "Integrating Community Service and Classroom Instruction Enhances Learning: Results From an Experiment." *Educational Evaluation and Policy Analysis* 15:410-419.

McCarthy, M.D. (1996). "One-Time and Short-Term Service-Learning Experiences." In *Service-Learning in Higher Education: Concepts and Practices*. Edited by B. Jacoby and Associates, pp. 113-134. San Francisco, CA: Jossey-Bass.

Morton, K. (1996). "Issues Related to Integrating Service-Learning Into the Curriculum." In *Service-Learning in Higher Education: Concepts and Practices*. Edited by B. Jacoby and Associates, pp. 276-296. San Francisco, CA: Jossey-Bass.

Olney, C., and S. Grande. (1995). "Validation of a Scale to Measure Development of Social Responsibility." *Michigan Journal of Community Service-Learning* 2:43-53.

Palmer, P. (September/October 1987). "Community, Conflict, and Ways of Knowing: Ways to Deepen Our Educational Agenda." *Change* 19(5): 20-25.

Pardo, W. (1997). "Service-Learning in the Classroom: Practical Issues." In *Service-Learning: Ninety-Sixth Yearbook of the National Society for the Study of Education: Part I*. Edited by J. Schine, pp. 90-104. Chicago, IL: University of Chicago Press.

Patton, M. (1996). *Snapshots of Service in the Disciplines: Corporation for National Service Grants 1994-1995*. Providence, RI: Campus Compact.

Rubin, S. (1996). "Institutionalizing Service-Learning." In *Service-Learning in Higher Education: Concepts and Practices*. Edited by B. Jacoby and Associates, pp. 297-316. San Francisco, CA: Jossey-Bass.

Seigel, S.E. (1997). "Teachers of Service-Learning." In *Community Service-Learning: A Guide to Including Service in the Public School Curriculum*. Edited by R.C. Wade, pp. 197-213. Albany, NY: State University of New York.

Svinicki, M.D., and N.M. Dixon. (1987). "The Kolb Model Modified for Classroom Activities." *College Teaching* 35:141-146.

Wade, R.C. (1997). "Challenges to Effective Practice." In *Community Service-Learning: A Guide to Including Service in the Public School Curriculum*. Edited by R.C. Wade, pp. 301-313. Albany, NY: State University of New York.

Wutzdorff, A.J., and D.E. Giles, Jr. (1997). "Service-Learning in Higher Education." In *Service-Learning: Ninety-Sixth Yearbook of the National Society for the Study of Education: Part I*. Edited by J. Schine, pp. 105-117. Chicago, IL: University of Chicago Press.

Yelsma, P. (1994). "Combining Small Group Problem Solving With Service-Learning." *Michigan Journal of Community Service-Learning* 1:62-69.

# Annotated Bibliography:
## Service-Learning and Communication

by Irene Fisher and Ann Wechsler, updated by April R. Kendall with permission of the primary authors

## Print Resources

Boss, J. (1994). "The Effect of Community Service Work on the Moral Development of College Ethics Students." *Journal of Moral Education* 23(2):183-198.
Seventy-one University of Rhode Island undergraduate students participated in an ethics class experiment designed to test the effect of a community service component on their level of moral reasoning. A pretest/posttest control group design was used, and results were measured using Rest's Defining Issues Test. Results supported the hypothesis that community service, combined with discussion of relevant moral issues, enhances moral reasoning ability.

Campus Compact. (1991). "The Project for Public and Community Service." President's statement. Providence, RI: Brown University.

————— . (1994). *Participatory Action Research: Merging the Community and Scholarly Agendas*. Providence, RI: Campus Compact, Project on Integrating Service With Academic Study.
This monograph defines action research and examines the relationship between *participatory* action research (PAR) and service-learning. The experiences of seven colleges and universities that have experimented with PAR give insights into the possibilities for assisting special populations with community-based research.

Cohen, J. (Fall 1994). "Matching University Mission With Service Motivation: Do the Accomplishments of Community Service Match the Claims?" *Michigan Journal of Community Service-Learning* 1(1): 98-104.
The author tempers the enthusiasm for and rapid growth of community service on campus with trenchant questions about the role of community and public service in academia. He also explores the motives of service-learning advocates and examines the compatibility

of service goals in relation to the mission of higher education. The article provides a historical perspective on service-learning and urges scholarly documentation of outcomes.

Cohen, J., and D. Kinsey. (Winter 1994). "'Doing Good' and Scholarship: A Service-Learning Study." *Journalism Educator* 48(4): 4-14.
This article defines and distinguishes service-learning from other forms of academic experience. Two hundred seventeen of 220 students in a Mass Communication and Society course engaged in service-learning projects. The authors conclude that service-learning is more than "doing good." Their results indicate that experiential learning, defined as individual contact between students and community members, is pedagogically superior to nonexperiential learning.

Coleman, J.S. (1976). "Differences Between Experiential Learning and Classroom Learning." In *Experiential Learning: Rationale, Characteristics, and Assessment.* Edited by M.T. Keeton and Associates, pp. 49-61. San Francisco, CA: Jossey-Bass.
The author compares experiential learning with the more common pedagogy, information assimilation, concluding that experiential learning is more effective. He discusses situations in which each type of learning is appropriate and advocates for incorporating experiential learning in school and college curricula.

Corporation for National Service. (1996). *Expanding Boundaries: Serving and Learning.* Columbia, MD: Cooperative Education Association.
A comprehensive publication from the Corporation for National Service that contains a section on building connections with the community, lessons learned, and program and assessment tools.

———. (1994). "Service-Learning: An Overview." In *Roles for Higher Education,* pp. 12-14. Washington, DC: Corporation for National Service.
This resource guide contains the definition of service-learning adopted in the National and Community Service Trust Act of 1993. The brief overview provides an excellent introduction to the concept of service-learning. It also contains a resource list of available organizations and publications that address service-learning and national and community service.

Council of Chief State School Officers. (1995). *Integrating Service-Learning Into Teacher Education: Why and How? Portraits of Improving Teacher Education Through Service-Learning.* Washington, DC: Council of Chief State School Officers.

This publication focuses on educating teachers to view teaching as vitally connected to the larger social context. Teacher education is, therefore, gradually being restructured to include firsthand service-learning experiences. Service-learning is seen as integral to an educational reform effort.

Della-Piana, C., and C. Bullis. (1991). "Exploring Service-Learning: A Journey Into the Realm of Education and Experience." Paper presented at the annual meeting of the Speech Communication Association, Atlanta, GA.

Using Delve, Mintz, and Stewart's theoretical framework to explain the purpose of service-learning, these two communication professors describe benefits of service-learning in the undergraduate curriculum. A service-learning course at the University of Utah is analyzed, and some implications for the field of communication are discussed.

Delve, C.I., S.D. Mintz, and G.M. Stewart. (Summer 1990). "Promoting Values Development Through Community Service: A Design." *New Directions for Student Services.* San Francisco, CA: Jossey-Bass.

The authors provide a theoretical framework to conceptualize the service-learning experience and to design service-learning programs. They posit a five-phase service-learning model incorporating key developmental variables: exploration, clarification, realization, activation, and internalization. Their service-learning model has served as a foundation for developing service-learning programs in numerous institutions of higher education. Research progress on service-learning echoes these five phases of the service-learning model.

Falbo, M.C. (1993). *Serving to Learn: A Faculty Guide to Service-Learning.* Columbus, OH: Ohio Campus Compact.

This guide, developed for the Ohio Campus Compact by the director for community service at John Carroll University, contains the "principles of good practice for combining service and learning" (the industry standard) and a valuable section on reflection and practice, with 20 questions to ask about service-learning.

Galura, J., R. Meiland, R. Ross, M.J. Callan, and R. Smith, eds. (1993). *Praxis II. Service-Learning Resources for University Students, Staff, and Faculty.* Ann Arbor, MI: OCSL Press, University of Michigan.

Giles, D.E., Jr., and J. Eyler. (1994). "The Impact of a College Community Service Laboratory on Students' Personal, Social, and Cognitive Outcomes." *Journal of Adolescence* 17:327-339.

The authors surveyed 72 undergraduates in a required course for an interdisciplinary major for impact of a required service component on attitudes of social responsibility. The civic and cognitive aspects of social responsibility were measured, as well as the long-term commitment to community service. Results showed an increase in empathy toward clients after service; they were more likely to attribute problems to circumstances beyond the control of clients. Student evaluations noted an increased understanding of social problems (knowing) and the value of community service (serving).

———. (Fall 1994). "The Theoretical Roots of Service-Learning in John Dewey: Toward a Theory of Service-Learning." *Michigan Journal of Community Service-Learning* 1(1): 77-85.

In this article, the authors review aspects of John Dewey's educational and social philosophy that they identify as relevant to the development of a theory of service-learning. They include learning from experience, reflective activity, citizenship, community, and democracy. The article concludes with a set of key questions for research and theory development.

Goldsmith, S. (1995). *Journal Reflection: A Resource Guide for Community Service Leaders and Educators Engaged in Service-Learning.* Washington, DC: The American Alliance for Rights and Responsibilities.

This complete guide to writing journals elucidates the role of journalkeeping in reflecting on service-learning, ways to get started, and useful exercises. The material is presented in a very friendly format.

Gray, M., S. Geschwind, E. Ondaatje, A. Robyn, S. Klein, L. Sax, A. Astin, and H. Astin. (1996). *Evaluation of Learn and Serve America, Higher Education: The First Year Report, Vol. I.* Los Angeles, CA: UCLA Higher Education Research Institute.

This report documents extensive research conducted regarding the value and effects of service in higher education and is performed by researchers associated with UCLA and RAND. This comprehensive research includes a national longitudinal study of nearly 3,500 students at 42 institutions. The major findings are related to three constituents involved in service-learning: the community, the academy, and students engaged in service-learning. Results include: community organizations found student service effective and valuable; institutions are increasing the number of service-learning courses taught and improving their relationships with the community; and students who participate in service-learning display advancement in learning and development and an increase in civic responsibility, academic achievement, and life skills.

Hesser, G. (Fall 1995). "Faculty Assessment of Student Learning: Outcomes Attributed to Service-Learning and Evidence of Changes in Faculty Attitudes About Experiential Education." *Michigan Journal of Community Service-Learning* 2:33-42.

This article contains an excellent review of the literature on student learning. It proceeds with two hypotheses: faculty conclude that learning derives from field study and service-learning; faculty have shifted from skepticism to positive affirmation concerning the integration of service-learning into course curricula.

Honnet, E., and S. Poulsen. (1989). *Principles of Good Practice for Combining Service and Learning*. Wingspread Special Report. Racine, WI: Johnson Foundation.

The principles of good practice for combining service and learning were formulated in a working group at Wingspread, convened by NSEE and the Johnson Foundation. These principles have become the industry standard for service-learning.

Howard, J., ed. (1993). *Praxis I: A Faculty Casebook on Community Service-Learning*. Ann Arbor, MI: OCSL Press, University of Michigan.

Jacoby, B., and Associates, eds. (1996). *Service-Learning in Higher Education: Concepts and Practices*. San Francisco, CA: Jossey-Bass.

This book is a comprehensive guide to developing high quality service-learning experiences both in the curriculum and through student affairs programs. It gives many practical examples from campuses and lists national organizations that support service-learning programs. It also lists resources that are useful in helping students make postcollege service and career choices.

Kendall, J., and Associates, eds. (1990). *Combining Service and Learning: A Resource Book for Community and Public Service*. 3 vols. Raleigh, NC: National Society for Experiential Education.

Edited by former NSEE executive director Jane Kendall, this three-volume resource book is a classic. Volume I contains the principles for effectively practicing service-learning, as well as rationales, theories, research, and history surrounding service-learning. Volume II contains comprehensive practical advice on specific issues in effective programs and courses; it provides more than 80 case studies of programs based in college, K-12, and community settings. Volume III is an annotated bibliography edited by Janet Luce of Stanford University (see below).

Kendall, J. (1990). "Principles of Good Practice in Combining Service and Learning." In *Combining Service and Learning: A Resource Book for Community and Public Service, Vol 1.* Edited by J. Kendall and Associates, pp. 37-55. Raleigh, NC: National Society for Experiential Education.
    This article in Volume I of *Combining Service and Learning* lists and explains the 10 principles of effective service-learning. The Bennion Center has based its Service-Learning Program for the University of Utah upon these principles.

Kettering Foundation. (1992). *Politics for the Twenty-First Century: What Should Be Done on Campus?* Dubuque, IA: Kendall/Hunt.
    This concise 44-page booklet focuses on education for citizenship and examines four ways in which higher education can fulfill this mission: (1) through involvement in service programs, (2) through public deliberation (the process by which people come to understand their differences and commonalities), (3) through creation of an egalitarian, participatory campus, and (4) through academic rigor.

Kolb, D.A. (1984). *Experiential Learning: Experience as the Source of Learning and Development.* Englewood Cliffs, NJ: Prentice-Hall.

Kraft, R.J., and M. Swadener, eds. (1994). *Building Community: Service-Learning in the Academic Disciplines.* Denver, CO: Colorado Campus Compact.
    The editors summarize results from general surveys, social growth investigations, psychological development investigations, moral judgment studies, intellectual learning investigations, community impact, and effects on those served. Actual results from an evaluation of Colorado Service-learning Programs are included in the text. The essays also contain a wealth of citations useful to service-learning practitioners.

Krupar, K. (1994). "Service-Learning in Speech Communication." In *Building Community: Service-Learning in the Academic Disciplines.* Edited by R.J. Kraft and M. Swadener, pp. 105-115. Denver, CO: Colorado Campus Compact.
    While reflecting on service-learning as a cooperative learning para-

digm, the author provides a detailed account of integrating service-learning into a speech communication course on aging. Teacher-student learning contracts are discussed and a thorough sample syllabus, specifying learning objectives in a service-learning course, is included.

Lempert, D.H. (1996). *Escape From the Ivory Tower: Student Adventures in Democratic Experiential Education.* San Francisco, CA: Jossey-Bass.
The book describes in detail an experiential approach that combines discussion and interaction, laboratory and field learning, community involvement and service, civic training, and student initiated participatory learning. It gives examples of learning beyond the classroom, at a community, national and international level, in terms of "adventures."

Luce, J. (1988). *Service-Learning: An Annotated Bibliography. Linking Public Service With the Curriculum.* Raleigh, NC: National Society for Experiential Education.
This 81-page annotated bibliography is fully indexed.

Markus, G.B., J.P.F. Howard, and D.C. King. (Winter 1993). "Integrating Community Service and Classroom Instruction Enhances Learning: Results From an Experiment." *Educational Evaluation and Policy Analysis* 15(4): 410-419.
This article reports results of an experiment in integrating optional community service into a large undergraduate political science course. In a postcourse survey, students in service-learning sections were significantly more likely than students in the control sections to report that they had performed up to their potential in the course, had learned to apply principles from the course to new situations, and had developed a greater awareness of societal problems.

Marriott, M. (August 4, 1996). "Taking Education Beyond the Classroom." *New York Times Education Life* 4A: 22,25,38,39.
This journalist gives concrete and current examples of campuses that are extending their mission to include the betterment of surrounding communities while, at the same time, providing a more comprehensive education for their students.

————. (August 4, 1996). "Colleges Setting Moral Compasses." *New York Times Education Life* 4A: 23,24,31.
This essay cites institutions that are promoting moral development along with intellectual life. Combining classroom learning with ser-

vice activity is seen as an appropriate way to foster personal responsibility toward a larger community.

Melchior, A., and L. Bailis. (Spring 1996). "Assessing Service-Learning." *Network: Constitutional Rights Foundation* 5(4): 1-4.

Miller, J. (1994). "Linking Traditional and Service-Learning Courses: Outcome Evaluations Utilizing Two Pedagogically Distinct Models." *Michigan Journal of Community Service-Learning* 1(1): 29-36.
This study examined the community service outcomes of students who selected a service option in two advanced introductory classroom-based courses in psychology. Four hypotheses were tested. Students did not differ either in their reports concerning gains in personal development, general mastery of course concepts, or in final course grades received, but participants reported an enhanced ability to apply concepts outside the classroom. Implications of the findings for community service-learning experiences at the university level and future research are discussed.

Morton, K., and M. Troppe. (1996). "From the Margin to the Mainstream: Campus Compact's Project on Integrating Service With Academic Study." In *Two Cases of Institutionalizing Service-Learning.* Edited by M. Troppe, pp. 3-16. Providence, RI: Campus Compact.

Seidman, A., and C. Tremper. (1994). "Legal Issues for Service-Learning Programs." A Community Service Brief. Washington, DC: The Nonprofit Risk Management Center.
This handbook addresses concerns about liability, insurance, and risk management that may arise in service-learning programs such as: rules for imposing liability for harm your program may cause; laws that require or prohibit certain practices; risk management procedures to reduce the likelihood of a negative incident; and insurance arrangements to provide adequate coverage when needed.

Silcox, H.C. (1995). *Motivational Elements in Service-Learning: Meaningfulness, Recognition, Celebration and Reflection.* Philadelphia, PA: Brighton Press.
This book is first in a three-part series on service-learning compiled by Harry Silcox, director of the Pennsylvania Institute for Environmental and Community Service-learning. The Institute focuses on training teachers in service-learning, producing educational packets, conduct-

ing workshops, and initiating innovative approaches to service-learning. This book addresses meaningful service, celebrating and recognizing service, motivating service participants, and reflection.

————. (1994). *Design, Leadership and Models: The Change Agents of School Service-Learning Programs.* Philadelphia, PA: Brighton Press.
The second book in the Silcox trilogy examines the planning and organization of service-learning programs. It focuses on institutional change agents and the state of the discipline today. It borrows from business management models and gives special attention to the work of Senator Harris Wofford and John Briscoe in organizing the state of Pennsylvania for service and service-learning. Models of four highly cognitive service-learning programs are described in the areas of environmental education, literacy, intergenerational historical studies, and citizenship.

————. (1995). *A How-To Guide to Reflection: Adding Cognitive Learning to Community Service Programs.* Philadelphia, PA: Brighton Press.
This book examines one of the core elements of a service-learning program — reflection. Through reflective teaching methodology, service to the community is blended with academic learning in schools, promoting more meaningful forms of learning. The book dissects reflective teaching methods, offers learning guideposts for facilitators and commentators, and addresses the need for empirical research on reflection activities.

Smith, M. (1994). "Community Service-Learning: Striking the Chord of Citizenship." *Michigan Journal of Community Service-Learning* 1(1): 37-43.
This study revealed that Campus Compact leaders and sponsors of the National and Community Service Act of 1990 stress citizenship as the most important student outcome of service participation. However, students, faculty, staff, and administrators at one institution did not share this emphasis. Smith, therefore, recommends a more collaborative process of goal setting to ensure that strategies connecting service-learning to citizenship are developed.

Stanton, T.K. (January 1990). *Integrating Public Service With Academic Study: The Faculty Role.* Providence, RI: Campus Compact, Brown University.

Troppe, M. (1996). "From Skeptic to Proponent: Faculty Involvement in Service-Learning." In *Two Cases of Institutionalizing Service-Learning, How Campus Climate Affects the Change Process.* Edited by M. Troppe. Providence, RI: Campus Compact, Brown University.

This article contains a very personal account of a faculty member's incorporation of service-learning into her class and her experience on a service-learning committee at Loyola College. The most compelling feature of this account is the faculty member's initial opposition to offering credit for service, and her eventual conversion to a supporter. The article also offers an excellent discussion on reflection.

Wechsler, A., and J. Fogel. (Summer 1995). "The Outcomes of a Service-Learning Program." *National Society for Experiential Education Quarterly* 20(4): 6.

The service-learning concept, introduced at the University of Utah by the Lowell Bennion Community Service Center, views community service and service-learning as a way to meet the needs of the community while enhancing learning. The article describes the development and preliminary findings of a three-year teaching and research project with student service involvement as a tool of regular instruction in university courses across disciplines.

Yelsma, P. (1994). "Combining Small Group Problem Solving With Service-Learning." *Michigan Journal of Community Service-Learning* 1:62-69.

This article combines the principles of small group problem solving with service-learning, drawing on 15 years of experience using this pedagogy. Techniques of small group problem solving are discussed and incorporated into successful group service-learning projects. Student reports of their service-learning experiences are qualitatively reported.

# Electronic Resources

Communications for a Sustainable Future
*http://csf.colorado.edu/sl/*

The most extensive collection of resources, this collection contains a wealth of information about service-learning programs at colleges and universities throughout the United States, as well as current research in the field, publications, and other information. This site also can be used to access the service-learning listserv.

American Association for Higher Education (AAHE)
*http://www.aahe.org*
> One of the leading organizations in the service-learning movement, this organization sponsors the monograph series and has other information.

American Association of Community Colleges (AACC) Service Learning Clearinghouse
*http://www.aacc.nche.edu/spcproj/service/service.htm*
> AACC is the primary advocacy organization for the nation's two-year degree-granting institutions. This website contains information on AACC projects as well as references and workshop information.

Campus Compact
*http://www.compact.org/*
> The "parent" organization in the service-learning movement, Campus Compact sponsors a number of funded programs and awards. The Compact is currently promoting a vision of "the engaged campus" as a next step in the movement.

Campus Outreach Opportunity League (COOL)
*http://www.cool2serve.org/*
> COOL is a national nonprofit that helps college students start, strengthen, and expand their community service.

National Society for Experiential Education (NSEE)
*http://www.nsee.org*
> NSEE is primarily composed of practitioners. Many of their programs, however, feature service-learning, and this site contains information on those programs.

National Communication Association (NCA)
*http://www.natcom.org*
> NCA is the most up-to-date source on programs in service-learning in communication studies.

Partnership for Service-Learning
*http://www.studyabroad.com/psl/pslhome.html*
> This partnership has originated, designed, and implemented intercultural/international service experiences since 1982.

# Contributors to This Volume

**James L. Applegate** is a professor and the chair, Communication, at the University of Kentucky. He is the second vice-president of the National Communication Association.

**Christine M. Bachen** is an assistant professor of communication at Santa Clara University.

**Mark J. Bergstrom** is an assistant professor of communication at the University of Utah.

**Connie Bullis** is an associate professor and the chair, Communication, at the University of Utah.

**Robbin D. Crabtree** is an assistant professor of communication studies at New Mexico State University.

**David Droge** is an associate professor of communication and theatre arts at the University of Puget Sound.

**Irene Fisher** is director of the Lowell Bennion Community Service Center at the University of Utah.

**Chris Wood Foreman** is an associate professor of communication and theatre arts at Eastern Michigan University.

**Jeff Harder** is an associate professor of communication at Loyola University Chicago.

**Peggy Hashemipour** is director of community service-learning at California State University, San Marcos.

**April R. Kendall** is a graduate student in communication at the University of Utah.

**Virginia Keller** is an assistant professor of communication at Loyola University Chicago.

**Virginia Kidd** is a professor of communication studies at California State University, Sacramento.

**Katherine N. Kinnick** is an assistant professor of communication at Kennesaw State University.

**Craig Kois** is an instructor in communication at Loyola University Chicago.

**Sherwyn P. Morreale** is associate director of the National Communication Association.

**Bren Ortega Murphy** is an associate professor and the chair, Communication, at Loyola University Chicago.

**Eleanor Novek** is an assistant professor of communication at Monmouth University.

**Sally Perkins** is an associate professor of communication studies at California State University, Sacramento.

**Mark A. Pollock** is an associate professor of communication at Loyola University Chicago.

**Gerri Smith** is an assistant professor of communication studies at California State University, Sacramento.

**Michael F. Smith** is an assistant professor of communication at La Salle University.

**Paul A. Soukup, S.J.,** is an associate professor of communication at Santa Clara University.

**Tasha Souza** is an assistant professor of communication at the University of Wisconsin-Parkside.

**Kathleen H. Stacey** is an associate professor of communication and theatre arts at Eastern Michigan University.

**Lynne A. Texter** is an associate professor of communication at La Salle University.

**Angela Trethewey** is an assistant professor of communication at Arizona State University.

**Kristin Bervig Valentine** is a professor of communication at Arizona State University.

**Ann Wechsler** is an administrative assistant at the Lowell Bennion Community Service Center at the University of Utah.

**Paul Yelsma** is an associate professor of communication at Western Michigan University.

**Sara Weintraub** is an assistant professor of English at Bentley College.

**Edward Zlotkowski** is professor of English at Bentley College. Founding director of the Bentley Service-Learning Project, he also is senior associate at the American Association for Higher Education.

## About AAHE

**AAHE's Vision** AAHE envisions a higher education enterprise that helps all Americans achieve the deep, lifelong learning they need to grow as individuals, participate in the democratic process, and succeed in a global economy.

**AAHE's Mission** AAHE is the individual membership organization that promotes the changes higher education must make to ensure its effectiveness in a complex, interconnected world. The association equips individuals and institutions committed to such changes with the knowledge they need to bring them about.

## About AAHE's Series on Service-Learning in the Disciplines

Consisting of 18 monographs, the Series goes beyond simple "how to" to provide a rigorous intellectual forum. *Theoretical essays* illuminate issues of general importance to educators interested in using a service-learning pedagogy. *Pedagogical essays* discuss the design, implementation, conceptual content, outcomes, advantages, and disadvantages of specific service-learning programs, courses, and projects. All essays are authored by teacher-scholars in the discipline.

Representative of a wide range of individual interests and approaches, the Series provides substantive discussions supported by research, course models in a rich conceptual context, annotated bibliographies, and program descriptions.

See the order form for the list of disciplines covered in the Series, pricing, and ordering information.

# Yes! Send me the following monographs as they are released.

| **Price per vol.** (includes shipping*): | **List** $28.50 ea | **AAHE Member** $24.50 ea |
| --- | --- | --- |

**Bulk prices** (multiple copies of the *same* monograph only):
**10-24 copies** $22.50 ea;  **25-99 copies** $21.00 ea;  **100+ copies** $15.00 ea

| | Quantity | Price | Subtotal |
| --- | --- | --- | --- |
| Complete Series (all 18 vols.) | | $405 | |
| Accounting | | | |
| Biology | | | |
| Communication Studies | | | |
| Composition | | | |
| Engineering | | | |
| Environmental Studies | | | |
| History | | | |
| Management | | | |
| Medical Education | | | |
| Nursing | | | |
| Peace Studies | | | |
| Philosophy | | | |
| Political Science | | | |
| Psychology | | | |
| Sociology | | | |
| Spanish | | | |
| Teacher Education | | | |
| Women's Studies | | | |

**Total** _____

## Shipping*

Price includes shipping to U.S. destinations via UPS. Call AAHE's Publications Orders Desk at 202/293-6440 if you need information about express and/or foreign delivery.

## Payment (F.I.D. #52-0891675)

All orders must be prepaid by check, credit card, or institutional purchase order; except AAHE members may ask to be billed.

❑ Please bill me; I am an AAHE member. (Provide member # below)
❑ Enclosed is a check payable to AAHE.
❑ Enclosed is my institutional Purchase Order: #_____.
❑ Please bill my:  ❑VISA ❑MasterCard ❑AmEx

_____
Cardholder's Name (please print)

_____
Cardholder's Signature

_____
Card Number                                          Exp. Date

**Bill This Order To** (if "Ship To" address is different, please provide on an attached sheet) :

_____        _____
Name                                     AAHE Member #  __ __ __ — __ __ __ __

_____
Address

_____
City                               State         Zip

_____
Phone/Email                        Fax

**Mail/Fax this order to:** AAHE Publications Orders Desk, Box SL03, One Dupont Circle, Suite 360, Washington, DC 20036-1110; fax 202/293-0073; www.aahe.org. Visit AAHE's website to read excerpts from other volumes in the Series. Need help with your order? Call 202/293-6440.